The Gratifications of Whiteness

The Gratifications
of Whiteness

*W. E. B. Du Bois and the Enduring Rewards
of Anti-Blackness*

ELLA MYERS

OXFORD
UNIVERSITY PRESS

Oxford University Press is a department of the University of Oxford. It furthers
the University's objective of excellence in research, scholarship, and education
by publishing worldwide. Oxford is a registered trade mark of Oxford University
Press in the UK and certain other countries.

Published in the United States of America by Oxford University Press
198 Madison Avenue, New York, NY 10016, United States of America.

© Oxford University Press 2022

Library of Congress Control Number: 2022937696

ISBN 978-0-19-755677-1 (pbk.)
ISBN 978-0-19-755676-4 (hbk.)

DOI: 10.1093/oso/9780197556764.001.0001

3 5 7 9 8 6 4 2

Paperback printed by Marquis, Canada
Hardback printed by Bridgeport National Bindery, Inc., United States of America

For M. and S., with love

Contents

Acknowledgments

This book would not have been possible without the community of readers, colleagues, and compatriots who saw me through.

I am indebted to those who read and commented upon the manuscript in its various stages of becoming, most especially Mark Schwarz and Demetra Kasimis. Mark has read nearly every iteration of this book, beginning with the earliest, most inchoate drafts. His incisive comments and probing questions, along with his unwavering belief in my abilities, helped me figure out what I wanted to say, and how to say it. Deme provided invaluable feedback on this project over many years; I am grateful to be in continual conversation with her, about political theory and everything else. I deeply appreciate those who have thoughtfully and seriously engaged with parts of this book: Paul Apostolidis, Lawrie Balfour, Mark Button, Edmund Fong, Adom Getachew, Patchen Markell, Marcel Paret, and Melvin Rogers. Zach Stickney provided much-needed research assistance. Thanks also to my editor Angela Chnapko for affirming this project from the very start and to the three astute anonymous readers at Oxford University Press who helped me sharpen it. An earlier version of Chapter 4 was published as "Beyond the Psychological Wage: Du Bois on White Dominion," *Political Theory* 47, no. 1 (2019) and I thank SAGE Publications for their permission to reprint this material. I am also grateful to Chris Anton for allowing his photograph of the Robert E. Lee Monument in Richmond, VA, taken in the summer of 2020, to be used in the cover design.

I have been fortunate to be able to present portions of this book to many smart audiences over the years. In particular, I am grateful to the attendees of the UCLA Political Theory Colloquium, the Cornell Political Theory Workshop, the University of Chicago Political Theory Workshop, the Yale Humanities Program Colloquium, and the "Race and Populism in the Age of Trump" workshop hosted by Ohio State University. I especially want to thank the participants in these events who read my work closely and asked tough questions that helped refine my analysis: Wendy Brown, Joshua Dienstag, Andrew Dilts, Lisa Disch, Jason Frank, Bryan Garsten, Laura Grattan, Nazli Konya, Alex Livingston, Benjamin McKean, Jeanne Morefield, Paul North,

Davide Panagia, Caleb Smith, Inés Valdez, and Joseph Winters. In addition, American Political Science Association meetings, Western Political Science Association meetings, and especially Association for Political Theory conferences offered crucial opportunities to think in the company of talented theorists. I benefited from discussing aspects of this project with Libby Anker, Courtney Berger, Mark B. Brown, Michael Dawson, Jodi Dean, Thomas J. Donahue, Laura Ephraim, Clifton Granby, Michael Hanchard, Onur Ulas Ince, Jill Locke, Nancy Luxon, Lida Maxwell, John McMahon, Charles Mills, Alex Moon, Jeannie Morefield, Timothy Pachirat, Heather Pool, Shalini Satkunanandan, George Shulman, Linda Zerilli, and Lena Zuckerwise.

I am lucky to have a job that provides me with the stability and material support to complete a long-term project like this. The University of Utah and its Department of Political Science and Division of Gender Studies provided crucial leave time along with research and travel funds. I am thankful to work with sharp, creative colleagues with whom I can share ideas and commiseration. I so appreciate Matt Basso, Erin Beeghly, Juliet Carlisle, Beth Clement, Ben Cohen, Jim Curry, Lisa Diamond, Nadja Durbach, Lezlie Frye, Sarita Gaytán, Claudia Geist, Lela Graybill, Claudio Holzner, Steven Johnston, Wanda Pillow, Susie Porter, Richard Preiss, Paisley Rekdal, Angela Smith, Brent Steele, Kathryn Stockton, and Jessica Straley, many of whom are also close friends. And to my students: thank you for making me feel less like a brain in a vat. I am grateful for the time we get to spend together and especially for your curiosity and your desire to create more just ways of living. Especially in dark times, thinking and talking with you has sustained me.

Some of the students I have taught during my years at the University of Utah have made a lasting impact on me. Thank you to Allyson Berri, Karolyn Campbell, Stephen Michael Christian, Nadine Cobourne, Jake Garrett, Chris Jensen, Jordan Jochim, Kasen Scharmann, Lacey Slizeski, Zach Stickney, and Nikila Venugopal for asking such interesting questions and for allowing me to explore them with you. Jess Esplin, Tillie Fowles, and Lucy Williams were exceptional students who have since become peers and friends.

I am grateful to dear friends in Salt Lake who supported the writing of this book and, more importantly, helped me live a life outside of it. Thank you to Gretchen Dietrich, Monty Paret, Henry Paret, and Julian Paret, who are beloved chosen family. Jen Prehn Kious has buoyed my spirits over many long talks and walks; she is warm, wise, and hilarious. Extra thanks to her for organizing the amazing camping trips to Southern Utah. Candace Lach is both extremely cool and extremely kind. Thank you also to Jen Lingeman, who is whip-smart and, amazingly, usually more outraged than I am. Marcel and Jessie, Erin and Josh, Claudia and Rachel, and Sarita and Gwyn provided delicious food and even better company.

I have incredible friends who, despite living far away, are vital parts of my life: Paul Adelstein, Alisa Barnes, Martine Hyland, Demetra Kasimis, Nick Markos, Jon McCoy, Laura Scott, Heather Simons, Mike Simons, David Singer, and Eva Yusa. I am so lucky to have each of you in my corner. I want to especially thank the inimitable Christine Pirrone for a lifetime of extraordinary friendship. I don't know what I would do without you.

Thank you to my family, especially my parents, Robyn New-Wagner and Tom Myers, for their faith in me. My mom's unstoppable creativity and inquisitiveness continually inspire me. My dad was the first to show me what it means to be an excellent teacher, and he also shows me how to keep on learning. Thanks to them both for filling their homes with books, even when money was tight.

Part of this book was completed during the (still-unfolding) COVID disaster, including periods of lockdown. That experience was brutal, but also clarifying. It turns out there's no one else I'd rather be trapped in a small house with than Mark Schwarz and Solomon (Sol) Schwarz, my very favorite people. Sol: You bring indescribable fun, wonder, and energy to every single day. I love getting to know you, and I am thrilled to be your mom. Mark: Your wit, patience, and kindness are everything to me. Thank you for believing in this project and also for continually drawing me into the world that lies beyond it.

1

The Gratifications of Whiteness

Long-standing questions about how the stratifications of class and race shape American politics were suddenly and dramatically revived on November 8, 2016.[1] More precisely, the "white working class" immediately emerged as a central category in public discussions of Trump's largely unexpected victory in the US presidential election. The day after the election, "Why Trump Won: Working-Class Whites" in the *New York Times* and "How Trump Won: The Revenge of Working-Class Whites" in the *Washington Post* announced the prominent place that would be granted to this classed and raced category in subsequent election commentary.

According to many analysts, "working-class whites" proved decisive for Trump, particularly in the so-called Rust Belt states, where narrow margins secured his Electoral College win. Of course, this group's exact impact was much disputed: was the outcome best explained by how many members of this demographic turned out to vote for Trump or by how many others abstained from voting or opted for a third-party candidate? Was this just the latest development in a long-standing shift rightward by a once-reliable Democratic voting bloc, the most recent installment of *What's the Matter with Kansas?* Or was this in some important sense an unprecedented "revolt," as some argued?[2] While pundits debated the precise role played by this demographic in the historic election, others warned that the persistent focus on the "white working class" and their motivations left many economically marginalized Americans (the majority of whom had not voted for Trump) unseen and unacknowledged.[3] Others cautioned that focusing on this category obscured the fact that the "vast majority of Trump supporters were not working class."[4] Still, the national conversation around the Trump election remained fixated on this collective political subject.

A striking feature of the initial debate centering on the "white working class" was the attempt to determine whether this group's support for Trump was driven primarily by economic concerns *or* by racial animus. That is, despite the construction of the category itself, simultaneously class and race specific, discussions of motivations frequently played out along either/or

The Gratifications of Whiteness. Ella Myers, Oxford University Press. © Oxford University Press 2022.
DOI: 10.1093/oso/9780197556764.003.0001

lines. Did Trump win this group's vote because his promise to "fight for every last American job" spoke to this group's sense of economic vulnerability or because his virulent public condemnations of President Obama, Mexicans, and Muslims and the promise to "Make America Great Again!" spoke to their sense of white entitlement?[5] In other words, was Trump's win *really* about class or was it *really* about race?[6]

This framing, questionable from the start, began to falter as more election data appeared. Most notably, this data indicated that Trump's white supporters were not particularly economically vulnerable. For example, although Trump was preferred two to one over Clinton by white voters without a college degree (often problematically defined as the "white working class"),[7] members of this group who were personally experiencing economic hardship were actually more likely to vote for Clinton.[8] Moreover, in the 2016 general election, as in the primaries, two-thirds of Trump voters earned household incomes *above* the national median of $57,000.[9] When "working class" is more usefully defined as those who do not hold a college degree *and* report annual household incomes below the median, then 31% of Trump's voters were white working class (almost the same as Mitt Romney in 2012). And the "typical Trump voter was relatively affluent."[10] If low income and economic insecurity on their own were not predictors of preference for Trump, what else might explain his appeal to whites without a college degree, who favored him by 35 percentage points[11]—or, for that matter, to white voters at large, who favored Trump over Clinton by at least 15 percentage points?[12]

The idea that Trump was ushered in by a "whitelash" having less to do with voters' actual economic conditions than with a perception of social and political displacement was publicized on live election night coverage when CNN commentator Van Jones characterized Trump's surprise win: "This was a whitelash. This was a whitelash against a changing country, it was a whitelash against a black president in part." Jones's remark actually summed up what Gallup polling during the campaign had indicated. For white Trump supporters, the perception of their diminished relative status within the US social order seemed to be a significant factor in their preference for Trump.[13] Surveys prior to the election suggested that personal experiences of economic distress or poverty among whites did not predict support for Trump. Rather, "the Trump voter is driven not by simple economic self-interest but by something deeper and more psychological . . . Trump voters are whites who feel that their privileged place in America is threatened by forces they don't really understand."[14] As Carol Anderson shows in her prescient 2016 book, American history evinces a clear pattern: "the trigger for white rage, inevitably, is black advancement." The 2008 election of Barack Obama, she suggests, was the most recent "trigger" in a long line that includes Reconstruction, the Great Migration, *Brown v. Board of Education,* and the civil rights movement. Anderson argues that the enactment of white rage—which does not necessarily take the form of overt violence but can also appear as "institutional backlash"—began well before Trump's presidential campaign, most notably with a "new intensified wave of voter suppression" following Obama's win in 2008.[15]

Studies of the 2016 election results seem to confirm that white Trump voters were spurred not by their personal economic situation but by what is sometimes euphemistically referred to as "cultural anxiety" or "fear of societal change."[16] Put in terms of group position theory, in 2016 the dominant racial group in the United States, believing themselves to hold a "proprietary claim to certain areas of privilege and advantage," seemed to respond defensively in the face of perceived advances by subordinate racial groups.[17] (A mass media public lament over so-called white "despair deaths" starting in 2015 offered a dramatic, corroborating narrative of "racial declension."[18]) Trump's vow to "Make America Great Again" promised a return to a time when white people ruled.

In an analysis of American National Election Survey (ANES) data, political scientist Ashley Jardina argues that a significant number of white Americans regard themselves as "outnumbered" and "disadvantaged." She finds that Donald Trump was attractive to whites for whom "an erosion of whites' majority status and the election of America's first black president . . . signaled a challenge to the absoluteness of white dominance."[19] Similarly, in *Identity Crisis: The 2016 Presidential Campaign and the Battle for the Meaning of America,* political scientists John Sides, Michael Tesler, and Lynn Vavrick argue that although economics shaped white voters' behavior, it was "not through concern about their individual financial situations, but through racialized perceptions of deservingness." White Trump voters tended to believe that "hardworking [white] Americans were losing ground to less deserving minorities."[20] (This was also the sentiment documented, though suppressed, in Arlie Hochschild's popular book, *Strangers in Their Own Land.*[21]) Nell Irvin Painter summed up the dynamic identified by these researchers: Trump was favored by Americans who saw themselves "*as* white" and felt they had experienced a "demotion" relative to other racial groups.[22]

In this context, W. E. B. Du Bois's famous account of US whiteness as a "public and psychological wage" acquired new life. Mainstream media outlets, ranging from the *Washington Post* to the *Guardian* to the *Boston Globe*, ran pieces that turned to various aspects of Du Bois's work to probe the present political moment. It was the idea of the metaphorical wage, however, that took center stage.

In *Black Reconstruction: An Essay Toward a History of the Part Which Black Folk Played in the Attempt to Reconstruct Democracy in America, 1860–1880* (1935), Du Bois argues that Reconstruction was overthrown and "racial caste" re-established in the United States, partly because the "theory of laboring class unity" had no purchase in the American context.[23] Why not? Du Bois explains:

> It must be remembered that the white group of laborers, while they received a low wage, were compensated in part by a sort of public and psychological wage. They were given public deference and titles of courtesy because they were white. They were admitted freely with all classes of white people to public functions, public parks, and the best schools. The police were drawn from their ranks, and the courts, dependent upon their votes, treated them with such leniency as to encourage lawlessness. Their vote selected public officials, and while this had small effect upon the economic situation, it had great effect upon their personal treatment and the deference shown to them.[24]

A defining feature of Du Bois's conception of the "public and psychological wage" is that it theorizes whiteness as a favored *status* within the US regime of racial capitalism. In multiple works, using a varied conceptual vocabulary, Du Bois argues that across regions and time periods—in the North and the South, before and after the Civil War—whiteness functioned as a socially legible mark designating superiority, one which depended upon a "badge of inferiority" attached to Blackness.[25] He observes that classification as white regularly supplied status to *all* those so categorized, yet carried special significance for poor whites, whose "vanity," Du Bois says, was "fed" by an "association with their masters."[26]

On the face of it, it might seem strange that those seeking to understand Trump's victory would turn to Du Bois's idea of the "public and psychological wage," since election results seemed to debunk the idea that the poorest whites were responsible for Trump's win. But it is important to recognize that Du Bois makes more than one claim with his formulation. He not only suggests that whiteness operates as "compensation" for otherwise exploited workers (a claim examined in detail in Chapter 2) but also throughout *Black Reconstruction* documents how passionately and violently whites of all economic classes mobilized to *defend* the status benefits of whiteness—"the public and psychological wage"—against perceived encroachment by Blacks. The "wage" not only reveals "a wedge between the white and black workers" but also exposes the political power borne of white solidarity.[27]

Recent popular-cultural deployments of Du Bois's idea of the wage emphasize both points: the attempt to defend racialized advantages in response to advances by nonwhites and the political significance of what Du Bois called a "white alliance."[28] In *Politico* Joshua Zietz argued that the "psychological, even spiritual payoff" Du Bois associated with whiteness remains salient today; its perceived diminishment shaped the 2016 election outcome, as Trump played on the "psychological benefits of being white more than any other major candidate in 100 years."[29] As the Trump presidency unfolded, the Du Boisean wage remained a touchstone. In late 2018, Joan C. Williams warned in *The Atlantic* that Democrats needed to create a compelling economic agenda if they hoped to compete with Trump's appeal to the "psychological wage" of whiteness.[30] In the summer of 2019, following a series of raucous Trump rallies that featured exuberant "Send her back!" chants directed at Representative Ilhan Omar of Minnesota, Jamelle Bouie turned to Du Bois's *Black Reconstruction* in a column in the *New York Times*. Bouie reminded readers that Du Bois understood anti-Black violence including lynching in the early 20th century partly as a defensive reaction by whites to the presumed loss or devaluation of the "public and psychological wage." He linked Du Bois's insight to the recent Trump rallies, where "the worst of our past play[s] out in modern form." The crowds of white Americans who were "united in frenzied hatred of a black woman" were responding to what they regarded as "a threat to a racialized social order."[31]

In addition to shaping these narratives of a contemporary "whitelash," Du Bois's idea of American whiteness as a metaphorical wage has also been mobilized to reflect on the cross-class "coalition" of white Americans who elected Trump.[32] Adam Serwer, writing in the *Atlantic,* argued that Trump "intuited that Obama's presence in the White House decreased the value of what W. E. B. Du Bois described as the 'psychological wage' of whiteness across all classes of white Americans, and that the path to their hearts lay in invoking a bygone past when this affront had not taken place, and could not take place."[33] In the *New York Times* Charles Blow argued that Trump's presidency—"a correction to Barack Obama"—delivered a familiar white supremacist message: the least qualified white man is better than the most qualified Black man. Developing this claim, Blow looks to Du Bois's account in *Black Reconstruction* of how white racial solidarity was forged in the United States through a system of both tangible and intangible rewards. Du Bois helps Blow illuminate what he describes as "the pact that America has made with its white citizens from the beginning: The government will help to underwrite white safety and success."[34]

Like these writers, I believe Du Bois's work can speak to us here and now. Yet I will show that his distinctive analysis of whiteness in the United States stretches well beyond the idea of the "wage" and offers insights into far more than the Trump presidency. More specifically, Du Bois's work fruitfully and provocatively conceptualizes American whiteness as the site and source of plural *gratifications* for its bearers. Although the well-known idea of the "public and psychological wage" plays a part in this account, it is only one of the ways Du Bois conceptualizes the rewards attached to whiteness. Indeed, as this book shows, the racialized gratifications Du Bois's writings illuminate include not only material goods and status benefits but also pleasures derived from gratuitous Black suffering and the faith-like conviction that the world belongs to those marked as "white."

Du Bois provides a fuller, more textured understanding of white racialization in America than has been appreciated. While other important studies, most significantly David Roediger's *The Wages of Whiteness: Race and the Making of the American Working Class,* have engaged and extended Du Bois's account of the "public and psychological wage," few if any have explored how Du Bois conceptualizes whiteness in ways other than the wage.[35] This book aims to deepen our understanding of his thought and to reveal that his complex account of whiteness, though developed in response to the social and political conditions of his time, can offer critical purchase on the present.

Du Bois's writings invite us to recognize that whiteness is not one thing but many; it cannot be reduced to a single expression, function, or meaning. At the same time, Du Bois's work suggests that there is good reason to analyze whiteness specifically in terms of the varied *gratifications* it offers those within its bounds. This book explores the gratifications of whiteness that Du Bois uncovers. This means returning to the oft-cited notion of the "public and psychological wage" but also tending to other, lesser-known, but no less incisive ways that Du Bois thinks and talks about the workings of whiteness. In the chapters that follow, I examine three key motifs in Du Bois's work—wage, pleasure, dominion—that push us to think about whiteness as a polyvalent formation delivering gratifications in multiple registers: material, psychological, affective, libidinal, existential, spiritual.

Gratifications

What is at stake in addressing whiteness in terms of its gratifications? What value might this approach, modeled in Du Bois's extensive writings, hold for us now? There are two key claims I want to make about the value of this conceptual framing. First, it productively counters several prevalent ways of thinking about whiteness today: as privilege, as ignorance, and as indifference. The academic and popular discourse of "white privilege" in the United States emphasizes benefits that accrue by virtue of being classified as white.[36] It points out unearned advantages reserved for those socially marked as "white." Importantly, as it usually circulates, the notion of "white privilege" characterizes such benefits as automatically conferred rather than purposely sought and actively enjoyed. This formulation positions whites in a passive, unwitting role, as the accidental beneficiaries of an abstract system, and fails to ask whether (some? most? all?) white Americans—and not just those who are obviously racists—seek and receive multiple gratifications from their whiteness, and from the anti-Blackness that undergirds it.

Other influential accounts of contemporary American whiteness posit crucial deficits, such as ignorance and indifference, on the part of those who are categorized and interpellated as white, which in turn help to maintain white-over-Black hierarchies in the United States. In Charles Mills's work, "white ignorance" refers to a "group-based cognitive handicap" that works to insulate whites from the reality of white supremacy and its racialized distribution of advantages and disadvantages.[37] "White ignorance," Mills says, denotes "an ignorance among whites—an absence of belief, a false belief, a set of false beliefs, a pervasively deforming outlook" that is causally linked to "being socially categorized as white."[38] In her bestselling book *The New*

Jim Crow, Michelle Alexander proceeds differently, insisting that most white Americans do *know*, for example, that mass incarceration maintains racial caste in America; the problem is rather white *indifference* to this reality—the "failure to care, truly care, across the color line."[39] In place of Mills's "not-knowing,"[40] Alexander posits "not-caring" as a defining feature of American whiteness, which helps sustain the unequal distribution of life chances along the color line.

"White privilege" stresses the automatic, unwitting conferral of benefits, while "white ignorance" and "white indifference" posit cognitive and moral deficits. Yet Du Bois's thinking—and the notion of "gratifications" I draw from it—should provoke us to ask whether whiteness really is best understood as a set of unsought advantages ("privilege") or as an absence—a matter of not-knowing or not-caring. Du Bois urges us to (re)consider the ways that white Americans—and not only Trump supporters!—have been actively invested in and positively attached to racialized gratifications that depend on the material and symbolic devaluation of Black existence.

This book does not refute the usefulness of the conceptual tools sketched above, but it seeks, via Du Bois, to refocus attention on the complex forms of comfort, reassurance, and even pleasure that anti-Blackness has delivered to those marked "white." In other words, rather than suppose that the continuation of white supremacy is accidental, incidental, or the result of a lack or error on the part of its beneficiaries, the concept of *white gratifications* requires confronting how anti-Blackness delivers an array of rewards that are desired, sought, and defended.

Second, *gratifications*—purposely pluralized—signals an anti-reductive approach to whiteness, one that productively defies conventional oppositions that have long governed debates over racialization in the US context (and which have affected the reception of Du Bois's work). Du Bois exposes how whiteness, itself dependent upon the practices and affects of anti-Blackness, generated multiple, varied rewards for its bearers in the early to mid-20th century. This layered analysis traverses a number of familiar binaries; it challenges the presumed antagonism between realist and symbolist approaches, Marxist and Freudian paradigms, and frameworks that stress material interests vs. latent desires. The complex analysis found in Du Bois's writings scrambles such apparent divides and invites us to look at whiteness, both past and present, as a protean formation capable of generating multiple forms of gratification.

Why Whiteness?

This book centers "whiteness." This is a term Du Bois himself used and one that has become more commonplace since then. But what is the value of investigating something called "whiteness," as this book does?

First, to focus on the meaning of whiteness counters the (understandable) tendency to emphasize how racism affects those who are most harmed by it. Many studies of the United States' distinctive racial order, for example, track how racist, and especially anti-Black, practices have affected the life experiences of nonwhite Americans. Yet as Toni Morrison argues in *Playing in the Dark: Whiteness and the Literary Imagination,* it is important to counter the habit of thinking about racism exclusively in terms of the consequences for its victims. Morrison characterizes her book's intent: "My project is an effort to avert the critical gaze from the racial object to the racial subject; from the described and imagined to the describers and imaginers; from the servers to the served."[41] *Gratifications of Whiteness* is animated by a similar spirit: it seeks to examine the varied rewards enjoyed by those who are racially dominant in the United States, those who inhabit "whiteness."

Du Bois's work is a fecund resource for this examination because his writings, beginning around 1920, offered a sustained analysis of the workings of whiteness. His oeuvre undeniably foregrounds the experiences of Black Americans and "darker peoples" throughout the world—not only documenting the oppression they face but also celebrating their fortitude, creativity, and humanity. However, as this book reveals, his writings also offer a specific, developed, and valuable account of whiteness.

This brings me to the second reason this book has the shape and focus that it does. It is interested in what bell hooks calls "representations of whiteness in the black imagination."[42] The project examines how Du Bois, a formidable Black political theorist, "represented whiteness." It tacitly affirms, as hooks and other theorists of race have argued, that Black people have " 'special' knowledge of whiteness." hooks characterizes this knowledge as the product of Black people watching white people "with a critical 'ethnographic' gaze."[43] Du Bois characterizes his own understanding of "The Souls of White Folk" in even more intimate terms:

> Of them I am singularly clairvoyant. I see in and through them. I view them from unusual points of vantage. Not as a foreigner do I come, for I am

native, not foreign, bone of their thought and flesh of their language. Mine is not the knowledge of the traveler or the colonial composite of dear memories, words and wonder. Nor yet is my knowledge that which servants have of masters, or mass of class, or capitalist of artisan. Rather I see these souls undressed and from the back and side. I see the working of their entrails.

This book takes seriously Du Bois's declaration that he sees "in and through" the souls of white folk. And it turns to his middle-period writings (roughly 1920–1940) to examine the "unusual points of vantage" on whiteness that he offers. In so doing, the project differs from much of the "whiteness studies" scholarship that gained prominence in the 1990s, which often did not "include serious consideration of black voices."[44]

Third, I believe "whiteness" remains an important object of inquiry, despite the legitimate questions that have been raised about its scholarly and political value. The boom in "whiteness studies" mentioned above took place throughout the humanistic disciplines in the United States but was especially notable in the field of history. Spurred in part by the Reagan presidency and catalyzed by Roediger's 1991 book *The Wages of Whiteness*, work on "whiteness," which frequently traced its lineage to Du Bois's *Black Reconstruction*, proliferated.[45] Yet this development was questioned by some scholars, even those committed to the study of racialized inequality in the United States. Chief among the concerns was that "whiteness" was too broad to be analytically helpful and, relatedly, that the term wrongly implied the existence of a fixed, almost timeless identity.[46] These claims point out real risks that attend the examination of "whiteness" but do not fairly describe much of the actual scholarship produced, then or now.[47] The majority of that work does not treat whiteness as an a priori monolith but instead scrutinizes how "whiteness"—as a key site of racial identification in the United States—has been made and remade on the shifting terrain of politics. Exemplary scholarship of this type includes Roediger's book, Alexander Saxton's *The Rise and Fall of the White Republic: Class Politics and Mass Culture in Nineteenth Century America*, and Grace Elizabeth Hale's *Making Whiteness: The Culture of Segregation in the South, 1890–1940* in the field of history, as well as subsequent work in other disciplines that examined "whiteness" from a range of philosophical perspectives without ever reifying it, such as Charles Mills's *The Racial Contract*, Shannon Sullivan's *Revealing Whiteness*, and Joel Olson's *The Abolition of White Democracy*.[48]

Studying "whiteness" remains a worthwhile endeavor. However vexed the term may be, it is currently the best name we have for what has been a powerful and enduring, if also plastic, source of meaning and identification in the United States for at least 300 years.[49] The term helps track both continuities and discontinuities in what it has meant (and means) to have membership in the dominant racial group in the United States.[50] Provided one guards against oversimplification, inquiring into "whiteness" is important and necessary. Such investigations have already contributed to our understanding of race-making and to recognizing how race is (re)constituted over time, in particular socio-political contexts, and with real effects. Grasping the powerful-yet-changeable character of whiteness also opens up more overtly political questions: can whiteness be abolished, or at least dramatically transfigured?

Finally, I am thinking and writing about whiteness as a white person who was born and raised in the United States. I have been perceived, and moved through the world, as "white," ever since that word appeared on my birth certificate. And of course, that has meant that I have had the luxury of *not* thinking about my racialization in many contexts. Yet the impetus for this project is to bring whiteness into critical focus. More specifically, I aim to investigate how those traveling under the sign "white" have been variously *gratified*, in the past and in the present, by the workings of white supremacy, and by anti-Blackness in particular. As I explained above, this is a different approach from those that track white privilege, ignorance, or indifference. It raises the disturbing proposition that many whites in the United States, perhaps even those who are avowedly "anti-racist," remain positively attached to whiteness as an enduring source of esteem, enjoyment, and license. This unsettling inquiry, I believe, is one that implicates most white people, myself included. The hope that guides the project, however, is that grasping these dynamics is a necessary step toward the radical, creative action that might loosen these investments and forge alternative sources of gratification that can sustain more equitable forms of life.

American White Supremacy and the Black/White Paradigm

Before offering a roadmap of the upcoming chapters, there are two more aspects of the book's overarching analysis that should be noted. First, the book primarily seeks to understand the gratifications of whiteness in the

US context. Second, as the book's title and subtitle indicate,. the project understands American whiteness to be intimately bonded to anti-Blackness. It employs what has been called a "Black/white paradigm," focusing primarily on the effects of this specific dichotomous, hierarchical construction, rather than on other racialized divisions that have (re)shaped the meaning of whiteness in the US case.[51] Because these authorial decisions might seem to strain against features of Du Bois's thought, I want to explain them.

First, this project seeks to better understand the workings of whiteness within the specific terms of US political history, that is, in relation to the afterlife of slavery as it has been lived in this country. Like other scholarship that investigates shifting practices of racialization (and the production of whiteness in particular) in specific times and places within the United States, such a focus need not imply that white supremacy is anything less than global. Du Bois was, at least by the end of World War I, committed to a view of white supremacy as a worldwide system of domination that called for transnational revolutionary action by "darker peoples" around the globe.[52] Moreover, much of his middle-period work (the primary archive for this book) elaborates a simultaneously anti-racist and anti-colonialist position that presents the Jim Crow regime in the United States and the Anglo-European imperialism of the early 20th century as mutually reinforcing programs of white supremacist capitalism.

The reading of Du Bois advanced here does not overlook these internationalist commitments. Chapter 4 on whiteness as dominion, for example, investigates Du Bois's account of the "divine" belief that the earth belongs to whites—a conviction that he finds substantiated in violent forms of exploitation and dispossession within and beyond the United States. The color line, he insists, "belts the world." Racialized entitlement, operating as a kind of existential faith, is evinced both in the US system of racial marks inherited from slavery and in practices of empire building carried out around the world, in which the United States is also implicated. This book is primarily focused on how whiteness gratifies within the space of American society, but as Du Bois's middle-period writings emphasize, this question calls for a political-historical analysis that situates the United States within the global dynamics of racial capitalism.

Next, the book addresses the gratifications of whiteness primarily in relation to Blackness. Du Bois's middle-period work often did so as well, particularly when analyzing the persistence of racial caste in the United States. But just as his middle-period work increasingly exposed white supremacy as a worldwide phenomenon, it also expanded the terms of that analysis to include its effects on "yellow, brown, and black" people.[53] And Du Bois frequently conceptualized a "white world" in relation to a "dark" or "darker" world that encompassed not only "black Africa" but also "yellow Asia" and the other targets of empire.[54] Given this, and given that part of this book's intention is to open up Du Bois's theorization of whiteness to reflect on the contemporary United States—where the shift toward a "minority white" population, primarily due to an increasing Hispanic and Latino population, is widely publicized—why retain a Black/white schema?[55]

The first crucial reason is that in the United States, as Joel Olson explains, the "archetype of non-whiteness has been blackness. This is due to the original function of the racial order, which was the maintenance of slavery."[56] In other words, it is impossible to seriously examine American whiteness without tending to its constitution over and against Blackness, in the context of slavery, where "race came to life primarily as the signifier of the master/slave relation."[57] Du Bois's account of the US racial order emphasizes the continuing relevance of these historical origins. In *Dusk of Dawn: An Essay Toward an Autobiography of a Race Concept* (1940) he writes that in the Jim Crow regime, dark skin remained an "unending, inescapable sign of slavery." And throughout his work, the "souls of white folk," no less than the "souls of black folk," reflect what he calls "the social heritage of slavery."[58]

The decision to focus on the relationship between whiteness and anti-Blackness in this book does not imply that Black people alone have suffered under American white supremacy, either in the past or in the present, nor does it entail an understanding of whiteness as solely or entirely forged in relation to (anti-)Blackness. The white/Black frame is instead a purposeful methodological choice, which, in the words of Cheryl Harris, seeks not to "accurately reflect racial demographics" but rather to "describe racial power."[59] This project thus recognizes that the boundaries of whiteness in the United States have shifted over time, as is well documented, yet maintains, per Lewis Gordon, that Blackness has consistently served as "the prime racial signifier."[60] In other words, although the contours of white racial identity can and do change, as Lani Gunier and Gerald Torres explain, "whiteness" in the United States remains a measure of "one's social distance from blackness."[61] To examine American whiteness thus requires tending to the way Blackness has served as a "fixed antithesis" over time, even amid dramatic political and social transformations.[62]

Overview

The following chapters explore the "gratifications of whiteness" that Du Bois conceptualizes in writings published between roughly 1920 and 1940. This is an especially fertile period, one that documents the radicalization of Du Bois's thinking since *The Souls of Black Folk* (1903) and includes Du Bois's famous break with the National Association for the Advancement of Colored People (NAACP) in 1934. Bookended by *Darkwater: Voices from Within the Veil* (1920) and *Dusk of Dawn* (1940), this period also includes the magisterial *Black Reconstruction* (1935) and many important essays published in *The Crisis* and elsewhere.

The next three chapters approach the "gratifications of whiteness" by exploring key motifs drawn from Du Bois's writings, which figure whiteness as a wage, as pleasure, and as dominion, respectively. While the investigation of these three motifs is not intended to provide a comprehensive account of Du Bois's views of whiteness, it illuminates Du Bois's multifaceted approach. In particular, these reflections reveal that Du Bois understood the US regime of racial capitalism as a necessary starting point for comprehending American whiteness in its full complexity but did not reduce whiteness to a simplistic "bribe" for maintaining capitalist rule. Instead, as we will see, he presents an intriguing, polyvalent account of the ways that American whiteness has served as a potent source of varied gratifications for its bearers.

The book interprets these three motifs—wage, pleasure, dominion—first and foremost in relation to the dynamic political conditions of Du Bois's time, yet it also brings these reflections into a creative encounter with the present. Although racial capitalism is lived today in the United States in forms Du Bois could scarcely have imagined, in the chapters that follow, I show that his account of anti-Blackness as a source of plural—and deeply disturbing—forms of white gratification also speaks to us here and now. Thus, Chapters 2, 3, and 4 each include a "coda" that inventively extends each of Du Bois's motifs in new directions, in order to reflect on contemporary conditions.

In Chapter 2, "Whiteness as Wage," I revisit Du Bois's most well-known formulation of whiteness as a "public and psychological wage" premised on the denigration of Blackness, which "feeds the vanity" of even the poorest white Americans, both before and after emancipation. I show first, contra some prominent interpretations, that Du Bois's formulation of the "wage" cannot be reduced to "economy first" dogma that understands racial division solely as a mechanism of capitalist social control. Rather, the Du Boisean wage, though "compensatory," is situated within a textured reading of American political history that emphasizes the persistent co-constitution of capitalism and racism and is reluctant to privilege either class- or race- based hierarchy as a more "fundamental" target for resistance. Next, I show that the wage argument has been further simplified in both scholarly and popular commentary, because "psychological" has taken precedence over "public." To redress this, I argue that the wage that accompanies the classification "white" is, for Du Bois, a *socialized* benefit—one that also denies Black citizens "rights of enjoyment and accommodation in the commonwealth." The third section explores how this wage has been passionately—and violently—defended by its recipients. I pay special attention to Du Bois's productively ambivalent account of responsibility, which suggests that when poor white people in particular fight to maintain their racialized advantages, they do so *both* as pawns of the capitalist class and as knowing oppressors of Black Americans. The chapter's coda reflects on decades-long opposition to proactive racial integration policies in K–12 public schooling in the United States. I contend that this political reality demonstrates, far more than Trump's narrow win, the extent to which whiteness has been widely defended as a "wage," one that is public no less than psychological, well into the 21st century.

Chapter 3 investigates a dimension of Du Bois's thinking about white subjectification that is less familiar than the wage. In "Whiteness as Pleasure" I bring into focus the way Du Bois figures American whiteness as an affective investment in Black pain. First, across multiple works, and most pointedly in *Dusk of Dawn*'s essays, Du Bois wrestles with what he refers to as the "irrationality" of anti-Black racism. I show that the "subconscious," "unconscious," "irrational," and "habitual" forces that Du Bois references are linked to anti-Black violence in particular. His writings suggest that racial caste persists in the United States in part because of the "sadistic" enjoyment and "vindictive joy" that anti-Black brutality delivers to whites (both as perpetrators and observers). Beginning around 1917, Du Bois emphasizes the gratuitous nature of such violence and the apparent pleasure it generates, thereby challenging strictly political-economic explanations of such acts. I further elaborate the problem of white sadism Du Bois's work raises by considering his relationship to a particular event—the 1899 lynching of Sam Hose in Alabama—that looms large in his later autobiographical reflections. Hose's public murder represents for Du Bois an appetitive, festive form of cruelty that seems to defy functionalist explanations. Ultimately, I contend

that Du Bois *simultaneously* argued that race hatred helped maintain capitalism by facilitating the subjugation of Black Americans as a "lower proletariat" (delivering benefits not only to white bosses but also to white
workers) *and* that anti-Black white supremacy, particularly in its most brutal
manifestations, was not merely a side effect of the economic order but a powerful source of pleasure in its own right. To build on this insight, the chapter's
coda considers how Du Bois's both/and approach speaks to contemporary
left debates over the character of anti-Black racism in the United States,
which tend to be divided sharply between political-economic interpretations and afropessimist assessments. I suggest that Du Bois's work invites us
to reject these seemingly opposed views as a false choice: today's anti-Black
practices, including targeted incarceration, are matters of the American political economy as well as its libidinal economy.

The fourth chapter, "Whiteness as Dominion," continues to explore how
anti-Blackness, according to Du Bois, has supplied multiple forms of gratification to whites. As the previous chapters showed, in addition to conceptual-
izing a "public and psychological wage" that secures social standing, Du Bois
also links whiteness to sadistic pleasure derived from Black pain. This chapter
examines a third motif: whiteness as dominion. In the same body of work in
which the other motifs appear, Du Bois presents "modern" whiteness as a proprietary orientation toward the planet in general and toward "darker peoples" in
particular. This "title to the universe" is part of chattel slavery's uneven afterlife
in which the historical fact of "propertized human life" endures as a racialized
ethos of ownership. I examine how this "title" is expressed and reinforced in
the 20th century by the Jim Crow system of racial signs in the United States
and by violent "colonial aggrandizement" worldwide. The analytic of white dominion, I argue, allows Du Bois to productively link phenomena sometimes
regarded as discrete, namely, domestic and global forms of white supremacy
and practices of exploitation and dispossession. Ultimately, the chapter argues
that the entitlement Du Bois associates with whiteness is best understood as
a quasi-theological worldview, a meaning-making horizon that may facilitate
the transaction of the "wage" as well as sadistic circuits of pleasure, but which
is not identical with either. I conclude by reflecting on two recent examples
of racialized dominion: the Bundy standoffs in Nevada and Oregon and multiple incidents in which white Americans have contacted law enforcement to
report the presence of Black people in everyday spaces—the criminalization of
"living while Black." These phenomena suggest that embodied belief in whites'
"divine" claim to "ownership of the earth" persists here and now.

In Chapter 5, I ask the questions: If the gratifications of whiteness are many, as this inquiry suggests, then what does this mean for anti-racist struggles? What strategies can interrupt the varied, plural forms of racialized reward that have long helped sustain white supremacy? If Du Bois exposes diverse gratifications attached to whiteness in the postemancipation United States—where it has offered a sense of superior social standing, especially for the poor; served as a modality of sadistic pleasure; and provided a comprehensive, aggrandizing worldview—and if such gratifications persist in altered form in the 21st century, can these patterns ever be undone? How? This chapter takes up this important question in two steps. I first examine Du Bois's persistent interest in "propaganda" as an indispensable tool for combating white-over-Black domination. Exploring the term's multiple meanings in Du Bois's work, the chapter focuses in particular on its significa-tion in *Dusk of Dawn*. Here Du Bois repeatedly insists that typical methods of education and persuasion favored by liberals cannot effectively reach the "subconscious" and "unconscious" forces that support white supremacy. In other words, the gratifications of whiteness operate in ways that are not reachable by "appeal or argument." Rather, in place of conventional reform tactics, "a persistent campaign of propaganda," Du Bois posits, is necessary. I show that Du Bois uses the word in this context to name a wide-ranging and multifaceted collective project, one still to be defined but which is simultane-ously political, aesthetic, and economic, and therefore capable of addressing the wide-ranging and multifaceted reality of white supremacy. Although his layered commentary on "propaganda" remains suggestive rather than defin-itive, it presents an invitation that I take up in the second part of the chapter. I inquire into the strategies and tactics of resistance of the Black Lives Matter (BLM) movement in the United States, paying special attention to the range of creative protest practices undertaken in its name. I suggest that their varied repertoire—placed in the service of what Du Bois called "the right of black folk to love and enjoy"—resonates with his vision of an inventive, protean politics of Black liberation. Finally, while BLM's innovative actions are rightly centered on the defense and celebration of Black existence, their efforts also unsettle some of the default presumptions and habits of anti-Blackness that have long fed the gratifications of whiteness.

The Epilogue considers recent signs—in public opinion, protest activity, and popular culture—indicating that more white Americans are alert to problems of racial domination than in the recent past. Although this ap-parent shift is ambiguous and fraught, it nonetheless presents an opening for potential radicalization, I argue. Borrowing from Du Bois's political theory of racial capitalism and his radical-utopian vision of a free society, as well as later Black Power models of white political agency, the Epilogue affirms bold emancipatory projects such as contemporary abolitionism as sites for organizational and coalitional work by whites. The patterns of racialized reward that lie at the center of the book impede, without entirely foreclosing, the transformed society Du Bois long imagined.

2

Whiteness as Wage

Reaping the Rewards of Racial Capitalism

The most well-known formulation of American whiteness found in the writings of Du Bois is that of the "public and psychological wage." In *Black Reconstruction*, he uses this memorable phrase to comment on the tenacity of racial caste in the United States. Explaining in 1935 why the country had so consistently defied "the theory of labor class unity," Du Bois points to the tendency of white workers in the late 19th and early 20th century to identify with other whites on the basis of race rather than with other workers on the basis of class. He suggests that they were incentivized to do so because their "low wage" was supplemented by a different sort of payment. Even though white workers were exploited as laborers, they were rewarded as whites. Americans marked as "white" enjoyed special social standing, regardless of their economic position, a standing that depended upon the "badge of inferiority" attached to Black persons.[1] Key claims embedded in Du Bois's idea of the wage—whiteness provides meaningful "compensation" (Du Bois's term) for citizens otherwise exploited by the organization of capitalism, the value of whiteness depends on the devaluation of Black existence, and the racialized benefits enjoyed by whites are "public and psychological" as well as material—shaped subsequent efforts to theorize white identity and to grasp the (non)formation of political coalitions in the United States.

This chapter begins to explore Du Bois's pluralistic account of the gratifications of whiteness by investigating the wage, the first and most recognizable of the three motifs examined in this book. Yet while the metaphorical wage is the most familiar, it is also the most misunderstood. Most problematically, Du Bois's idea of whiteness as wage has often been severed from the important, anti-reductionist account of racial capitalism in which it is embedded. As a result, it has sometimes been deployed in overly simplistic ways that render it as nothing more than a bribe—a social control mechanism that secures capitalist domination. While there is a kernel of truth in this reading, it will not suffice.

The Gratifications of Whiteness. Ella Myers, Oxford University Press. © Oxford University Press 2022.
DOI: 10.1093/oso/9780197556764.003.0002

To better understand how the "public and psychological wage" gratifies—or "feeds the vanity" of—its recipients, this chapter proceeds in four steps. First, rather than focusing directly on the "wage" idea, I begin by analyzing the account of (what has become known as) *racial capitalism* found in Du Bois's middle-period writings. I show that he makes a compelling case for the co-constitution of racism and capitalism, one that resists placing greater analytical or political weight on either term. The chapter argues that in order to comprehend the "public and psychological wage" as a lasting source of white gratification, it must be situated within Du Bois's trenchant reading of the political history of racial capitalism in the United States. With this context in place, the inquiry returns to the "wage" motif in its specificity. My reading stresses its dual public *and* psychological character, which has been overlooked by commentary that neglects the first descriptor. The chapter reveals that the racialized esteem Du Bois envisions as a metaphorical wage is bound up with the enjoyment of socialized goods—access to a "commonwealth" that is (de jure or de facto) for whites only. The third section explores how this wage has been passionately—and often violently—defended by its recipients. I pay special attention to Du Bois's productively ambivalent account of responsibility, which suggests that when poor white people in particular fight to maintain their racialized advantages, they do so *both* as "tools" of the capitalist class and as willing dominators of Black Americans. The chapter concludes by exploring long-standing opposition to school integration since *Brown v. Board of Education*—a potent reminder of the extent to which white citizens have consistently organized, in varied and innovative ways, to maintain this wage.

Both/And: Du Bois's Anti-Reductionist Account of Racial Capitalism

Du Bois's understanding of the "public and psychological wage" as a source of white gratification, unpacked in detail in the next section, is embedded in a distinctive account of *racial capitalism*. This term does not appear in Du Bois's vast oeuvre; however, I follow Cedric Robinson's usage in *Black Marxism: The Making of the Black Radical Tradition*, where it names a key political-theoretical claim at the center of Du Bois's work since at least the 1930s: capitalism and racism are inseparable.[2] At its most fundamental, "The term 'racial capitalism' requires its users to recognize that capitalism *is* racial capitalism," in the words of Jodi Melamed.[3] Du Bois's middle- and late-period work does so, first, by emphasizing the key role that chattel slavery played in the emergence and expansion of capitalism: it was Negro slavery in America, Du Bois writes, upon which "modern commerce and industry was founded."[4] Yet the concept of racial capitalism nascent in Du Bois's thought is not limited to a thesis about historical origins. He shows that the partitioning by "race" that facilitated enslavement and the growth of modern capitalism continued to structure postemancipation capitalist society, where Black workers, "the ultimate exploited," were subjected to distinctive, coercive forms of surplus extraction.[5] His writings explore the ongoing imbrication of racial domination and capitalist accumulation in the 20th century, confirming Ruth Wilson Gilmore's pithy declaration, "Capitalism: never not racial."[6]

The work by Du Bois that lies at the center of this book (roughly 1920–1940) challenged two prominent perspectives of his era: anti-racist liberals' commitment to capitalism and the Left's myopic focus on class exploitation to the exclusion of racial oppression.[7] Although Du Bois's writing in this period is strongly influenced by his reading of Marx and presents a powerful critique of capitalism as a (changeable) source of human misery, he also objects, again and again, to the tendency of the Left to reduce racism to a subsidiary effect of class-based domination. In place of that reductivist view, Du Bois stresses that while racism and capitalism cannot be thought of (or effectively resisted) in isolation from one another, neither can they be collapsed together nor rank-ordered in terms of conceptual or political priority. They are effectively "conjoined twins," as Ibram X. Kendi puts it.[8] Yet Du Bois's both/and style of thought is at times obscured by his passionate and consistent calls for economic revolution in writings from this period. Below I explore the meaning of those calls, in order to shed light on Du Bois's powerful account of racial capitalism, which ultimately refutes any simple economy-first framework.

Black Reconstruction's narrative tells the story of a nascent socialist revolution. Most obviously, Du Bois depicts Black Union soldiers as participants in a "general strike" and describes the democratizing Reconstruction governments of the South as instances of the "dictatorship of labor." Even more broadly, however, the book centers on the drama of a thwarted economic revolution. In Chapter 14, titled "Counter-Revolution of Property," Du Bois notes that "the sudden enfranchisement of a mass of laborers threatens fundamental and far-reaching change, no matter what their race or color." Specifically, Du Bois notes, this shift in power threatens changes to the "prevailing manner of holding and distributing wealth." Yet this transformation was never realized, Du Bois laments. The struggle for suffrage was just and important, Du Bois charges, but "Negro and White labor . . . ought to have tried to change the basis of property and redistribute income" and did not. Pointedly, Du Bois attributes this inaction to a fundamental flaw within liberal thought: "Liberalism did not understand," Du Bois says, that a truly democratic government in the United States that included all Black and white people on equal terms required a "revolution [that] was economic and involved force." A well-meaning anti-racist like Charles Sumner might be forgiven, Du Bois grants, because "that other Charles—Karl Marx—had not yet published *Das Kapital* to prove to men that economic power underlies politics." Still, the stakes of liberal misunderstanding were high: abolitionists "did not know that when they let the dictatorship of labor be overthrown in the South they surrendered the hope of democracy in America for all men."[9]

This conviction—that rule by labor rather than by capital is the best way to secure "general wellbeing" for all citizens and is a prerequisite for genuine democracy—also animates Du Bois's assessment of later political turning points in the United States. In an essay written in 1935, the same year that *Black Reconstruction* was published, Du Bois reiterates his account of Reconstruction as a "failure," one that "has simply made the fact more clear that without economic reconstruction freedom and power is impossible."[10] Yet this crucial lesson had still not been learned, Du Bois warned. While the goal of thoroughgoing "economic reconstruction" initially guided the New Deal, he notes, it succumbed to a more limited agenda: "instead of real reform, we are going to have restoration of capitalism."[11] Du Bois had already pinpointed the task that still awaited his country: "The rebuilding, whether it comes now or a century later, will and must go back to the basic principles of Reconstruction in the United States during 1867–1876—Land, Light and Leading for slaves black, brown, yellow and white, under the dictatorship of the proletariat."[12]

Du Bois's analysis sometimes presents class struggle as the hidden motor of what appear to be racial antagonisms. In *Darkwater*'s "Of Work and Wealth" (1920), Du Bois addresses the violent East St. Louis Riots of 1917 in which white mobs, reacting to an influx of Black workers (some of them "scabs"), killed up to 200 Black people and drove another 6,000 out of the city.[13] (See Chapter 3 for further discussion of Du Bois's interpretation of this event.)

Du Bois refocuses attention away from the immediate conflict between white and Black residents to other significant, though concealed, forces:

> Dislikes, jealousies, hatreds,—undoubtedly like the race hatred in East St. Louis; the jealousy of English and German; the dislike of the Jew and the Gentile. But these are, after all, surface disturbances, sprung from ancient habit more than from present reason. They persist and are encouraged because of deeper, mightier currents. If the white working-men of East St. Louis felt sure that Negro workers would not and could not take the bread and cake from their mouths, their race hatred would never have been translated into murder. If the black workingmen of the South could earn a decent living under decent circumstances at home, they would not be compelled to underbid their white fellows. Thus the shadow of hunger, in a world which never needs to be hungry, drives us to war and murder and hate. But why does hunger shadow so vast a mass of men? Manifestly because in the great organizing of men for work a few of the participants come out with more wealth than they can possibly use, while a vast number emerge with less than can decently support life.[14]

Beneath the "race hatred" on display in East St. Louis, Du Bois finds something "deeper, mightier" at work—class struggle. Many intergroup antagonisms, Du Bois suggests, are promoted by a capitalist order that rewards only a "few." In places like East St. Louis, conditions are ripe for racial hostility because all workers—white and Black—suffer from existential insecurity (though not equally). A "shadow of hunger," endemic to capitalism itself, haunts those who must sell their labor power to survive, making them nervous and desperate, and inclined to lash out. Yet "surface disturbances"—Black workers' "underbidding" white workers, anti-Black violence carried out by white mobs—conceal a more profound question, according to Du Bois: "why does hunger shadow so vast a mass of men?"

Similarly, the interpretation of Reconstruction in *Black Reconstruction* alleges that what appear to be conflicts between racial groups are actually class conflicts. When summarizing the "counter-revolution" by capitalists that ended Reconstruction, Du Bois writes:

> Beneath the race issue, and unconsciously of more fundamental weight, was the economic issue. Men were seeking again to reestablish the domination of property in Southern politics. By getting rid of the black labor vote,

they would take their first and substantial step. By raising the race issue, they would secure domination over the white labor vote, and thus the oligarchy that ruled the South before the war would be in part restored to power.[15]

Class domination is key; it explains the push to disenfranchise Blacks. "Beneath" what look obviously like practices of race-based exclusion, Du Bois posits another dynamic: the effort to resurrect oligarchy. It was in pursuit of this aim, he says, that "the race issue" was invoked so consistently in the Reconstruction era. Class struggle seems primary in this formulation: white supremacist beliefs and practices are effective tools for the ruling class's exercise of broad social control.

In "The Concept of Race" (1940), Du Bois anticipates later historiographical arguments concerning the origins of racism, when he states that anti-Black racism did not lead to chattel slavery so much as it was developed to justify that profitable institution.[16] He explains that his visits to Africa led him "more clearly to see the close connection between race and wealth." More specifically, Du Bois describes

> a realization that the income-bearing value of race prejudice was the cause and not the result of theories of race inferiority; that particularly in the United States the income of the Cotton Kingdom based on black slavery caused the passionate belief in Negro inferiority and the determination to enforce it even by arms.[17]

Here Du Bois alleges that "passionate belief in Negro inferiority" was instrumentally useful for the justification and maintenance of chattel slavery, a system that he also places at the heart of American capitalism and the growth of modern industry.[18] Capitalism seems to be the prime mover in this formulation; "theories of race inferiority" fulfilled an important function, enabling the owners of the "Cotton Kingdom" to become rich. Anti-Black racism, Du Bois seems to say, emerged largely because it served the needs of capital. Although he does not delve into the thorny question that would preoccupy later historians—how to explain the "initial act of differential treatment that does not invoke racism . . . as a causal factor"[19]—it is clear that Du Bois believes white supremacy, and specifically "belief in Negro inferiority," served the economic interests of capitalists in the formative days of what would become the United States.

Du Bois contends that the "recognition and preservation of so-called racial distinctions" was indispensable to capitalism's development—a crucial insight that has shaped later scholarship on racial capitalism.[20] Robinson's *Black Marxism*, for example, emphasizes the tendency of burgeoning European capitalism "not to homogenize but to differentiate," emphasizing and consolidating regional and cultural variations into "racial" types.[21] Michael C. Dawson explains, "Understanding the formation of capitalism requires a consideration of . . . the ontological distinction between superior and inferior humans—codified as race—that was necessary for slavery, colonialism, the theft of lands in the Americas, and genocide," the violent practices of accumulation that built modern capitalism.[22] When Du Bois describes theories of racial inferiority as "income-bearing" and argues that "belief in Negro inferiority" served the purposes of amassing wealth in the "Cotton Kingdom," he places racial differentiation at the center of capitalism. As Melamed explains, "Capital can only be capital when it is accumulating, and it can only accumulate by producing and moving through relations of severe inequality among human groups." In other words, "racism enshrines the inequalities that capitalism requires."[23]

Du Bois maintains that the fabrication of "so-called racial distinctions"— the partitioning of the world's people in accordance with a scale of human value—is an *ongoing* and *constitutive* feature of capitalism, not limited to its origins. Differentiation and hierarchization according to "race" facilitate the division between "free labor and less than free labor," in the words of Nikhil Singh, even after the formal end of slavery.[24] Stressing that "racial distinctions" remain central to the workings of capitalism, Du Bois commented repeatedly in the 1930s that the "black proletariat is not a part of the white proletariat." Although white and Black workers both have legitimate grievances against capitalists, Du Bois insists that the exploitation experienced by Black workers is qualitatively distinct: it is "more fundamental and indefensible."[25] Black workers in the Jim Crow era are targets of super-exploitation, a particular form of subordination by "organized capital" that reinforces the color line.[26] Racial differentiation remains integral to capitalism over time, according to Du Bois, finding expression in phenomena ranging from "chattel slavery to the worst paid, sweated, mobbed, and cheated labor" in the 20th century.[27]

Capitalism relies upon and benefits from racialized partitioning, enabling what Saidiya Hartman calls "modern forms of bonded labor," even after the official end of slavery.[28] In 1935 Du Bois describes a "dark and vast sea of human labor" who are "enslaved in all but name." He writes, "Out of the exploitation of the dark proletariat comes the Surplus Value."[29] The super-exploitation of the "dark proletariat" in the postemancipation United States, he shows in *Black Reconstruction*, relies on an array of coercive techniques, including debt peonage, compulsory labor schemes, vagrancy statutes crimi-nalizing those not holding labor contracts, split labor markets, and discrimi-nation and exclusion (both de jure and de facto).[30]

Still, while Du Bois clearly argues that the workings of anti-Black racism in the United States cannot be understood apart from an analysis of capitalism, he also challenges the idea that racial stratification is only or simply an ep-iphenomenon of class domination. He explicitly and repeatedly rejects the notion that economic transformation could, in itself, establish racial equality. His writings from the period under discussion take aim at this conceit often:

> Socialists and Communists assume that state control of industry by a ma-jority of citizens or by a dictatorship of laborers, is going in some magic way to abolish race prejudice of its own accord without special effort or special study or special plan; and they want us Negroes to assume on faith that this will be the result.[31]

Such faith, Du Bois insists, is unwarranted. Racial hierarchy will not crumble "automatically" with the demise of capitalism—a point he returns to again and again.[32] Although the "dogma of class struggle" instructs that a socialist or communist revolution will inevitably abolish racism, Du Bois labels this a groundless assumption, nothing more than a kind of "magical" thinking.[33] The "dogma" that Du Bois refutes treats racism as a mere side effect of capi-talist exploitation, a view that is especially untenable, he says, in the case of the United States. In essays from the 1930s, Du Bois often advises that those concerned with "the Negro problem" would benefit from certain insights of Marxism, yet he argues that the race-blindness of Marxism calls for major revision, especially if it is to address the American social order. He writes that while he is "convinced of the essential truth of Marxian philosophy . . . I must ask myself seriously, as must every Negro, 'Is there any automatic power in socialism to override and suppress race prejudice?'"[34] And he continues, quipping that there is certainly no proof of this in America. Indeed, if Marxism is to have any critical purchase on US society, it must be "modi-fied," Du Bois argues in his important "Marxism and the Negro Problem" essay (1933). Granting that Marx's philosophy may offer a "true diagnosis of

19th century Europe," Du Bois declares that it must be altered and amended "in the United States of America and so far as Negroes are concerned." The oppression of Black people, he continues, is carried out "equally" by "white capitalists" and "the white proletariat."[35] Black people are not only subject to exploitation by capital but also harmed by a race-specific form of hate that is not restricted to any economic class of whites.

Even though Du Bois calls for an economic alternative to capitalism, be believes that anti-Black racism is so formidable—and so valuable to dispossessed whites—that it has prevented the kind of alliance necessary for revolutionary action against capitalism. Organizations of the early 20th century that were meant to serve as sites for class-based solidarity—labor unions and socialist and Communist political parties—were direct targets of Du Bois's critique. As he remarked more than once, the "black proletariat is not a part of the white proletariat."[36] And this exclusion is not accidental; for Du Bois it is evidence of the tenacity and reach of "race hate." He puts the point starkly: "No revolt of a white proletariat could be started if its object was to make black workers their economic, political, and social equals."[37] And no theory of working class unity, however elegant, can get around the fact that, on the ground, a formidable and unacknowledged project remains: "we have to convince the working classes of the world that black men, brown men, and yellow men are human beings."[38]

Du Bois's critique is attached to an alternative conceptualization of the dynamics of race and class that contends that anti-Blackness and capitalism are simultaneously connected *and* irreducible. From this both/and perspective, struggles for Black liberation are, in the words of David Roediger, "not separate from or subsidiary to the question of class conflict."[39] Du Bois illustrates this difficult point in more than one essay with the idea of "vertical and horizontal" social divisions. Writing of Communist thought, he says, "This philosophy did not envisage a situation where instead of a horizontal division of classes, there was a vertical fissure, a complete separation of classes by race, cutting square across the economic layer."[40] The image of cross-cutting lines expresses Du Bois's conviction that capitalism and racism intersect and interact, while also carrying independent force; neither is simply a side effect of the other.

Not all readers of Du Bois embrace—or even acknowledge—his important efforts to conceptualize the co-constitution of race and class and address their entanglement without collapsing one into the other. Theodore W. Allen, for example, cites Du Bois as the major influence upon his important

two-volume work, *The Invention of the White Race*. Yet Allen's argument—
that the "white race was invented as a social control formation" in the United
States—draws selectively on aspects of Du Bois's thought that support Allen's
central thesis that anti-Black racism was and is *entirely* a device for ensuring
class domination, beginning in the 17th century, and extending into the 20th
century. Allen's account of white supremacy treats "class society" as the unquestioned starting point of analysis and racism is explained completely in
terms of its efficacy in stabilizing rule by capital. As we saw above, elements
of Du Bois's writings can be marshaled in support of such a view, but to do so
in the unqualified way Allen does requires overlooking Du Bois's trenchant
challenges to socialist and communist orthodoxy and his various efforts to
link capitalism and white supremacy without ranking them as primary and
secondary.[41]

David Roediger's scholarship, also principally indebted to Du Bois, affirms
rather than conceals the complexity of Du Bois's thought. Confronting
Marxist approaches like Allen's that posit race as merely ideological and class
as "objective," Roediger writes that this view advances "the notion that class
(or 'the economic') is more real, more fundamental, more basic, or more
important than race."[42] Du Bois's genius, Roediger argues, lies precisely in
his "attention to how race and class interpenetrate" in the United States.[43]
Roediger's groundbreaking book, *The Wages of Whiteness*, directly borrows
and develops Du Bois's idea of a whiteness as a "public and psychological
wage" forged within a capitalist class structure. Yet Roediger, citing Du Bois,
stresses that racial stratification is not only a tool of class domination.[44] Du
Bois understood that white-over-Black hierarchies in the United States,
firmly entrenched by centuries of formal and informal enforcement, were
sustained not only by "economic exploitation" but also by "racial folk-lore."[45]
While Allen cites Du Bois to argue that class relations are bedrock in ways
that race relations are not, Roediger finds in his work a different lesson: "To
set race within social formations is absolutely necessary, but to reduce race to
class is damaging."[46]

I turn in the remainder of this section to three specific points Du Bois makes
in his 1920–1940 writings that capture his both/and approach, according to
which racism is neither "separate from" nor "subsidiary" to class oppression.
First, although Du Bois (as we saw) argued in *Darkwater* that confronting
and ending the oppression of Black people requires challenging capitalism,
this claim is attached to the seemingly opposite argument presented in the
same text (and others)—that resisting class-based oppression depends upon

directly organizing against anti-Black racism. Second, as his image of "horizontal and vertical" divisions implied, Du Bois often grants equal weight to class hierarchies and racial hierarchies and at times even suggests that racial stratification is a more powerful force in his contemporary United States than class stratification. Finally, Du Bois disturbs the tendency among leftists to think of race-based oppression as superstructural by locating racialization *within* the economic "foundation" of society.

By 1920, Du Bois was adamant that capitalism must be overturned and that an economic revolution was necessary for remaking white/Black relations in the United States. We saw this clearly in his "Of Work and Wealth" essay, which argued that material suffering ("the shadow of hunger") generated racial animus and violence such as the anti-Black riots in East St. Louis. However, even as he seeks to locate the "deeper, mightier currents" driving racial conflict, Du Bois does not present class relations as the privileged site of political intervention. Indeed, immediately after arguing that a remedy for racial injustice requires economic transformation, Du Bois insists that the reverse is also true. Noting that "the great and real revolution" of industry—both necessary and inevitable, he says—will raise difficult questions about which human wants ought to be satisfied, how industry ought to be organized, and who will be authorized to make these judgments, he continues: "But this is not the need of the revolution, or indeed, perhaps its real beginning. What we must decide sometime is who is to be considered 'men.' "[47] The "real beginning" of economic revolution, Du Bois says, lies not with formulating a program for the practical reorganization of industry, but with confronting a more basic and profound question: who counts as human, and therefore as entitled to the benefits of socialization, in the first place.

Du Bois's move here implies that economic revolution cannot bypass the problem of racial domination. He makes this point even more emphatically in the form of a demand and a threat: "These disinherited darker peoples must either share in the future industrial democracy or overturn the world."[48] For the full inclusion of "darker people" to occur, direct efforts to combat race hatred are required. Indeed, recognizing and responding to racism, Du Bois believes, is the prerequisite for the economic transformation he and others on the left call for. He writes in 1920, "Do we want the wants of American Negroes satisfied? Most certainly not, and that negative is the greatest hindrance today to the reorganization of work and redistribution of wealth, not only in America, but in the world."[49] If economic transformation is necessary to achieve racial equality, so too is some measure of racial equality necessary to achieve economic transformation. While those on the left regularly advanced the first portion of this proposition without the second, Du Bois insists upon a reciprocal dynamic. In another essay written 16 years later, he re-emphasized this point. Having defined the pressing task for socialists and communists in the United States in 1936 to be fostering class consciousness among workers, he writes that the "first proof of conversion" to class consciousness is "the abolition of race prejudice."[50] The constitution of workers as a class is not a given, and the project of constructing such a class requires directly attacking racialized hierarchies.

A second important intervention conveys Du Bois's refusal to treat class stratification as more real than the cleavages of race. "The Colored World Within," published in *Dusk of Dawn* in 1940, extends the metaphor of a social order split both horizontally and vertically and goes further to suggest that racial division may be the most significant social reality at present. "The Communist philosophy" in the opening decades of the 20th century has to face the fact, Du Bois writes, that "the split between white and Black workers was greater than that between white workers and capitalists; and this split depended not simply on economic exploitation but on racial folk-lore grounded on centuries of instinct, habit, and thought and implemented by the conditioned reflex of visible color."[51] Not only does Du Bois insist upon the continuing power of anti-Black racism, but he also specifies that its recalcitrance cannot be explained by its economic value alone; notions of white superiority and Black inferiority are part of a shared inheritance that is lived perhaps bodily, operating as "instinct" and "reflex." Du Bois thus grants to anti-Blackness an independent vitality that is absent from formulations that treat American racism as secondary to, and wholly explicable in terms of, capitalist profiteering.

Finally, Du Bois posits the irreducibility of racial oppression by modifying the familiar metaphor of an economic structure/superstructure. We saw before that in *Darkwater*'s "Of Work and Wealth" and *Black Reconstruction*, class struggle was sometimes presented as an underlying mechanism that explained apparently racial conflict, including the 1917 East St. Louis riots and the "counter-revolution" that brought Reconstruction to an end. However, in addition to suggesting that economic relations lie "beneath" seemingly racial relations, Du Bois makes a different and striking claim in *Dusk of Dawn*: "The economic foundation of the modern world was based on the recognition and preservation of so-called racial distinctions."[52] This statement is provocative and important because it simultaneously references the conventional Marxist notion of "economic foundation" yet radically revises it so that "racial distinctions" are incorporated into the founding structure rather than cast as effects of it. When Du Bois continues, "In accordance with this, not only Negro slavery could be justified, but the Asiatic coolie profitably used and the labor classes in white countries kept in their places by low wages," he makes clear that capitalism *is* racial capitalism.

Collecting the Public and Psychological Wage

Black Reconstruction, where the idea of the "public and psychological wage" appears, offers a historical materialist analysis of the struggle over slavery, epitomized by Du Bois's rendering of slaves' actions during the war as a "general strike." Yet he insists that the domination of Blacks by whites, both before and after the Civil War, was never simply a matter of profiteering in a conventional economic sense. To be sure, anti-Black racism "pays," as Du Bois knew, as when white-only labor unions in the late 19th and early 20th century excluded Black members and secured better jobs and higher wages for themselves.[53] But the insight that has captured so many readers' attention is Du Bois's identification of a payment made to white workers that is less tangible but perhaps no less significant than a padded paycheck.

The oft-cited passage appears in Chapter 16 of *Black Reconstruction,* where Du Bois traces the South's trajectory since 1876 "back toward slavery" (the chapter's title). Reflecting on the tenacity of racial caste in the United States, Du Bois argues that the country has consistently defied "the theory of labor class unity." Rather than white and Black labor seeing themselves as "one class" with shared interests, a "wedge" has divided them. To explain the estrangement between Black and white workers, Du Bois continues:

> It must be remembered that the white group of laborers, while they received a low wage, were compensated in part by a sort of public and psychological wage. They were given public deference and titles of courtesy because they were white. They were admitted freely with all classes of white people to public functions, public parks, and the best schools. The police were drawn from their ranks, and the courts, dependent upon their votes, treated them with such leniency as to encourage lawlessness. Their vote selected public officials, and while this had small effect upon the economic situation, it

had great effect upon their personal treatment and the deference shown to them.[54]

This passage reflects Du Bois's view that both before and after the Civil War, poor working whites in the United States reaped real, and not only monetary, benefits linked to the degradation of Black persons. In *Black Reconstruction* and other texts written between 1920 and 1940, Du Bois analyzes whiteness as an enduring form of compensation made available under the terms of racial capitalism in the United States.

The distinctive "wage" bridges North and South, antebellum and postbellum societies, but its initial conceptualization appears in relation to "poor whites" in the slave South. Long before the phrase "public and psychological wage" appears in Chapter 16, Du Bois introduces the concept of whiteness as compensation and attributes to it a pivotal disciplinary role within the system of chattel slavery. Poor white Southerners, Du Bois alleges, held the system of slavery intact, acting as its "special police force." For the propertyless white, performing the role of enforcer "fed his vanity because it associated him with the masters."[55] In other words, even the poorest whites were rewarded with the sense that they shared a *status* with their economic superiors. This status depended upon a cross-class "association" among those with "pale" skin united on the basis of their shared identity as nonslaves.[56]

What this meant, according to Du Bois, was that class struggle to contest the planter class was effectively foreclosed, "nullified by deep-rooted antagonism to the Negro, whether slave or free."[57] Moreover, this dynamic was not restricted to the South. Du Bois dramatizes the missed opportunity for lasting cross-racial solidarity in *Black Reconstruction* when he presents Abolition and the Free Soil Party (both based in Northern cities) as "two movements" whose union in the mid-19th century, he says, would have been "irresistible." Yet instead of "forming one great party of free labor and free land," the two projects diverged: "poor whites and their leaders could not for a moment contemplate a fight of united white and black labor against the exploiters."[58] The prospect of abolition-democracy dedicated to the political equality and economic well-being of all was summarily thwarted, according to Du Bois: "it was stopped and inhibited by the doctrine of race."[59]

White identities in both the North and South were forged in contradistinction to Blackness, which, Du Bois says, was seen as an "unpardonable crime.[60] The hierarchy of white over Black, however, had special meaning for those whites who were poor, because it helped assuage the painful and often degrading terms of advancing industrial capitalism in the 19th-century United States. Citing Du Bois, David Roediger explains:

> Statuses and privileges conferred by race could be used to make up for alienating and exploitative class relationships, North and South. White workers could, and did, define and accept their class position by fashioning identities as "not slaves" and as "not Blacks."[61]

Du Bois's analysis demonstrates that this tendency among white workers—to see themselves as "not Black"—persisted past abolition and helped to undermine the radically egalitarian potential of Reconstruction. "Race philosophy" made "labor unity or labor class-consciousness" impossible and assured that white supremacist interests, backed by terror, would destroy Reconstruction's promise of equality between Blacks and whites.[62] Poor whites and rich whites, Du Bois alleges, sustained an alliance "by the shibboleth of race despite divergent interests," destroying the prospects of genuine emancipation for Blacks while also reinforcing the exploitation of all workers and ensuring that no serious opposition to "exploitation by capitalists" would develop in the United States.[63]

The defining feature of Du Bois's conception of the "public and psychological wage" is the identification of whiteness as a form of favored *status* within American racial capitalism. Across regions and time periods—in the North and the South, before and after the Civil War—whiteness functioned as a socially legible mark designating superiority. Classification as white supplied status to all those so categorized, but as noted above, Du Bois argued that being marked as "white" held particular significance for those Americans without economic power, for whom it functioned as a "consolation prize," in the words of Cheryl Harris, keeping them from the very bottom of the social order.[64] In *Black Reconstruction,* speaking of poor whites in the slave South and of poor whites in the postbellum United States at large, Du Bois separately describes each group as having their "vanity" fed through their social positioning as "white."[65]

Describing anti-Black violence during Reconstruction, Du Bois writes of the "poor white": "He joined eagerly secret organizations, like the Ku Klux Klan, which fed his vanity by making him a co-worker with the white planter."[66] The leveling effect Du Bois describes here—in which a poor laborer sees himself as a "co-worker" alongside his capitalist boss—is crucially important. It captures the dualistic character of whiteness as status. As Joel

Olson writes, the "wage" paid to whites provides white citizens "with an air of both equality and superiority: equal to all white people—even the rich—yet superior to all Black people—even the rich."[67] Du Bois conceptualizes whiteness in the 19th- and early 20th-century United States as a form of social currency within a capitalist "economic order that seriously delimits material well-being" (in the words of Cedric Robinson).[68]

An overlooked aspect of Du Bois's account of compensatory whiteness is his characterization of the wage as *both* public and psychological. The second adjective has taken precedence over "public" in most readings and deployments of Du Bois's wage thesis. But Du Bois's phrasing should caution against an overly narrow understanding of "psychological," which might individualize the gratifications of whiteness, by conceiving of them too simplistically in terms of personal (in)security and self-esteem. The "public" quality of the wage directs attention to the existence of a *shared* racial hierarchy—both material and symbolic—in accordance with which the "badge of inferiority" stamped on Black persons has as its flipside a badge of superiority for whites. The nonmonetary wage Du Bois identifies is paid openly and is legible to everyone.

Du Bois's conceptualization of whiteness as a wage that is public as well as psychological partly anticipates group position theory, developed by Herbert George Blumer beginning in the 1950s. Blumer's crucial intervention into the sociological study of racism at the time was to contest the "common presupposition" across most scholarship that racial prejudice belonged to the "realm of individual feeling." The group position theory that he advanced built upon Du Bois's indispensable insight in *Black Reconstruction* (though Du Bois was never cited by Blumer): that racial identification—in particular, seeing oneself as white—is a *collective* process that involves "an image or conception of one's own racial group and of another group, inevitably in terms of the relationship of such groups." Du Bois's pairing of "public" with "psychological" captures the resolutely *social* character of the transaction he identifies; if whiteness can "compensate" poor whites, this is because the descriptor "white" designates a position within a stratified schema of classification that is widely shared. The nonmonetary wage he conceptualizes depends for its value upon this schema. Blumer noted this in a decidedly Du Boisean formulation: "vis-à-vis the subordinate racial group the unlettered individual with low status in the dominant racial group has a sense of group position common to that of the elite of his group."[69]

At the same time, Du Bois's formulation of the wage as "public" also exceeds the terms of group position theory. Why? The wage that whiteness delivers is, for Du Bois, not just about an inflated "image or conception" of one's own group vis-à-vis another. That image is itself produced and reinforced by the government's delivery of a set of communal goods for the enjoyment of whites only. In *Black Reconstruction*'s famous passage referring to the "wage" (quoted earlier in this section), Du Bois points to a specific, identifiable set of provisions—parks, schools, police, and other "public functions"—that ought properly to be shared by all but are in fact exclusive to whites. Du Bois describes a bundle of resources that are public, not private. They are collectivized and shared, but only among whites. The regime Du Bois describes, though far from the socialist economic model he advocated at the time, nonetheless provides socialized benefits—but only to one portion of the population, those designated white. These benefits do not only materially enrich their recipients; they also signify standing, belonging, and deservingness.

Whiteness acts like a wage thanks to the existence of a perverse—that is, racialized—commonwealth. The collective goods Du Bois references in the passage are like fun-house versions of the real thing; they purport to be "public" yet are horded on one side of the "color line." Socialized benefits like parks, schools, and police do not serve the general welfare; they are monopolized by whites as a class at the expense of Blacks. This practice of "social closure" allows the dominant group, with the aid of the state, to secure advantages, for themselves through the exclusion of others.[70] These advantages are at once "public and psychological"; the selective provision of collective goods on the basis of race communicates to the whole of society who deserves "deference" and "courtesy." Du Bois illustrates the dynamics of this racialized commonwealth in *Black Reconstruction* by juxtaposing the "public" *wage* that belongs to whites as a group with the "public" *insult* to which Blacks are subject as a group.

When Du Bois speaks of the wage, he draws attention to the existence of a *partial* public that distributes collectivized resources on the basis of racial classification, affirming the worthiness of whites as a group. Another passage, in the "Founding the Public School" chapter, dramatizes the gap between a genuine (inclusive) commonwealth and a disfigured (exclusive) commonwealth. Addressing fierce battles over public schooling for Black people in the South during Reconstruction, Du Bois juxtaposes two claims—one that joins Blacks and whites together and one that severs them from one another when imagining the community and the public ends it serves. The back-to-back quotes read: "'A due regard for the public weal imperatively requires that the Negroes be educated'" (from an 1865 editorial in a Selma, Alabama, newspaper) and "'The sole aim should be to educate every white child in the commonwealth'" (from an 1865 editorial in a Charleston, South Carolina, newspaper).[71] The first statement invokes the idea of a "public weal" that includes "Negroes," while the second tacitly but obviously excludes them from it.

In an important 1944 essay, he returns to this dynamic when reflecting on the meaning of "Negro freedom."[72] After stating that freedom for Black persons means "full economic, political and social equality with American citizens, in thought, expression and action, with no discrimination based on race or color," Du Bois comments that the meaning of economic and political freedom are well understood, referring to the right to work for a wage that allows for a decent standard of living and the right to vote and have a "voice" in government, respectively. It is the meaning of "social equality"—a historically contentious, charged term—that remains "vague" to many.[73] In what follows, Du Bois explains its significance in part by illuminating the import and character of truly "public services."[74]

Du Bois's commentary affirms and deepens *Black Reconstruction*'s critique of a racially exclusive commonwealth. "Public services and opportunities," properly understood, are shared by all citizens. Du Bois says of these goods: "the whole social body is joint owner and purveyor." Yet this principle is openly violated by the kinds of arrangements Du Bois linked to the "public and psychological wage." Social equality forbids any discrimination or segregation that "compels citizens to lose their rights of enjoyment and accommodation in the commonwealth."[75] The regime Du Bois depicts in the "wage" passages are marked by this very compulsion and loss. Where a corrupt version of the common weal reigns, there is no "just sharing."[76]

"Tools and Accomplices" in Defense of the Wage

Throughout his writings, Du Bois insists that the public-psychological economy of race, carried over from slavery and into the postemancipation era, is tragic, and not only for Black Americans.[77] Alliances among whites across class lines may spare poor whites from occupying the very bottom rung of the social hierarchy, yet the repeated failure to unify "poor against rich" or "worker against exploiter" constitutes a loss for the majority of whites, in Du Bois's view.[78] Continual (re)drawing of the color line preserves unjust economic arrangements and prevents the establishment of genuine democracy in the United States. When Du Bois recounts how Reconstruction was brought to an end by a "combination of planters and poor whites in defiance of their economic interests," he specifies the political-economic stakes of this turning point: "it was not simply the Negro who had been disenfranchised in 1876, it was the white laborer as well."[79]

Who is responsible for this tragic state of affairs? What explains such seemingly enduring white solidarity across class?[80] Du Bois's writings do not provide an easy answer to this question. He casts white workers in the United States simultaneously as "accomplices" and "tools," to paraphrase Marx.[81] They are knowing collaborators in the enforcement of white supremacy and they are the pawns of the rich who manipulate them to ensure capitalist control.[82]

At times *Black Reconstruction*'s narrative implies white capitalists are the prime movers, because they draw poor whites into an alliance that strengthens capitalist rule. Here white property owners seem to be acting *upon* poor whites. In response to the threat of universal suffrage that would "outbid landed interests," for example, "landholders had one recourse, and that was to draw the color line and convince the native-born white worker that his interests lay with the planter-class."[83] Capitalists seems to be the primary agents: they "draw" the line between Black and white and "convince" poor whites to unite on the basis of race. The Southern white worker, on this account, was "induced to prefer poverty to equality with the Negro."[84]

Du Bois tells a similar story about racialized labor politics in the first part of the 20th century. In essays in the *Crisis* published in 1918 and 1920, he characterizes capitalist bosses as "breeders" of racial animosity and violence and as "ringmasters" who "play" white and Black workers "off each other."[85] He even describes workers as "helpless pawns" in the hands of their employers.[86] When addressing the St. Louis riots in *Darkwater*, he says industry leaders were engaged in a "deliberate effort to divert the thoughts of men, and particularly of workingmen, into channels of race hatred against blacks."[87] In later essays from the 1930s, he argues similarly that employers "foment racial prejudice" among workers and thereby strengthen their class position.[88] And it is due to this "sinister influence" that the white worker has "swallowed the white employer's race prejudice, lock, stock, and barrel."[89]

Some of Du Bois's readers emphasize the idea that white workers have been tricked by capitalists. Noel Ignatiev, for example, cites Du Bois in writings over many decades in order to argue that "white skin privilege" is a kind of "poison bait" that reconciles white workers to exploitation by allowing them to think they are part of the master class.[90] The "racial ploy" is a concept central to Derrick Bell's account of the "permanence of racism" in the United States—where it refers to a maneuver whereby a "mass of whites . . . accept large disparities in respect to economic opportunity in respect to other whites as long as they have priority over blacks."[91] Like Ignatiev's "poison bait," Bell's "racial ploy" borrows from the Du Boisean plot above, in which capitalists lure poor whites into a coalition by dangling the carrot of whiteness as status, a reward that comes at the profound cost of securing the conditions of capitalist domination.

Some of Du Bois's readers formulate this problem in terms of "interests," arguing that when white workers are "convinced" by capitalists to accept the "public and psychological wage," they effectively abandon their "real interests" in pursuit of "fancied," "counterfeit" interests. This is how Ignatiev characterizes the position of white workers in his 1967 essay, "White Blindspot," the title of which borrows a line from Du Bois.[92] Allen's *Invention of the White Race*, which he describes as an extension of Du Bois's work in *Black Reconstruction*, contrasts "actual" and "illusory" benefits. He contends that white workers in the United States have received the latter in the form of "white skin privilege" and foregone the former, insofar as the status rewards of whiteness have not truly provided an escape from "propertylessness."[93]

Du Bois occasionally speaks in this idiom, as when he states in *Black Reconstruction* that "the catastrophe of 1876" was brought about by "a combination of planters and poor whites in defiance of their economic interests."[94] But while Du Bois believes poor whites' economic interests suffer so long as capitalism endures, he does not discount the benefits they derive from a white supremacist order as merely "illusory." The notion of a nonmaterial wage conveys just this: even workers who are "propertyless" in the conventional sense nonetheless profit from what Cheryl Harris calls "property in whiteness."[95]

Du Bois's analysis challenges those accounts—some even claiming his imprimatur—that locate agency squarely in a clever capitalist class that makes use of poor whites as unwitting instruments of class domination. Even as Du Bois depicts capitalists as successfully manipulating white workers into bonding with them rather than fellow Black workers, he also simultaneously presents poor whites as active participants in the circulation of the "wage" and the debasement of Blackness on which it depends. Two important essays from the 1930s illustrate how Du Bois overcomes a dichotomy of activity vs. passivity to argue that white workers are not only "tools" but also "accomplices" in the maintenance of racial capitalism. In "The Negro and Communism" (1931), he rejects the usual explanation offered up for the failure of class solidarity in the United States:

> Socialists and Communists explain this easily: white labor in its ignorance and poverty has been misled by the propaganda of white capital whose policy is to divide labor into classes, races and unions and pit one against the other. There is an immense amount of truth in this explanation . . . But white American Laborers are not fools. And with few exceptions the more intelligent they are, the higher they rise, the more efficient they become, the more determined they are to keep Negroes under their heels.[96]

Du Bois continues on, describing how "intelligent white labor" has actively worked to exclude Blacks—from the trades, from decent housing, and from political power. Plainly, "white labor has been the black man's enemy, his oppressor."[97] "Marxism and the Negro Problem" (1933) similarly pins responsibility on poor whites for their vital role in enforcing racial hierarchy in the United States. Again disputing the simplified interpretation of white workers as the dupes of their bosses, Du Bois asserts, "It is no sufficient answer to say that capital encourages this oppression and uses it for its own ends . . . The bulk of American white labor is neither ignorant nor fanatical. It knows exactly what it is doing and it means to do it."[98]

Du Bois's language in *Black Reconstruction* is also productively ambivalent. In addition to characterizing landowners as "convincing" and "inducing" poor whites to identify with their bosses on the basis of whiteness, Du Bois ascribes willful action to poor white Americans as well. For example, he says that after the upheaval of the Civil War, poor whites in the South "sought redress by demanding unity of white against black."[99] The invocation of a "demand" subverts the image of poor whites as hapless marks and repositions them as political actors. Similarly, Du Bois describes what seems to be a conscious alliance forged during Reconstruction in which "the white laborer joined the white landholder and capitalist and beat the black laborer into subjection."[100] The people who here actively "join" others and "beat" Black Americans are not a different lot than those cast elsewhere as "pawns." White workers are both, Du Bois seems to say. They have been manipulated, no doubt, but they have also acted decisively on their own behalf, forging coalitions and enforcing the "badge of inferiority" placed on Black people—often by brutal means—in order to claim the rewards of whiteness for themselves.

With this account of white workers as simultaneously "tools" and "accomplices" in mind, the remainder of this section investigates the dynamism Du Bois attributes to the collection of the "wage." The social value of whiteness is not static or guaranteed. In order for the classification "white" to serve as meaningful payment, even amid seismic political shifts, the white-over-Black racial hierarchy initially forged in and through chattel slavery must be continuously renewed. Du Bois argues that the beneficiaries of the wage have repeatedly defended it—vigilantly and violently.

Du Bois's middle-period writings convey white supremacy's rough continuity over time, muddying the usual binaristic terms in which American racial history is told.[101] The relentless defense of the wage, for example, traverses even the cataclysmic event of emancipation. Despite the drama and import of the Civil War and Reconstruction—when millions "rose from the dead in the finest effort to achieve democracy for the working millions which this world had ever seen"—this historic upheaval was insufficient to break the "habit" of anti-Black violence.[102] In contrast to those who thought abolition would offer a clean slate upon which to reorder American political life, Du Bois stresses the enduring nature of white supremacy and the lengths to which white citizens went to protect their status.

This reality was not initially perceived by Karl Marx, who thought the end of slavery would usher in a new era of worker unity and create the conditions necessary for revolutionary action. When Marx drafted a letter on behalf of the First International to President Abraham Lincoln in November 1864, he was convinced that a Union victory would be a decisive win for a still-larger global struggle against capitalism. The letter announced that the "working men of Europe" recognized the American Civil War as an event that would determine the "destiny of their class." It declared that workers in the United States had once "boasted it the highest prerogative of the white-skinned labourer to sell himself and choose his own master" and therefore had failed to achieve "the true freedom of labor." Yet the tide had turned, Marx thought: "this barrier to progress has been swept off by the red sea of civil war."[103]

Just six years later, however, Marx seems to have glimpsed the very problem that Du Bois would name—white workers' attachment to their status-bearing racialized identity remained a formidable obstacle to class-based coalition, even after the historic rupture of the American Civil War. In a letter to Sigfrid Meyer and August Vogt in 1870, focused on the "domination of England over Ireland," Marx notes that the working class in England is "*divided* into two *hostile* camps, English proletarians and Irish proletarians." He continues, describing the "ordinary English worker":

> In relation to the Irish Worker, he feels himself to be a member of the *ruling nation*, and, therefore, makes himself a tool of his aristocrats and capitalists *against Ireland*, thus strengthening their domination *over himself*. He harbors religious, social and national prejudices against him. His attitude towards him is roughly that of the POOR WHITES to the NI****S in the former slave states of the American Union. The Irishman PAYS HIM BACK WITH INTEREST IN HIS OWN MONEY. He sees in the English worker both the accomplice and the stupid tool of *English rule in Ireland*.[104]

Although Marx mentions the US case only briefly here, and by way of analogy with England, he importantly characterizes poor whites in America as persons who, by virtue of their classification as white, see themselves as members of a "ruling nation" vis-à-vis Black Americans, no matter the outcome of the Civil War.

Du Bois develops this point with more precision, suggesting that the "public and psychological wage" paid to whites has endured not *despite* the steps made toward racial equality but perhaps *because* of them. In other words, the wage has been reasserted and defended by whites, Du Bois says, who believe that any advance made by Black Americans constitutes a loss for whites.[105] Thus, efforts to protect this valuable source of social status are especially energetic precisely at moments when Black Americans seem to be gaining some ground. Du Bois identifies this dynamic first in the context of the Civil War, when large numbers of escaped slaves fled to the North or joined the Union cause. Du Bois states that "blacks became a new and living threat as they became laborers and soldiers . . . If the Negro was to be free where would the poor white be?"[106] As fugitive slaves acquired new power as "laborers and soldiers," poor whites in the South became anxious about their own fates, and this sense of uncertainty only grew with the end of the war. If Blacks' prospects were improving, Du Bois says, this was experienced by many poor whites as a demotion of their own standing: "Suppose that freedom for the Negro means that Negroes might rise to be landholders, planters, and employers? The poor whites thus might lose the last shred of respectability."[107] Writing of the contemporary labor movement in 1939, Du Bois identifies a similar push-and-pull action. The white worker, he says, usually excludes the Black worker from organizing efforts because "long cultural training" has instructed him to see the Black person's treatment as an equal as "a degradation of his own status."[108] This zero-sum outlook, though neither natural nor inevitable, according to Du Bois, motivates the presumed recipients of the "public and psychological wage" to passionately defend it, sometimes violently.

Du Bois's analysis of the anti-Black brutality carried out in defense of the wage makes a striking claim about the misplacement of "bad" affects within America's racial capitalist order. The violence routinely directed at Black persons is animated, at least in part, by white citizens' feelings of "hatred" and "fear" fostered by the unforgiving realities of capitalism. These emotions, Du Bois theorizes, are routinely altered and redirected in accordance with racialized structures of feeling that position Black people as the default targets for the expression of negative sentiment.

Two versions of this idea appear in Du Bois's writings. In the first, a feeling of hatred is "transferred" from an initial object—capitalists or capitalism—to a substitute object, Black persons, who become targets of violence. This is how *Black Reconstruction* describes the animosity poor whites in the slave South felt toward Blacks: "To these Negroes he transferred all the dislike and hatred which he had for the whole slave system."[109] Here, poor whites are depicted as deeply dissatisfied with the terms of the capitalist-slave economy, yet this is not expressed directly; instead, their hatred is rerouted toward a different and familiar target—"Negroes." Du Bois identifies this process of substitution again when discussing the Civil War draft of 1863. When the draft law was passed in New York, he says, it meant that "soldiers were going to be poor men who could not buy exemption. The result throughout the country was widespread disaffection that went often as far as rioting." But this resistance, Du Bois, says, quickly changed shape: "it was easy to transfer class hatred so that it fell upon the black worker" until "at last the whole force of the riot turned against the Negroes. They were the cause of the war and, and, hence the cause of the draft." This "transfer" of hatred galvanized anti-Black mob violence, Du Bois reports, in which Blacks were "brutally murdered by hanging on trees and lamp posts . . . cruelly beaten and robbed," their houses burned and sacked.[110] As for why this transfer was so "easy," Du Bois says little in this passage, but it surely was facilitated by what he calls elsewhere the "world campaign beginning with the slave trade" that has "unconsciously trained millions of honest, modern men into the belief that black folk are sub-human."[111] So many were taught for so long to "despise colored peoples" that it operated as a default disposition and orientation, making Black persons readily available, all-purpose targets for white grievances of all sorts.[112]

The second process Du Bois analyzes, whereby whites' negative feelings wrought by capitalist arrangements are displaced onto Black people, is more complex. In addition to the outright "hatred" that shifts from one target to another, Du Bois also conceptualizes a kind of transmogrification of affect. Here, emotions that are not consciously felt as hatred at all—anxiety, worry, and, most notably, *fear*—sometimes manifest as violent rage against Black persons.

Addressing the "guerilla warfare" that undermined Reconstruction,[113] Du Bois writes in a fascinating passage that mob brutality against Blacks, including that of the Ku Klux Klan (KKK), was not the result of "total depravity" or "human hate."[114] Rather, he says a "nucleus of ordinary men" help form the mob. He explains:

> . . . these human beings at heart are desperately afraid of something. Of what? Of many things, but usually of losing their jobs, being declassed, degraded, or actually disgraced; of losing their hopes, their savings, their plans for their children; of the actual pangs of hunger, of dirt, of crime. And of all this, most ubiquitous in modern industrial society is that fear of unemployment.[115]

Without excusing the suffering inflicted by the "mob spirit," Du Bois suggests that the racial animosity evinced in acts of anti-Black terror following abolition was at least partly an expression of fear in disguise, specifically the fear induced by capitalist competition and exploitation.[116] Du Bois thus establishes a link between whites' (legitimate) fear of economic insecurity and (illegitimate) practices of anti-Black brutality.

In his earlier 1920 essay in *Darkwater*, "Of Work and Wealth," Du Bois reads the 1917 mob violence in St. Louis similarly. The mass migration of Black workers north, Du Bois says, made white workers fearful that they were losing their chance at upward mobility. This worry over their own fates within an economic order that pitted worker against worker to maximize capitalists' profit was expressed, however, in the form of "unbridled anger against 12,000,000 humble, upstriving" Black workers."[117]

Du Bois's account certainly presents such anti-Black violence as misdirected. Yet he notes that this transformation (of fear into rage) and re-direction (of energies toward Black workers, not white bosses) was, if not rational, then certainly predictable. The anger expressed in the 1917 riots occurred, Du Bois says, according to "the logic of the broken plate, which, seared of old across its pattern, cracks never again, save along the old de-struction."[118] In other words, the "pattern" established under slavery, in which cross-class white solidarity was forged on the basis of anti-Black op-pression, was readily available for re-enactment in response to new events, particularly those that activated economic anxieties.

Coda: The White Commonwealth and the Long Fight Against School Integration

I have argued that the Du Boisean wage names a kind of collective esteem forged in relation to a racially exclusive commonwealth. With this concep-tualization in mind, there is perhaps no clearer example of the lengths to which payees will go to secure this "public and psychological wage" than the unending resistance to equitable multiracial public schooling in the United States in the 20th and 21st centuries. The specific means by which white Americans have sought to—in the words of Du Bois—"arrogate to them-selves exclusive rights of public service" have varied, but organized opposi-tion to racially integrated schools, conjoined with efforts to horde valuable public educational resources for whites, has continued unabated since *Brown v. Board of Education* found segregated educational institutions unconstitu-tional in 1954.[119]

This chapter closes with a condensed analysis of how white Americans have sought to secure quality K–12 public education as a socialized benefit for whites in the post-*Brown* era. I argue that the largely successful effort to preserve racial segregation in the public education system and concen-trate resources on one side of the "color line" is a prime example of how the "public and psychological wage" has been actively pursued and protected over time.[120] Three key moments illustrate this pattern: (1) massive resist-ance in the South (1954–1965)—a sweeping, multipronged, and sometimes violent movement that opposed federal school desegregation measures;

(2) euphemistic "anti-busing" organizing in major Northern cities in the 1960s and '70s that likewise fought desegregation measures;[121] and (3) widespread resegregation and resource grabs by whites under the regime of "school choice" that became dominant once the US government largely abandoned the enforcement of desegregation requirements, beginning in the 1970s. These examples reveal the impressively wide range of tactics developed by whites to retain the preferential status tied to racially specific "public" goods.

To the extent that massive resistance is remembered today, it is usually associated with the top-down political manipulation of "fringe mobs." Yet this picture conceals the fact that for a decade beginning in 1954, many whites throughout the South—including "moderates"—actively opposed the integration of public schools, using every tool imaginable.[122] Their practices of defiance included intimidation and violence but also policy initiatives at the state and local level. Indeed, the defining characteristic of this movement—which helps distinguish it from the South's long tradition of enforcing white supremacy—is its "scope and scale."[123] As George Lewis has documented, massive resistance was marked by a "breath-taking diversity" of resistance efforts:

> The devices that they chose to employ ranged from race-free appeals to the sanctity of states' rights to playing upon latent fears of miscegenation that were saturated in brutally racist rhetoric; legislative and legal rejoinders that varied from subtle and effective stalling tactics to poorly thought-through obstructions that reeked of short-term expediency; attempts to undermine southern segregationists' opponents as "outsiders"[;] . . . legislative committees and subcommittees that hid their racist agendas under the banner of "state sovereignty" or "security" issues; threats of economic and violent reprisal; and, of course, sporadic descents into mob rule . . . [124]

Massive resistance cannot be explained away in terms of elite opportunism or minoritarian extremism. Rather, it was a mass movement, made up of large numbers of "ordinary people" who drew upon a "diverse array of ploys and strategies" in the hopes that the (better-funded and better-resourced) public schools they enjoyed would continue to serve whites only.[125]

As Mark Golub has argued, massive resistance is typically not recounted this way; the "full range of southern strategies of defiance" is suppressed in favor of an image of an unruly minoritarian outburst. The "truth" of massive resistance, he persuasively argues, is disavowed so that the alternate story of rogue extremists can support an American ideology of "racial redemption." Put differently, massive resistance is narrated so as to obscure the fact that the majority of Southern whites were determined to hold onto white-only schools as part of the "public and psychological wage" paid to them.[126]

Organized opposition by white Americans to school desegregation is also minimized when it is depicted as a strictly Southern phenomenon. This misperception is aided, first, by the distinction often made between Jim Crow de jure segregation in the South and de facto segregation in the North and, second, by reliance on "busing" as the default vocabulary for talking about Northern opposition to de-segregation policies in the 1960s and '70s.[127]

The distinction between "southern-style" and "northern-style" segregation was initially used by civil rights activists in the mid-20th century to "build a political consensus against Jim Crow laws in the South," as Matthew Desmond explains, but the de jure–de facto dichotomy also allowed politicians, courts, and citizens in the North to deflect responsibility and "shored up the myth that segregation in the North was innocent rather than the product of decades of local, state, and federal policies."[128] In fact, however, "racially-motivated and explicit public policy," especially concerning housing, meant that residential and school segregation in the North were never simply accidental.[129]

"Busing," a "race-neutral euphemism" that was taken up by mass media, provided white activists in the North cover. Talk of disputes over "busing" concealed organized opposition that actually looked "a lot like war."[130] White parents could claim that they were not opposed to integration at all but simply wanted their children to attend local neighborhood schools.[131] But this explanation was disingenuous, at best, since busing was a widespread, accepted practice in all parts of the United States, prior to court-ordered busing programs intended to desegregate public schools.[132] Additionally, the story of "busing crises" in Boston, Chicago, New York, and other Northern cities is usually told in reactive terms, as though white citizens were responding to overreach by the civil rights movement and the federal government.[133] But this overlooks the extent to which white Northerners had long opposed school desegregation—for example, by successfully lobbying to include a provision in the 1964 Civil Rights Act that sharply differentiated between "segregation" by law in the South and "racial imbalance" in the North, and was intended "to keep federal civil rights enforcement of school desegregation focused away from the North." The "white backlash" story covers up how "preemptive white protests" shaped key legislation with the express purpose of impeding school desegregation.[134]

The history of "busing"—court-ordered school desegregation—is most often cast as a "failure." Apart from the fact that there was only a relatively brief period of time (roughly 1964–1971) when the US government undertook significant desegregation efforts—thus making lasting "success" unlikely—the narrative of past failure does meaningful political work in the present. Today, American public schools remain largely "separate and unequal." Since 1988, the highpoint of school integration in the United States, "the gains of *Brown* have been almost entirely reversed."[135] Beginning in the 1990s, hundreds of school districts were released from court-ordered desegregation plans, re-entrenching divisions along race and class lines in public education.[136] For example, schools in the South, once the most segregated in the country, had actually become the most desegregated by the 1970s, thanks to federal court orders. But as judges have released these districts from court-enforced desegregation plans, they have moved "back toward segregation."[137]

Resegregation here signifies inequality, not merely physical separation. In the case of public education, resources and opportunities closely track "the spatial distribution of race."[138] High-poverty, majority-nonwhite schools are less likely to offer a full range of math and science courses than other schools, for example, and more likely to suspend and expel students.[139] Nationwide, the "achievement gap between black and white students, which greatly narrowed during the era in which schools grew more integrated, widened as they became less so."[140] School districts that predominantly serve students of color received $23 billion less in funding than mostly white school districts in the United States in 2016, despite serving the same number of students.[141] According to data from the Department of Education, "the whiter the school, the more resources it has."[142] These arrangements persist, despite research showing that students of all races and incomes do worse in segregated schools.[143] In this context, the now-conventional wisdom that "busing failed" encourages people to accept "the ongoing racial and socioeconomic segregation of schools in the United States as inevitable and unchangeable."[144] It fosters resignation in the face of injustice.

By the mid-1970s government-backed desegregation efforts were mostly abandoned in the wake of widespread white resistance and major political and legal shifts, with subsequent legal decisions enshrining an extremely "minimalist" approach to desegregation into law.[145] Since the Reagan administration, "school choice" has become the dominant logic of American public education. School choice policies—vouchers, charter schools, and open enrollment plans—have a complex history, having been advocated by both segregationists and their opponents.[146] Today school choice is largely justified in terms of "fostering competition" in the "free market" and operates in ways that facilitate resegregation: "Mounting evidence suggests that 'color-blind' school choice policies, which are not designed to promote racial integration, generally lead to greater stratification and separation of students by race and ethnicity across schools and programs."[147] These segregative effects result from the decisions parents—especially white parents—make. Studies have found, for example, that among middle- to upper-class white parents who express concern over racial and socioeconomic segregation in schools, this concern is outweighed by a desire to see "their children win the 'race to the top' of a highly competitive and stratified system."[148] Other findings suggest that regardless of what they say when asked, in practice white parents have a "strong preference" for schools in which their children are alongside more white peers.[149]

Some recent efforts to secure the best public educational resources for whites—to hold onto this "public and psychological wage"—are plainer.[150] In Howard County, Maryland, a 2019 plan, "Equity in Action," aimed to balance low-income students throughout the county by transferring 7,400 of the district's 58,000 students to different schools. The proposed change would have affected the racial makeup of some schools because the majority of poor students in the county are Black or Hispanic. Opposition to the plan was swift, even in the largely liberal area. Thousands of letters and emails, many openly racist, flooded the superintendent's office. The main opposition group, Howard County Families for Education Improvement, composed of many self-professed Democrats and "social justice" advocates, purposely distanced themselves from past anti-integration struggles in the 1960s and '70s, even as they adamantly opposed the plan. For example, their website instructed supporters to avoid the language of "forced busing," although references to "long" bus rides were permissible and, even more tellingly, their members regularly advanced a "charitable" narrative to explain their stance. Protesters acknowledged that they did not want their children transferred to different schools (schools that would be more racially and economically mixed), yet their criticisms of the plan emphasized "other people's children—those with less advantage—who they believed would suffer under the plan."[151] They thus defend their own enjoyment of better-resourced and higher-performing schools under the guise of philanthropy. It is out of concern for others, they implied, that they must act so as to reinforce their own advantage.[152]

Since *Brown*, white Americans in all parts of the country and in differing legal and policy contexts have found ways to ensure that an ostensibly public good—state-funded education—continues to be unfairly distributed along racial and economic lines. Whether by openly opposing school integration plans (in the name of "tradition," "the right to attend a neighborhood school," or purported concern for marginalized communities) or by engaging in savvy resource grabs within the architecture of "school choice," white citizens have consistently acted to consolidate and protect their advantaged position within a deeply hierarchical schooling system. Following Du Bois, we can recognize these moves as reinvestments in a racialized "public and psychological wage," a payment that delivers valuable resources as well as meaningful social status. Public schools were one of the social benefits exclusively enjoyed by whites that Du Bois named when elaborating on the meaning of the nonmonetary wage in *Black Reconstruction*. Although today's public schools no longer serve whites exclusively, American schools are seriously and unequally divided along racial lines. This is not accidental or incidental; whites have acted decisively for decades since *Brown* to secure the most valuable public educational goods for themselves, at the expense of nonwhite community members. "The presence of the past" is evident in the public schooling system today: what Du Bois called "the best schools" are still primarily for the benefit of white students, and poorly funded majority-minority schools retain the racialized "badge of inferiority" Du Bois identified in 1935.[153]

Contra some analyses, passionate defense of the "public and psychological wage" of whiteness did not dramatically reappear on the American political scene in the 2016 election. Rather, it has been a persistent feature of the polity since before Du Bois gave it a name. And as Du Bois highlighted, this wage is produced partly by ongoing practices of collective resource allocation that simultaneously advantage white Americans and penalize communities of color, reinforcing racialized conceptions of standing and belonging in the US polity. The recent history of public schooling in the United States is especially relevant because equitable socialized education is at the heart of abolition-democracy itself, as Du Bois maintained: "the education of *all children together at public expense* is the best and surest path to democracy."[154] The story of white mobilization against the meaningful integration and equalization of public schools since 1954 demonstrates a long-standing refusal to establish a truly multiracial commonwealth in the United States.

3

Whiteness as Pleasure

Anti-Black Brutality and Sadistic Enjoyment

The narrative arc most often applied to W. E. B. Du Bois's long and pro-lific intellectual life is one of increasing political radicalization, in the pe-riod following *The Souls of Black Folk* and becoming more pronounced around the First World War. This account focuses on Du Bois's growing interest in Marxist thought and his eventual departure from the National Association for the Advancement of Colored People (NAACP) in 1934 over the organization's fidelity to liberal reforms that failed to address "the organization of industry" and capitalism's role in the maintenance of racial caste. *Black Reconstruction* (1935) cemented this shift by famously declaring, "The emancipation of man is the emancipation of labor and the emancipa-tion of labor is the freeing of that basic majority of workers who are yellow, brown, and black."[1] Du Bois—who frequently retold his own life story—also commented directly on the changes his political thought and action under-went, recounting often how he grew to see the necessity of "economic rev-olution" for the emancipation of "darker peoples" in the United States and around the world.[2]

There is another shift evident in Du Bois's middle-period writings, however—one that he points out, but that is missing from most accounts of his "radicalization." In addition to coming to see racial caste and capitalist exploitation as inextricably linked, Du Bois reveals that he recognizes, contra his prior views, that there is something "irrational" about the workings of racism. The essays collected in 1940's *Dusk of Dawn* repeatedly raise the problems of the "white world's" irrationality and the tenacious character of an American racial order sustained, Du Bois suggests, at least partly by "unconscious" and "subconscious" forces. Here Du Bois explicitly describes a significant transformation in his thinking: away from the social-scientific conviction that racism was sustained by ignorance that could be remedied by information and toward the unsettling conclusion that racism was (also?) a matter of "reflex," unreachable by such argument. In other places Du Bois

The Gratifications of Whiteness. Ella Myers, Oxford University Press. © Oxford University Press 2022.
DOI: 10.1093/oso/9780197556764.003.0003

does not announce this reorientation so explicitly, but his commentary—particularly concerning anti-Black brutality—suggests that by 1920 he was repeatedly confronting what he later calls in *Dusk of Dawn* the "irrationality" of racism and its implications for political action.

This chapter examines how those reflections on "irrationality" reveal a form of white gratification distinct from the "wage" addressed in Chapter 2. More specifically, as I will show, Du Bois's preoccupation with the "subconscious" and "unconscious" dimensions of white supremacy—and his corresponding analysis of racialized violence against Black people in particular—figures whiteness as a source and site of sadistic *pleasure*. If, as Du Bois is famous for arguing, whiteness in the United States has delivered meaningful status benefits to its bearers, it has also offered something more nebulous and unsettling: *enjoyment* derived from Black denigration.

I begin by considering how the question of racism's "irrationality" emerges in *Dusk of Dawn*, where it seems to mark the limit of social-scientific methods for redressing injustice. Although Du Bois's claims about "irrationality" and related terms are somewhat elusive, I argue that he uses this vocabulary to address anti-Black violence specifically. In major works spanning 1920–1940, and seemingly sparked in part by the Red Summer of 1919, Du Bois repeatedly analyzes whites' brutality against Blacks in ways that stress its gratuitous, excessive character, thereby complicating strictly political-economic interpretations of white supremacist violence. The specter of white sadism—racialized pleasure derived from Black pain—looms especially large in Du Bois's recounting of a particular event—the 1899 lynching of Sam Hose in Alabama. Hose's public murder, I show, represents for Du Bois an appetitive, festive form of cruelty that raises grave doubts about the prospects of a genuinely abolition-democracy.

Importantly, as this chapter demonstrates, Du Bois's reflections on the potentially sadistic dimensions of anti-Black violence exist alongside political-economic interpretations, illustrating his pluralistic approach to the gratifications of whiteness. He understands anti-Black violence to be *both* a means of defending a "public and psychological wage" within the terms of American racial capitalism *and* a potent source of enjoyment that cannot be fully accounted for in instrumental terms.

Exploring Du Bois's figuration of whiteness as pleasure renders more complex received understandings of Du Bois's political-theoretical trajectory, because it considers his "radicalization" not only in terms of a critique of capitalism but also as a growing attunement to the seemingly gratuitous, excessive, "irrational" qualities of anti-Blackness itself. Tending to this neglected feature of Du Bois's writings may also offer a new angle on contemporary left interpretations of the US racial order. The first of these holds that anti-Black racism operates primarily as a tool of capitalist social control that rewards whites, however poor, for their allegiance to an abusive economic regime. This interpretation is challenged by the thesis that contends that anti-Black racism obeys no such "logic" and is animated instead by base cruelty directed at Black persons who remain symbolically marked as "enslaveable." Popular debates over Trump's 2016 election, especially on the left, played out partly along these lines, between commentators who mobilized a simplified "wages of whiteness" argument to address Trump's appeal to some voters seemingly disadvantaged by his policies and those who rejected this class-based analysis to argue that sheer racist animus, fueled by generations of white supremacy that traverses economic divisions, enabled Trump's election.[3] Might Du Bois help us think less dichotomously about such propositions? This chapter shows that Du Bois's writings resist the false choice between political economy and libidinal economy.

Dusk of Dawn and Racism in the "Twilight Zone"

The essay collection *Dusk of Dawn* (1940) is especially concerned with the tenacity of "race hate," and in particular, with the possibility that such hate may be impervious to the strategies of education and moral suasion pursued by the NAACP and similar organizations. More specifically, references to the "irrationality" of anti-Blackness appear frequently, and across multiple essays. The precise meaning of this concept (and those with which it often appears—"unconscious" and "subconscious") remains somewhat opaque, yet it clearly flags what is for Du Bois a vexing problem, one that leads him to doubt whether full citizenship for Blacks in the United States is possible, even "many years, many generations" into the future.[4] In a characteristic passage from "The White World," Du Bois writes:

> The present attitude and action of the white world is not based solely upon rational, deliberate intent. It is a matter of conditioned reflexes; of long followed habits, customs, and folkways; of subconscious trains of reasoning and unconscious nervous reflexes.[5]

Du Bois here juxtaposes a collection of phenomena—reflex, habit, custom, folkways, subconscious trains of thought, unconscious reflexes—with "rational, deliberate intent" to contend that "the white world's" beliefs are shaped by any array of factors that defy a rationalist paradigm. As this passage illustrates, Du Bois often relies on a constellation of terms, some of which carry different valences (most notably the terms "habit," "customs," and "folkways," which arguably register differently than "irrationality," the "unconscious," and the "subconscious"), rendering his meaning even more obscure.[6] This chapter, however, focuses on the irrational-unconscious-subconscious nexus as it appears in Du Bois's thought.

In *Dusk of Dawn*, Du Bois uses these terms often when giving an account of himself and important changes in his thinking. That is, a growing awareness of the "subconscious," "unconscious," and "irrational" dimensions of white supremacy is part of the "autobiography of a race concept" that Du Bois claims to provide in *Dusk of Dawn*. Several of the essays contain before-and-after reflections that contrast a prior understanding of racism's operation with the one he holds in 1940. For example, Du Bois describes the perspective he held when he first helped found the NAACP in 1909 and began to serve as editor of *The Crisis* in 1910:

> My basic theory had been that race prejudice was primarily a matter of ignorance on the part of the mass of men, giving the evil and anti-social a chance to work their way; that when the truth was properly presented, the monstrous wrong of race hate must melt and melt quickly before it. All human action to me in those days was conscious and rational. There was no twilight zone.[7]

Yet Du Bois reports that around 1930 he began to "look back critically at the twenty years" that had passed since he left his academic position to work full time for the NAACP. From this point on, he seems to wrestle with the existence of this twilight zone, in which "race prejudice" is not simply "a matter of ignorance to be cured by information."[8]

Second, the shift that appears in these writings as Du Bois's awakening to the "irrational" elements of racism also represents a loss of faith in the social sciences. He explains that his schooling at Fisk, Harvard, and the University of Berlin had "emphasize[d] science and the scientific attitude" and that in his academic career he was "determined to put science into sociology through a study of the condition and problems of my own group."[9] He characterizes himself during this period as "casting about to find a way of applying science to the race problem."[10]

On Du Bois's telling, the first problem that caused Du Bois to question this scientific project was the "determination of certain people to suppress and mistreat the darker races." Yet at that point (the period of 1910–1920, according to Du Bois), he still held out hope for a social-scientific approach that relied on information and education to combat racial hierarchy: "I believed that this evil group formed a . . . small minority and that once the majority of well-meaning folk realized their evil machinations, we should be able to secure justice." But a "further," even more unsettling realization awaited Du Bois: that there are "actions of men which are not due to lack of knowledge nor evil intent," and therefore the world cannot be transformed using the methods he had previously supposed. This instigated, he says, nothing short of a "revolution in my thought."[11]

Third, this "revolution" in thinking carries significant political meaning. Du Bois, looking back on his life in 1940, sees his varied career, both academic and activist, as persistently directed at a "utilitarian object": dismantling racial caste.[12] But the confrontation with the "irrational" dimensions of racism would seem to place that object even further out of reach. The essays in *Dusk of Dawn* return again and again to the problems of "irrational and unconscious habit" and the "reflexes of race hate," which seem to defy the best efforts of anti-racist organizers and agitators.[13] The NAACP's "campaign against Negro prejudice," Du Bois notes, was based on two assumptions, the validity of which he now doubts: "on the one hand that most race prejudice is a matter of ignorance to be cured by information and on the other hand that much discrimination is a matter of deliberate deviltry and unwillingness to be just."[14] But if "irrational and subconscious actions" are at play, as Du Bois insists, what does this mean for the "plight of the Negro"? Can "unconscious cerebration" be the target of political agitation? What are the prospects for genuine democracy in the United States if the obstacles are greater even than "ignorance and deliberate ill-will"?[15] At certain points in *Dusk of Dawn*, Du Bois seems pessimistic, as when he recounts in "Revolution" that despite the successes of the NAACP's educational and legislative campaigns, "the barriers of race prejudice were certainly as strong in 1930 as in 1910 the world over." It now appears to Du Bois that there are "stronger and more threatening forces, forming the founding stones of race antagonisms, which we had only begun to attack or perhaps in reality had not attacked at all."[16] But at other moments, Du Bois seems determined to imagine a new, ambitious political program: "Not science alone could settle this matter, but force must come to its aid. The black world must fight for freedom."[17]

Finally, *Dusk of Dawn*'s references to the "irrational" character of anti-Black racism are especially suggestive because Du Bois hints that Freud may have had some effect on the "revolution" in his thinking about the maintenance of racial hierarchy:

> . . . the meaning and implications of the new psychology had begun slowly to penetrate my thought. My own study of psychology under William James had pre-dated the Freudian era, but it had prepared me for it. I now began to realize that in the fight against racial prejudice, we were not facing simply the rational, conscious determination of white folk to oppress us; we were facing age-long complexes now sunk largely to unconscious habit and irrational urge . . . [18]

To be sure, Du Bois does not offer up a Freudian interpretation of "color caste," in this text or anywhere else, but it is notable that he cites the influence of "new psychology" when he claims that racism is at least partly fueled by "unconscious" and "irrational" forces. This is not the only time Du Bois suggests that Freudian thought has made an important imprint on his thinking about race, particularly in the US context. In the new preface or "Apologia" added to the 1954 republication of *The Suppression of the African Slave-Trade to the United States of America* (originally published in 1896 and based on Du Bois's PhD dissertation), Du Bois notes the analysis presented in the book was limited by "ignorance": "Freud and his companions and their epoch-making contribution to science was not generally known when I was writing this book, and consequently I did not realize the psychological reasons behind the trends of human action which the African slave trade involved."[19]

It is not possible to know precisely how Du Bois's account of phenomena such as the slave trade might have been reshaped by a sustained engagement with psychoanalytic thought. Yet digging further into the problem of racism's "irrationality," as it appears in Du Bois's writing, may still prove generative. What exactly seems to prompt Du Bois's references to the "subconscious" and "unconscious" dimensions of racialized human relations? What specific features of the social world is Du Bois seeking to name when he speaks in the language of "irrationality"?

The "Red Ray" of White Violence

Scrutinizing *Dusk of Dawn*, the text in which Du Bois narrates this "revolution" in his thought, it becomes evident that discussions of racism's "irrationality" and its "subconscious" and "unconscious" elements usually appear in connection with reflections on white supremacist violence. That is, ongoing, organized brutality directed at Black Americans appears to play a central role in Du Bois's changing understanding of the character of racism and the strategies best suited to combatting it. In this section I suggest that the term "irrational," as Du Bois uses it in *Dusk of Dawn*, and the accompanying terms "subconscious" and "unconscious," are inextricably linked to anti-Black cruelty, especially in the form of lynchings and race riots. More pointedly, this vocabulary seems to be mobilized to name violence carried out against Black persons that is gratuitous and perhaps even serves as a source of *enjoyment* for whites, both perpetrators and observers. It thus identifies a distinctive form of white gratification. Although the vocabulary of "irrationality" emerges only in Du Bois's 1940 book, I also show that the idea that anti-Black brutality is in some way excessive and may be pleasurable for whites is evident in his work as early as 1917. Du Bois's writings over this two-decade period repeatedly raise the possibility that white violence challenges the interpretive frameworks he otherwise uses to understand racial caste in the United States (namely, mass ignorance, minoritarian "evil," and, most significantly, the "public and psychological wage" of whiteness, addressed in Chapter 2).

Hope for a "scientific" approach to overcoming racism in the United States seems to diminish in relation to cumulative acts of physical violence against Black persons. In one of the *Dusk of Dawn* essays, "Science and Empire," Du Bois explains that as he embarked on his academic career, he hoped to find a way to "appl[y] science to the race problem," but he then immediately comments that "lynching . . . was still a continuing horror in the United States at the time of my entrance into a teaching career . . . and in the sixteen years of my teaching nearly two thousand persons were publicly killed by mobs, and not a single one of the murderers punished."[20] This essay also includes a personal recollection of Sam Hose's 1899 lynching in Georgia (discussed in detail later in this chapter): "At the very time when my studies were most successful, there cut across this plan which I had as a scientist, a red ray which could not be ignored." This "red ray" is nothing other than the excessive, even festive violence routinely enacted upon Black persons by white mobs— illustrated by, but not limited to, the death of Sam Hose. Du Bois explicitly cites his exposure to such violence as disruptive of his intellectual trajectory. He writes that a new realization "broke in upon my work": "one could not be a calm, cool, and detached scientist while Negroes were lynched, murdered, and starved."[21]

The reality of white supremacist violence seems to have led Du Bois in a more overtly activist direction, at least on this telling. According to his retrospective reflections, such violence pushed him to take up a role as a "master of propaganda" rather than a scholar.[22] Yet the problem of unrelenting physical violence reappears again and again, continually confronting Du Bois even during the years he spent with the NAACP. In the unconventional "autobiography" *Dusk of Dawn* provides, at nearly every point that gains for Black Americans seem to have been won by the NAACP, the menace of anti-Black cruelty reappears, undercutting apparent progress.

This pattern can be reconstructed chronologically across the essays included in *Dusk of Dawn*. For example, Du Bois explains that he was "ready to follow the steps that led from the Niagara Movement meeting of 1906 to the Negro conference of 1909." Yet he remarks that at the same time such promising institution building was underway:

> Lynching continued in the United States but raised curiously enough little protest. Three hundred twenty-seven victims were publicly murdered by the mob during the years 1910 to 1914, and in 1915 the number leaped incredibly to one hundred in one year. The pulpit, the social reformers, the statesmen continued in silence before the greatest affront to civilization which the modern world has known.[23]

Even as the NAACP became more established and could claim some successes, Du Bois's narrative stresses how anti-racists' optimism was repeatedly shattered by white violence. Recounting the NAACP's campaigns against disenfranchisement, he remarks that the 1915 *Guinn v. United States* offered a "decided note of hope. The Supreme Court of the United States, after having dodged the plain issue for a decade, finally at our insistence and with the help of our corps of lawyers . . . handed down a decision which outlawed the infamous 'Grandfather Clauses' of the disenfranchising constitutions of the South."[24] But any satisfaction this seeming breakthrough might have brought is almost immediately undone: "To overbalance this sense of hope there came, however, continued prevalence of lynching in unusually serious form." Du Bois recounts over the next two paragraphs a mass lynching of five

Black men in Georgia; a "horrible public burning" in Texas "before a mob of thousands of men, women, and children"; and the torture, mutilation, and murder of a Black farmer in South Carolina.[25]

Another apparent NAACP achievement is cast similarly by Du Bois. In October 1917, following the hard-won training and commissioning of the first-ever "six hundred-thirty nine" Black military officers who would serve in the world war, Du Bois says, "we felt tremendously uplifted." Yet in the "very hour of our exaltation, the whirlwind struck us again": "The very month that the Des Moines camp was authorized, a Negro was publicly burned alive in Tennessee under circumstances unusually atrocious." Du Bois recounts the gruesomeness of the event—its advertisement beforehand, the thousands who traveled to witness it, and the crazed gathering of "bits of his body, clothing, and the rope" as obscene souvenirs.[26]

The Red Summer of 1919 also appears in *Dusk of Dawn* as an overwhelming countermovement that threw into doubt the accomplishments of the NAACP and its allies. Although the "beautiful days" of the Amenia Conference of 1916 "marked the beginning of a new era" in which "the Negro race was more united and more ready to meet the problems of the world," Du Bois reports that in the same year there came "lynching, burning and murder" and "finally in 1919 the worst experience of mob law and race hate that the United States had seen since Reconstruction."[27] He returns to the "almost unbelievable" summer of 1919 later in the same essay, explaining that he had been planning a national celebration to take place that year to mark the 300 years since the first "permanent black settlers" came to America, "but, alas," there erupted race riots in Chicago and DC "which were among the worst" faced in "three hundred years of slavery and emancipation."[28]

Recurring acts of anti-Black brutality, which are tacitly—when not openly—sanctioned by most white citizens and authorities, loom large in the "autobiography of a race concept" that Du Bois provides. The seeming intractability of white supremacist violence seems to have had a profound impact, prompting Du Bois, first, to shift away from academic social science and toward political organizing and, later, at every turn, to call into question the apparent achievements and preferred strategies of that organizing. Moreover, confrontation with the fact of unending and frequently spectacular brutality seems to be closely related to Du Bois's growing sense that there is something "irrational" about racism in the United States. Indeed, the "revolution" by which Du Bois came to appreciate the significance of "those irrational and partly subconscious actions of men"—explained in relation to his disillusionment with science and later his dissatisfaction with the techniques of the NAACP—maps onto his narrative of repeated confrontations with the unrelenting, vicious physical violence carried out against Black persons in the United States. It seems, then, that when Du Bois speaks of the "unconscious habit and irrational urge" at work in the maintenance of white supremacy, he is at least in part signaling the enduring problem of anti-Black brutality.

The link between what Du Bois calls "irrationality" and white violence against Blacks becomes more pronounced and unsettling when one considers the ambivalent interpretations Du Bois offers of such violence, in *Dusk of Dawn* and earlier middle-period works as well. The primary framework Du Bois mobilizes to understand anti-Black brutality—which stresses an "economic motive" at work—is repeatedly complicated by depictions suggesting that such violence verges on sadism for those who enact and witness it.[29]

Recounting the Red Summer of 1919 in *Dusk of Dawn*'s "Propaganda and World War," Du Bois cites "two main causes" for the white violence that erupted in US cities. First, he notes that white workers were motivated by perceived economic "competition" resulting from Black workers' migration to the North. But he also cites a second reason: "The other cause was the resentment of American soldiers, especially those from the South, at the recognition and kudos which Negroes received in the World War; and particularly their treatment in France. In the last case, the sex motive, the brutal sadism into which race hate always falls, was all too evident." Du Bois does not elaborate upon the exact meaning of the "sex motive" or "brutal sadism" in this context, though he immediately reports that in 1919 alone, "seventy-seven Negroes were lynched . . . [O]f these, fourteen were publicly burned, eleven of them being burned alive."[30] Du Bois's remarks here suggest that these violent expressions of "race hate" cannot be explained away entirely in terms of a perceived economic threat—even as he acknowledges its role. Moreover, the references to "sex" and "sadism" implicate whites' *enjoyment* in the brutality Du Bois cites.

Du Bois's interpretation of white mob violence as sadistic is not confined to 1940's *Dusk of Dawn*. In *Darkwater*, published 20 years earlier, he was already analyzing the violence of 1919 in similar terms. There he describes "city after city drunk and furious with ungovernable lust of blood."[31] The reference to drunkenness and lust, linked to acts of anti-Black brutality, suggests that a passionate desire to hurt and a corresponding sense of pleasure may be at work in such violence. The problem of sadistic enjoyment appears in this text again when Du Bois characterizes mob violence as an "orgy," again raising the question of (sexual?) pleasure taken in Black suffering.[32]

To be sure, Du Bois also analyzes white violence against Blacks in terms of the cross-cutting relations of race and class that characterize the US regime of racial capitalism. For example, in *Black Reconstruction*'s account of the "terrorism" that helped overthrow Reconstruction, he emphasizes that such violence was fueled by whites' belief that free Blacks "threatened their future work and income."[33] Exploited white workers lashed out at Blacks in a misguided attempt to secure themselves against the economic vulnerability endemic to capitalism. As discussed in Chapter 2, Du Bois believes that mob violence, including that of the Ku Klux Klan (KKK), is at least partly driven by material insecurity.[34]

Yet there are times in *Black Reconstruction* when it seems as though anti-Black brutality cannot be fully explained by this interpretive framework. There is something more unnerving that seems to be at work in patterns of white violence. In the book's penultimate chapter, "Back Toward Slavery," where Du Bois forwards the economics-first analysis summarized above, he also describes in slow, excruciating detail over eight pages the "guerilla warfare" directed at Black citizens, recounting numerous particular cases, many involving prolonged torture and mutilation as well as death.[35] Although he continues to view such brutality as an extreme expression of how the "shibboleth of race" effectively pits white workers against Blacks, Du Bois also reads the horror he catalogs in a different way. He writes, "Inter-racial sex jealousy and accompanying sadism has been made the wide foundation of mobs and lynching."[36] This formulation, like Du Bois's commentary on 1919's anti-Black violence in *Dusk of Dawn*, portrays such brutality as *sadistic*—involving pleasure taken in the abuse of racialized others. The idea that whites' participation in, and witnessing of, Black suffering is enjoyable complicates Du Bois's narrative about economic anxiety driving white violence against Blacks.

Black Reconstruction also characterizes "mob violence and lynching" as a "sort of permissible Roman Holiday for the entertainment of vicious whites," further indicating that white supremacist violence operates in ways that exceed a strictly political-economic interpretation.[37] The depiction of organized anti-Black violence as a "Roman Holiday" here echoes an earlier piece on the East. St. Louis riots coauthored by Du Bois, which was published in *The Crisis* in 1917. The report by Du Bois and Martha Gruening quotes an eyewitness who described the activities in town as a "man hunt, conducted on a sporting basis." The witness continues, "It was like nothing so much as the holiday crowd . . . in the Roman Coliseum, except that here the shouters were their own gladiators, and their own wild beasts."[38] (In 1929, *The Crisis* published an article by William Pickens, with the title "A Roman Holiday," which documents the December 31, 1928 lynching of Charley Sheppard in Rome, Mississippi, and describes the crowd as "whetting their appetites on the spectacle."[39])

In that same 1917 essay, Du Bois offers an analysis of white violence that, much like his writing in *Dusk of Dawn* 23 years later, defies easy categorization. Du Bois and Gruening explain the gruesome events in East St. Louis partly in terms of a socioeconomic order that has long fostered interracial competition at the expense of class solidarity. As "special investigators of the recent outrages" that left 200 Black people dead and drove another 6,000 out of the city, Du Bois and Gruening reported that white workers in the city had been manipulated by labor leaders into villainizing and attacking Black workers.[40] Yet, as we saw above, they also included eyewitness accounts that stressed the festive, even jubilant mood of the attacks, likening them to "sport." There were "everywhere bodies, blood, hate, and terrible levity."[41] A resident of the city quoted in the piece described the violence in nearly Nietzschean terms, as having a "spirit of fun about it."[42] The article casts labor union leaders as "opportunists" who made a "direct appeal to prejudice" in order to mobilize white workers, who were eager to defend their "privileges." At the same time, the mobs are described as experiencing "pleasurable excitement" in carrying out bloody, savage violence (recounted in gruesome detail in the essay).[43]

An unforgettable passage captures the essay's both/and interpretation of the cruelty. First, Du Bois and Gruening begin by comparing the events in Missouri with the violence of the concurrent world war: "Germany has nothing on East St. Louis when it comes to 'frightfulness.'" They continue: "In all the accounts given of German atrocities, no one, we believe, has accused the Germans of taking pleasure in the sufferings of their victims. *But these rioters combined business and pleasure.* These Negroes were butchered to make East St. Louis a holiday."[44] This statement stresses the sadistic qualities of white mob violence in the United States through contrast with well-known contemporaneous "atrocities" that purportedly did not involve enjoyment in others' suffering. The passage further suggests that the anti-Black brutality carried out in East St. Louis blended "business and pleasure." Keeping with the article's broader argument, this phrase suggests that the violent attacks on Black people were simultaneously an attempt by whites (both bosses and workers) to secure economic advantages *and* something else—the infliction of cruelty for the sake of enjoyment.

Across writings over more than two decades, Du Bois seems to wrestle with the "irrational"—and specifically sadistic—character of white violence committed against Black persons. As can be seen in the examples above, at times pleasure-in-cruelty is cast as sexual in character—particularly in the later texts from 1935 and 1940. This is also around the time that Du Bois begins mentioning that Freud has influenced his thinking, as noted earlier in this chapter. It is perhaps unsurprising, then, that when Du Bois uses the specific word "sadism" (as opposed to other vocabulary that seems to refer to a similar phenomenon), he links it to "sex"—"sex jealousy" in *Black Reconstruction* and "the sex motive" in *Dusk of Dawn*. This association, albeit imprecise in both instances, is consistent with Freud's initial theorization of sadism as a sexual drive, according to which the "torture" of another is accompanied by "sexual excitation."[45] The association between violence and sexuality that Du Bois makes is not just broadly Freudian, however. It is also a way of speaking back to prevailing racialized and sexualized discourses that serve to justify racist violence, especially lynchings. Du Bois's writings, and especially the NAACP's anti-lynching campaign he helped guide, often followed the strategy established by Ida B. Wells in this regard. Du Bois and the NAACP took aim at the false claims accusing Black men of raping white women (frequently made with reference to what were actually consensual relationships between Black men and white women) that were used to foment rage and provoke lynchings. They also pointed out the hypocrisy of such faux moral outrage, given the prevalence of Black women's sexual abuse at the hands of white men.[46] The dominant mythology around lynching cast Black male sexuality as "savage," represented white women as sexually pure and passive, and called for white patriarchal defense in the form of (frequently emasculating) brutal attacks on Black men.[47] In this context, when Du Bois describes white violence against Black people as sadistic, he is pushing back against the sexualized and racialized myths that serve white supremacy. His provocative claim about the pleasure (sometimes coded as sexual) that whites appear to derive from Black pain both gestures toward and rejects the dominant racial-sexual narratives of the time.

Finally, although Du Bois most often explores the problem of sadistic pleasure in relation to examples in which whites actively inflict pain on Black persons, he also suggests that such enjoyment can be experienced more in-directly, by whites who are onlookers or in some sense third parties to anti-Black violence. For example, in "The Souls of White Folk," after describing the festive, orgy-like mood surrounding white mob violence in US cities in the later 1910s, he makes another distressing point: the taking of pleasure in Black suffering and death is potentially a more common affective re-sponse than these instances of dramatic public violence would imply. He declares:

> . . . today to the millions of my people no misfortune could happen,—of death and pestilence, failure and defeat—that would not make the hearts of millions of their fellows beat with fierce, vindictive joy! Do you doubt it? Ask your own soul what it would say if the next census were to report that half of black America was dead and the other half dying.[48]

Here Du Bois is addressing not the "girls with blood on their stockings [who] helped to kick in what had been black faces of the corpses on the street" in East St. Louis.[49] Rather, he speaks directly to "millions" of white Americans—including "you"—and asks how they would feel if they were to learn of the mass "failure and defeat" and "death" of Black citizens. Du Bois suggests a response to such news that is not merely indifferent or apathetic, but *joyful*. The passage confronts us with the suggestion that myriad forms of Black suf-fering may be enjoyed by those who are not directly responsible for the inflic-tion of pain and loss (e.g., those who hear of Blacks' mass death in a census report). Du Bois dares his white readers to consider whether they too might be *pleased* to learn of the extinction of Black people.

There are also hints that racialized pleasure may be felt not only in rela-tion to acts of physical violence but also in relation to less bloody practices of humiliation and debasement. This kind of routine racialized mistreatment is cataloged throughout Du Bois's writings, ranging from Black women's reg-ular subjection to "insult and degradation"[50] to the "jibes of children" who taunt and humiliate Black adults to the supposition that all Black people are servants to be treated "like furniture."[51] Such practices of disrespect, more-over, seem to be *enjoyed* by those marked as "white." As we saw in Chapter 2, *Black Reconstruction* argued that the socially sanctioned "public and per-sonal insult" of Black people in both the antebellum and postbellum eras served to "feed the vanity" of whites.[52] And in "The Souls of White Folk"

Du Bois points out how conditional this experience of gratification is; how contingent it is upon the acquiescence of Black people to their treatment as inferiors. There he notes, for example, that white people often confirm their sense of superiority and worthiness by positioning themselves as the benefactors of Black people: they perform "the obligation of nobility to the ignoble." And they *enjoy* the performance of this purported duty, provided that the desired script is adhered to. Du Bois explains, "So long, then, as humble black folk, voluble with thanks, receive barrels of old clothes from lordly and generous whites, there is much mental peace and moral satisfaction." This peace and satisfaction, derived from an affective display that affirms reigning racial hierarchies, is disturbed when the expectation of obsequiousness on the part of "ignoble" Black persons goes unfulfilled. Du Bois continues, "But when the black man begins to dispute the white man's title . . . when his attitude toward charity is sullen anger rather than humble jollity; when he insists on his human right to swagger and swear and waste,—then the spell is suddenly broken . . ."[53] The white "philanthropist" can no longer take pleasure in this relationship, Du Bois observes; the assertion of Black agency (in defiance of the white supremacist norm of servility) denies the benefactor the specific form of enjoyment he seeks, which is parasitic upon racialized humiliation.

Du Bois suggests that sadistic enjoyment of Black degradation is more widespread than anyone would like to admit. He does so by implying that such gratification may be derived indirectly—by witnesses in addition to perpetrators—and that it may not be limited to instances of physical pain. What if "vindictive joy" is neither restricted to white persons who directly harm Black others nor to acts of visible, bodily violence?

Although his work poses these fraught questions, it is also clear that beginning in the late 1910s and including his key texts *Darkwater, Black Reconstruction,* and *Dusk of Dawn*, Du Bois's work is preoccupied with—and repeatedly confronts—the phenomenon of gratuitous, racist violence. And as we have seen, in these confrontations, Du Bois presents political-economic readings that indict white capitalists and white labor for brutal attacks on Black citizens, while also repeatedly raising the unsettling prospect that such cruelty cannot be fully explained in those terms. The "barbarism" Du Bois describes almost seems to defy explanation. By 1940, when he publishes *Dusk of Dawn*, his writings seem to pointedly ask: is anti-Blackness libidinal rather than simply instrumental?[54]

The Ghost of Sam Hose

For at least 20 years before the publication of *Dusk of Dawn* in 1940, Du Bois seems to be vexed by persistent, gratuitous physical violence against Black Americans and to consider the possibility that such cruelty continues in part because it is *enjoyed* by whites. Perhaps the most striking way the question of racialized sadism appears in Du Bois's oeuvre is through the figure of Sam Hose.[55]

In April 1899, Sam Hose, a Black man who had been accused of killing his boss and raping his boss's wife, was chased for almost two weeks in the Georgia countryside by a white posse before being caught. He was then tortured and burned at the stake before a crowd of about 2,000 people in Newnan, Georgia, 30 miles outside of Atlanta. Although Hose's death was one of many suffered at the hands of white mobs in the time period, his lynching was particularly gruesome and was the subject of unusually wide-spread publicity, of all different types. Local and regional newspapers actively promoted the lynching in their columns during the 10 days Hose was on the run from the white mob. And following his death, the story of his pursuit, capture, and brutal public killing was widely reported, not only in the Southern press, but also by national and international newspapers.[56] Many of these reports recounted in exacting detail how Hose was physically abused and reported on the practice of attendees collecting "souvenirs," including body parts, from the event.[57] Photos of Hose's mutilated body were also sold in the days after the event. The case prompted Ida B. Wells and other anti-lynching activists to hire an investigator whose report on "the burning of Sam Hose" was included in Wells's pamphlet *Lynch Law in Georgia* published that year.[58] (Elsewhere Wells declared the Hose lynching to be "the crime of the century."[59]) For these reasons, the case of Sam Hose is sometimes regarded as marking a turning point in the history of white supremacist violence in the United States, establishing a "new and horrifying pattern," according to which lynchings would function as "modern public spectacles."[60]

Prior to 1938, Du Bois's writings and speeches make no mention of Sam Hose. Indeed, one could read the entirety of his scholarship published up to that date and have no idea that this man's death had affected Du Bois at all. Yet once Du Bois begins talking about his memory of Hose's lynching in 1938, he does not stop talking about it. When he writes and publicly speaks about Sam Hose (at least six times in six different works from 1938 to 1963), he casts Hose's brutal death—and Du Bois's own exposure to it—as a profound rupture, a point of no return in his experience of the American color line.[61] The lapse in time between the event and Du Bois's retelling, along with the charged and vivid yet slightly inconsistent quality of the recollections, certainly suggests the unfolding of a trauma. My point here, however, is not to psychoanalyze Du Bois but to consider how his recollections of Sam Hose's murder might be related to the politico-ethical problem of racism's "irrationality" that his work raises in other ways.[62]

The first public reference to Hose I have found in Du Bois's work appears in a speech he gave on the occasion of his 70th birthday in 1938, which was published as a pamphlet shortly after.[63] The narrative presented here is similar to that which appears in "Science and Empire" in *Dusk of Dawn* two years later. There Du Bois writes:

> At the very time when my studies were most successful, there cut across this plan which I had as a scientist, a red ray which could not be ignored. I remember when it first, as it were, startled me to my feet: a poor Negro in central Georgia, Sam Hose, had killed his landlord's wife. I wrote out a careful and reasoned statement concerning the evident facts and started down to the Atlanta *Constitution* office, carrying in my pocket a letter of introduction to [associate editor] Joel Chandler Harris. I did not get there. On the way news met me: Sam Hose had been lynched, and they said that his knuckles were on exhibition at a grocery store farther down on Mitchell Street, along which I was walking. I turned back to the University. I began to turn aside from my work.[64]

The two earliest references to Du Bois's personal encounter with the lynching of Sam Hose are not identical. The 1938 and 1940 narratives recount Hose's initial alleged crime differently (as having killed his landlord in a wage dispute and raping the landlord's wife [1938]); as having killed his landlord's wife [1940]). Du Bois also provides more sustained interpretation of the event's effects in the latter essay, explaining the "two considerations" that "broke in upon his work" as a result of this searing experience: first, that he could no longer strive to be a "calm, cool, and detached scientist" in the midst of such cruelty, and second, that he had to relinquish what he'd once regarded as "axiomatic": that "the world wanted to learn the truth" and that education could reliably undermine racial caste.

The common features of Du Bois's earliest recollections are striking, however. In both the 1938 and 1940 narratives, Du Bois introduces his memory of Sam Hose's lynching and his experience on the streets of Atlanta with reference to "a red ray of emotion" (1938) and "a red ray which could not be ignored" (1940). (This latter formulation reappears in Du Bois's 1961 autobiography in which he repeats, verbatim, the account of Sam Hose's lynching contained in *Dusk of Dawn.*) The "red ray" in all these instances precedes the story of Hose's death and Du Bois's startling experience of its immediate aftermath. The image, preceding the story itself, seems to sound a warning, signaling to the listener/reader the coming breach.

The breach, every time, across all six narratives, comes in the form of Sam Hose's knuckles. The "news" that stops Du Bois in his tracks in every instance is less Hose's death than the revelation that his body has been mutilated and put on display.[65] Although certain details of Du Bois's recollection shift over time (see below), what remains constant is Du Bois's confrontation with the fact of Hose's destroyed flesh on public view. *Excess* and *enjoyment* together seem to mark the event for Du Bois: the excessive character of the violence inflicted on Hose, evident in his annihilated body, and the celebration and commemoration of his suffering in the form of a material object presented for a white audience's viewing pleasure. His language stresses the element of spectacle: in four places he describes the knuckles as "on exhibition" or describes the store as "exhibiting" them; in two other narratives he says they were "on display." These characterizations emphasize that Hose's brutalized body was offered up for visual consumption and enjoyment. It was not enough, somehow, to torture and kill him in public; the gratuitous, festive character of the lynching itself was carried over to the postmortem treatment of his remains.[66]

The sadistic dimensions of Hose's death are brought into especially stark relief because in each recollection, the horrifying news of the "knuckles" on display in the grocery store *interrupts* Du Bois's delivery of a "careful and reasoned statement" about Hose's case to the local newspaper. That is, word of the grotesque artifact on display shatters Du Bois's plan to address the phenomenon of anti-Black mob violence through argument and persuasion. In every iteration of the Sam Hose episode, this dynamic reappears: Du Bois's attempt to speak to Sam Hose's predicament by presenting a well-argued case in writing in the newspaper—his reliance on the mechanisms of rationality—is completely undone by the "irrationality" of Hose's knuckles on exhibit.[67]

Du Bois's recollections of the Sam Hose incident are partly inconsistent, and it is difficult to independently confirm key details. First, it is notable that Du Bois does not begin telling the story of his encounter with the case of Sam Hose until 39 years after it occurred, which necessarily casts doubt on the specifics—if not the core meaning—of Du Bois's experience. As other readers have pointed out, Du Bois seems to misremember Hose's alleged crime (noted above). A central premise of Du Bois's tale is also in dispute: how likely would it have been for an artifact of Hose's lynching (the knuckles) to have traveled from Newnan to Atlanta as quickly as Du Bois's narrative implies?[68] Another complication, strangely unremarked upon in the secondary literature, is worth noting. In the three descriptions of the Hose incident Du Bois authors in 1938, 1940, and 1944, he reports that as he was walking to the offices of the *Atlanta Constitution*, he became aware of Hose's death and, more significantly, the gruesome relic: "the news met me . . . [T]hey said that his knuckles were on exhibition" and "on the way I learned that Hose had been caught and lynched; and I was also told that some of his fingers were on exhibit."[69] But in two of Du Bois's later retellings, from the 1960s, he says something different: he says he *saw* the display. In a 1960 oral history, he describes his walk to the newspaper offices and reports, "On the way down, I had to pass a meat market, and in the meat market, they were displaying the fingers of Sam Hose."[70] And in a 1963 interview (at age 95) with an *Atlantic Monthly* journalist, Du Bois explained, "Walking to [Harris's] office, I passed by a grocery store that had on display out front the drying fingers of a recently lynched Negro."[71]

What exactly did Du Bois experience on the streets of Atlanta in April 1899? It is probably impossible to know. And adjudicating the veracity of Du Bois's recollections is not what interests me. Rather, it is the way that the figure of Sam Hose seems to haunt Du Bois over the course of his life. More specifically, the festive brutality that is for Du Bois forever linked with Hose's name appears to have made an indelible mark; it is a "red ray" that was never forgotten, even though Du Bois remained silent about it for decades. The multiple references to Hose after 1938 would seem to confirm Joseph Winters's claim that "racial loss and trauma" play a much larger role in Du Bois's thinking than has generally been recognized.[72]

In the 1944 essay, Du Bois writes of that day in Atlanta: I was "told that some of his fingers were on exhibit at a butcher shop which I would pass on my way to town. I turned and never went home. I never met Joel Chandler Harris. Something died in me that day."[73] What died exactly? Perhaps, as this chapter has suggested, it was the belief that anti-Black racism could be combatted with reason, by way of factual and moral argument. It is not coincidental that Du Bois's memory of Sam Hose emerges in his writing at the same time that he begins to overtly raise the problem of racism's "irrationality." The knuckles mark a limit. And this limit throws into question the efficacy of the political strategies Du Bois had held fast to for many years. The educational and legislative campaigns of the NAACP seem, at the very least, ill-equipped to respond to the sadistic brutality that lies at the center of Du Bois's varied Sam Hose narratives.

When Du Bois summarized the aims of the NAACP in 1921, he explained that it was "organized to agitate, to investigate, to expose, to defend, to reason, to appeal. This is our program and the whole of our program."[74] But Du Bois's faith in this approach, as we've seen, was significantly shaken by the time *Dusk of Dawn* appeared; he now emphasizes the "vast areas of unreason at play" and the "powerful motives less open to reason or appeal" that seem to sustain anti-Black racism in the United States, especially its most brutal manifestations.[75] And the figure of Sam Hose in particular seems to cast further doubt on the idea that "exposing" and "arguing" against injustice can dismantle racial caste in the United States.

Perhaps the most unsettling implication of Du Bois's reflections on white sadism is the possibility that the measures intended to combat white supremacy are not merely ineffective or insufficient; rather, they may actually *feed* the "blood lust" of white Americans. For example, consider the "politics of sight" that animated the NAACP's anti-lynching campaign. As Du Bois explained in 1916, "The most important thing which can be done immediately toward stopping lynching is to gather all the facts of lynching and give them the widest publicity."[76] This was the same year that *The Crisis* published lynching photos for the first time, a practice that continued for many years and which Du Bois supported against some initial objections from the editorial board. The purpose of these images, and the detailed investigative journalism that often accompanied them, was, of course, to engage in the "politics of sight"—in the words of Timothy Pachirat, "to make visible what is hidden . . . in order to bring about social and political transformation."[77] But if—as Du Bois also contends in *Darkwater* (1920)—the belief in Black bestiality and subhumanity is so "passionate" as to be "moved by neither argument nor fact" and the prospect of mass Black suffering and death can elicit "vindictive joy" on the part of many whites, then the gruesome images of the torture of Black persons may not assuredly bring about the change the NAACP sought.[78] The reproduction and circulation of these photos, whatever the intent, runs the risk of affirming rather than contesting the notion that "blackness must be punished" and of providing viewers with a vicarious experience of "pleasurable excitement" derived from Black pain.[79]

It seems that Du Bois found the publication of lynching photos to be a worthwhile, if perhaps fraught, tactic during his time as editor of *The Crisis*. But the difficulties opened up by his growing attention to the sadistic dimensions of whiteness should perhaps give pause to contemporary practitioners of the "politics of sight." In particular, the circulation and consumption of photos and videos of anti-Black violence and death—though usually produced and distributed with the aim of documenting and exposing injustice—may be a more uncertain practice than is usually recognized.[80] Recent commentary has addressed the traumatizing effects that repeated exposure to such visuals can have on viewers of color but usually does not consider their reception by white audiences. Might these images tap into "subconscious urges" of the sort that concerned Du Bois, offering racialized pleasure to those invited to identify as (white) subjects over and against denigrated (Black) bodies?[81] Contra the "positivist fantasy" according to which photos and videos of anti-Black violence simply document "what happened,"[82] such imagery enters into a "historical-racial schema" (Fanon), a "racially saturated field of visibility" (Butler)—one that may entice whites to find gratification in violence inflicted on Black people.[83]

Coda: Crossing the Divide

The oft-cited radicalization of Du Bois's thought cannot be fully understood apart from the problem of anti-Black cruelty as a source of white pleasure.[84] In the body of work usually associated with Du Bois's increasing insistence that overcoming racial inequality would require economic revolution, he also wrestled with the possibility that there was something fundamentally irrational, sadistic even, about whites' attachment to the degradation of Black persons. Du Bois argued that whiteness within the racial capitalist regime of his day delivered benefits in the form of literal and metaphorical wages, yet his work also warned against mistaking the "wages of whiteness" thesis for an exhaustive account of racialized gratification. More pointedly, as I have tried to show, his work suggests that whiteness is also experienced, and even enjoyed, through ongoing practices of anti-Black brutality.

Du Bois anticipates contemporary debates over the American racial order, while defying the oppositional terms in which they often play out.

His thought stands as an important alternative to the temptation on the American left to interpret anti-Black racism in the United States as *either* rational (serving a legible function in support of capitalism) *or* irrational (driven by fantasy and enjoyment-in-suffering).

Barbara J. Fields's "resolutely materialist" scholarship is exemplary of the first approach.[85] In her work race *is* capitalist ideology. In the influential article "Slavery, Race, and Ideology in the United States of America," Fields argues that race—and specifically the classification of African-descended people as a race—emerged in the United States "at a discernable historical moment for rationally understandable historical reasons."[86] More pointedly, Fields draws on Edmund Morgan's history of Virginia to show that in the 17th century, both English indentured servants and African slaves were subject to the "grossest forms of brutality and exploitation" by the colonists for whom Virginia was a "profit-seeking venture."[87] On Fields's telling, these two groups of abused laborers came to be more strictly differentiated from one another, largely because Africans in early colonial Virginia "entered the ring alone" and were therefore "available for perpetual slavery in a way that English servants were not."[88] Additionally, the threat that a coalition of aggrieved poor freedmen, servants, and slaves might pose to the colonialists' property and profits—vividly communicated by Bacon's Rebellion in 1676— hastened the systematization of perpetual slavery and the supporting ideology of racial inferiority. Race, on this telling, began to be "invented" in 17th-century colonial America and coalesced as a "coherent ideology" in the revolutionary era of the 18th, where it served to legitimate slavery within a polity ostensibly committed to "inalienable" rights.[89] *Racecraft: The Soul of Inequality in American Life*, which is coauthored with Karen E. Fields, likewise argues:

> Racism and class inequality in the United Sates have always been part of the same phenomenon. Afro-Americans began their history in slavery, a class status so abnormal by the time of the American Revolution that it requires an extraordinary ideological rationale—which then and ever since has gone by the name *race* . . .[90]

On this understanding, "racecraft"—the conjuring of racial designations, particularly in order to distinguish "who is black and who is not"—is a national practice that has outlived the institution of slavery yet continues to operate in the service of economic domination.[91] Racism remains a powerful ideology for American capitalism in the 21st century because it provides an "explanation of why people do badly," according to Fields and Fields.[92] Material inequality, even for well-socialized capitalist subjects, might register as scandalous were it not for the "moral reinforcement" that the "doctrine" of racial superiority and inferiority offers.[93]

From within this framework, contemporary racialized violence such as police killings of Black citizens, for example, is explicable—though certainly not justified—because such brutality expresses and reinforces the hierarchical division between "who is black and who is not."[94] And this racial demarcation, renewed through both spectacular and quotidian acts, sustains capitalism, according to Fields and Fields. Racism today, as always, is a "propaganda weapon" for its elite beneficiaries.[95]

The everyday vocabulary of "race"—even when it is part of an "anti-racist" agenda—thus distracts from what Fields and Fields call "the nature of inequality" and "inequality in its most general form."[96] These terms refer to the material inequality that divides "working Americans" from "those at the top." This fundamental problem—the reality of class domination—is continually obscured by "a racial disguise," according to Fields and Fields.[97] Racecraft supplies an all-purpose discourse that "camouflages" class inequality. It "conceals the truth": that workers of every racial designation "suffer under the same regime of inequality."[98] Such obfuscation, Fields and Fields argue, buttresses a cruel economic order and leaves "working Americans" without an effective way to seek redress.[99]

There is perhaps no clearer counterpoint to the Fields' political-economic account of the US racial order than the work of Frank Wilderson III. Wilderson, like Fields and Fields, understands the specific division Black/not Black to be decisive, yet he rejects any interpretation of this division that places it in the service of capitalist domination. Wilderson criticizes Marxist- and Gramscian-influenced approaches, for example, on the grounds that they attempt to advance a "rational explanation" for anti-Blackness, instead of facing up to its "despotic irrationality."[100] To do the latter would mean acknowledging the existence of a "libidinal economy"—one that relies on Black suffering and death to promote the "psychic health and well-being" to everyone else. The libidinal economy is "irrational" for Wilderson because it does not conform to the logic of capitalist accumulation and because its workings are experienced primarily at the level of the unconscious. This libidinal economy nonetheless generates meaningful effects, on Wilderson's telling: Blacks' abjection has always "nourished" the rest of the world, most crucially by constituting them as human.[101]

Wilderson's theory, developed over the past 20 years, repeatedly advances several striking premises concerning "Blackness" across time and space: it is utterly unique, it is synonymous with "slaveness," and it is antithetical to humanness.[102] Rejecting any possible analogy with other forms of oppression (racialized or otherwise), Wilderson identifies anti-Blackness with a distinctive form of "structural suffering" that bears unparalleled significance.[103] Specifically, there is an "antagonism between Blacks and the world" that—unlike contingent "dustups between the worker and the capitalist," for example—is "the *essential* antagonism" of existence.[104] For Wilderson, what makes this antagonism essential is that it is necessary for the concept of the human to acquire its shape and coherence. The category of humanity, Wilderson maintains, can and does include those who are "degraded"—"an oppressed worker, a vanquished postcolonial subaltern, or a non-Black woman suffering under the disciplinary regime of patriarchy"—but never "the Black," who is the "antithesis of the human subject" and must be "banished" so that others can acquire human standing.[105]

Unsurprisingly, Wilderson understands anti-Black violence in a markedly different way than Fields and Fields. For them, police and vigilante brutality targeting Black Americans is part of a vast race-making project that helps preserve, partly by concealing, an unjust economic order that harms most citizens. Despite other shifts in his thinking over time, Wilderson has long maintained that there is no way to "make political or economic sense" of violence against Black people. There are "no rational explanations for this limitless theatre of cruelty."[106] Instead, this brutality is simply sadistic, a source of collective, ritualized pleasure born from Black pain. "Black death," he declares, is a "recreational pastime."[107]

The enjoyment taken in anti-Black violence is integral to the "Black/Human" division, as Wilderson conceptualizes it. Indeed, humanism itself is sadistic; it depends not simply upon the othering of Blackness, but upon a specific, potent pleasure taken in Black suffering and death.[108] Wilderson argues that "rituals of bodily mutilation and murder are necessary to securing . . . the division between the Human and the Black." Other subordinated social groups experience violent forms of oppression, Wilderson acknowledges, but their vulnerability, he insists, is of a different order; only the abuse and destruction of Black persons delivers "pleasure and psychic renewal for the Human race."[109] Indeed, within the libidinal economy, Black death is enjoyed by everyone who is not Black, on Wilderson's account:

> . . . activists want to make sense of the death of Sandra Bland, and the murders of Michael Brown, and Eric Garner; when what these spectacles require, in order to be adequately explained, is a theory of the *nonsense;* their absence of a tangible or rational utility . . . Black death does have a certain utility, but it's not subtended by the extraction of surplus value; not in any fundamental way. And it is certainly not subtended by the usurpation of land. Black death is subtended by the psychic integration of everyone who is not Black.[110]

The above passage intimates what Wilderson makes explicit elsewhere. Anti-Black violence stands alone in its "irrationality," even when compared to violence directed at other oppressed peoples, including those who are racialized as nonwhite. Since about 2015, Wilderson has differentiated between white supremacy and anti-Blackness, contrasting the "utility" of white supremacist violence with the "*nonsense*" of anti-Black violence, often using the death and dispossession of Native Americans to illustrate the former.[111] On this view, "White supremacy is conceptually coherent," while anti-Blackness is not. White supremacist violence, for example, affects "non-Black people of colour (POC) because White people need something tangible from them, such as land." Anti-Blackness, however, "can't be analogised with the violence that secures White supremacy," because it is "prelogical" and "conceptually incoherent," albeit *necessary* for the humanization of everyone else.[112] Native American genocide, "the murder of eighteen million people," surely entails "pre-logical or libidinal elements," Wilderson notes, yet he maintains that "land acquisition and usurpation give the genocide a kind of coherence and reasonableness" that is entirely absent from the violence inflicted upon Black people.[113]

This worldview understands anti-Black violence to be sadistic, "life-affirming," and indispensable—required for the construction not only of *white* identity, but human identity.[114] The enjoyment taken in Black suffering allows everyone else—"White and non-Black" subjects alike—to feel alive, confident in their humanness.[115]

A similar divergence, though perhaps less stark, can be found in contemporary analyses of the US carceral system. Abolitionist scholar-activists Angela Davis and Ruth Wilson Gilmore, for example, advance interpretations of the "prison industrial complex" that reveal how public punishment operates as a massive and profitable site of investment.[116] Although Davis's and Gilmore's analyses differ, both thinkers demonstrate that the "prison boom" in the United States was never a response to crime rates and ought instead to be understood in political-economic terms. For Davis, this means recognizing that incarceration is "big business."[117] Carceral expansion, which began in the 1980s, is a means of "concentrating and managing what the capitalist system had implicitly declared to be a human surplus."[118] It is a vast, innovative apparatus for generating "dividends" and "profits."[119] Gilmore's account takes a wider view of the phenomenon. She argues that in the United States, "a multi-decade crisis-driven political economy threw off surpluses that became prison expansion's basic factors: land, people, money-capital, and state capacity."[120] The "prison fix" was developed as a way of repurposing these surpluses, according to Gilmore, through "enclos[ing] people in situations where they are expected, and in many ways, compelled, to sicken and so die."[121] Both Davis and Gilmore present analyses in which racism performs a legitimating role in the creation, maintenance, and growth of the carceral apparatus in the United States. They agree that the devaluation of the lives of people of color, especially Black people, enables their overrepresentation in a lucrative system that functions by "discarding" human beings.[122] Davis contends that "ideologies of racism" facilitate the "stupendous profits" that punishment delivers.[123] And although Gilmore cautions against a myopic focus on anti-Black racism, especially when it comes to strategizing against "carceral geographies," she also grants racism a pivotal role. Americans' willingness to believe that "millions of people should spend part or all of their lives in cages" depends on pre-existing patterns of dehumanization. And racism, Gilmore says, is the customary way that "dehumanization achieves ideological normality."[124] In these accounts, mass incarceration is an abomination, but it also makes a certain kind of sense. For both Davis and Gilmore, the carceral regime serves a legible economic function within the contemporary American capitalist state; racism plays an important supporting role.

Jared Sexton advances an account of the American penal system that runs counter to the analyses developed by Davis and Gilmore. In work coauthored with Steve Martinot, Sexton contends that the policing and incarceration of Black people in the United States are only the most obvious examples of a fundamental, pervasive, and unrelentingly violent anti-Blackness that founds and sustains the US order, without serving any "functional role" within its political economy.[125] What they call "white supremacy"—the formal and informal regime that "owes its existence to killing and terrorising those it racializes for that purpose"—is held to be more or less autonomous, de-linked from the capitalist mode of production.[126] Against those who purportedly think the "color line," however brutally maintained, is mere "ideological subterfuge" for propping up the economic order, Sexton and Martinot insist otherwise. They reject any "approach to race [that] subordinates it to something that is not race."[127] Black subjection lacks all instrumental value; it is its own end. The routine punishment of Black Americans is driven by "animus" lacking any "rationale."[128]

The contrasts just outlined are reminiscent of the distinction Michael Rogin draws in his landmark account of American political demonology. Rogin identifies two prominent, divergent schools of thought for addressing the collective creation of (often racialized) monsters: the realist view, which holds that the practice fulfills rational purposes, and the symbolist view, which understands demonization to be driven by latent, unconscious desires. According to the first, which often mobilizes a Marxist conception of ideology, demonology serves identifiable material interests, while the latter interpretation, shaped by Freudian insights, argues that demonology operates at the level of unconscious fantasy and desire. The problem with this division, Rogin warns, is the refusal to acknowledge that *both* "interests and fantasies" are constitutive features of American racial politics, and they can neither be reduced to nor fully separated from one another.[129]

Du Bois's writings defy these either/or paradigms. As we have seen, Du Bois offers a trenchant analysis of the "income-bearing value of racial prejudice," yet he also warns that there are "irrational" dimensions of "race hate" that abide by no such logic.[130] Du Bois appears to hold these views simultaneously, suggesting that they need not be mutually exclusive and that each explanation on its own may be insufficient. (Du Bois hints at this willingness to think across typical boundaries in the preface written for the 1954 republication of *The Suppression of the African Slave-Trade to the United States of America*, originally published in 1896. He identifies the book's greatest limitation: "my ignorance in the waning nineteenth century of the significance of the work of Freud and Marx." Du Bois signals his both/and approach by suggesting that his investigation of the slave trade would have been enriched by a deeper knowledge of Freud, allowing him to probe "the psychological reasons behind the trends of human action which the African slave trade involved," *and* from "the application of Karl Marx to my subject" in order to better address the "influence of economic motives" on the slave trade.[131])

In the work examined here, Du Bois confronts anti-Black violence in its full complexity. He analyzes the brutality inflicted upon Black persons in ways that stress its gratuitous, excessive character, thereby complicating strictly political-economic interpretations of white supremacist violence. Advancing the unsettling possibility that such violence serves as a source of sadistic enjoyment for whites does not lead Du Bois to abandon his insights into the "economic motive" animating such acts, however. He holds these interpretations together. Anti-Black violence is a practice that serves to defend a "public and psychological wage" within the terms of American racial capitalism, and it is a potent source of enjoyment that cannot be fully accounted for in instrumental terms.

Du Bois's account of racial hierarchy in the 20th-century United States, especially its most violent expressions, breaks down the opposition between realist and symbolist approaches, Marxist and Freudian paradigms, and frameworks stressing material interests vs. latent desires. His work scrambles those apparent divides and invites us to look at whiteness, both past and present, as a polyvalent formation capable of generating multiple forms of gratification and therefore calling for varied strategies of resistance.

4

Whiteness as Dominion

The Racial-Colonial Ethos of Ownership

Du Bois's middle-period writings theorize whiteness as a polyvalent formation capable of delivering multiple gratifications to those who bear its sign.
This book's examination of the first motif—the wage—revealed a form of
gratification more complex than a "bribe" engineered by the ruling class.
Rather, as Du Bois illuminated, classification as "white" within the American
regime of racial capitalism has long provided a powerful sense of belonging
and standing—rewards that have been actively and aggressively defended
against perceived encroachment. The public esteem attached to whiteness, as we saw, has depended upon the existence of an exclusive, partial
commonwealth—one that has become less explicit over time, but nonetheless real. Analysis of the next motif—pleasure—further unsettled the tendency to identify Du Bois with a notion of "compensatory whiteness" that
reduces it to a buy-off securing allegiance to capitalism. Turning attention
to what Du Bois referred to as the "irrational" dimensions of "race hate," the
previous chapter explored how whiteness is also figured in his work from
this same period as a source and site of *pleasure* derived from Black suffering.
Reflecting on the gratuitous, excessive qualities of anti-Black violence, Du
Bois confronts the specter of sadism and suggests that whiteness is bound up
with a perverse form of enjoyment taken in Black pain. As I show, Du Bois
does so without abandoning his insights into the workings of the "wage."
That is, his pluralistic approach invites recognition that "whiteness" serves
as a source of material, psychological, affective, and libidinal gratifications.

This chapter further develops that account by addressing Du Bois's astute reading of what I call *whiteness as dominion*.[1] Du Bois locates in "the
souls of white people" a deep, unquestioned belief that the world—nay,
the universe—*belongs to* those with "pale, white" skin. To be white in the
early 20th century, according to Du Bois, is to inhabit a possessive, proprietary orientation—toward the planet in general and toward "darker peoples" in particular. Here he explores a form of racialized gratification that

The Gratifications of Whiteness. Ella Myers, Oxford University Press. © Oxford University Press 2022.
DOI: 10.1093/oso/9780197556764.003.0004

is distinguishable from both the public esteem of the wage and the visceral thrill of sadistic enjoyment. Alongside those motifs, Du Bois's work presents a third—dominion—and proposes that we *also* understand whiteness as an embodied faith with proprietorship at its center.

I argue that Du Bois provides a compelling analysis of a white *ethos of ownership* that deserves attention, both for the way it productively complicates received interpretations of Du Bois and for the way it speaks to the tenacity of white supremacy. As I show, his account of whiteness as dominion is valuable for several reasons. First, it reveals that whiteness is often lived as a comprehensive worldview or "religion" that casts the "darker world" as the default property of those marked "white," and therefore as both usable and expendable. Second, Du Bois's work traces this proprietary imaginary to the material practices and ideology of chattel slavery, while also suggesting that there is something distinctively "modern" about the whiteness he analyzes in the 20th century. This approach allows for recognition of continuity and discontinuity within the afterlife of slavery. Third, the racialized "title to the universe" is an analytic that links domestic and global forms of oppression and also connects practices of exploitation and dispossession, the "theft" of labor to the "theft" of land. Du Bois's incisive theory of white dominion, moreover, remains relevant here and now.

The argument proceeds in four steps. The first section introduces Du Bois's conceptualization of whiteness as dominion and shows how this formulation tethers 20th-century racial dynamics to the institution of slavery, even as Du Bois posits a specifically "modern" form of whiteness. The second and third sections examine how such dominion is enacted on the US and international stages of the 20th century, via practices that are vestiges of slavery and earlier colonialism *and* instantiations of something "new." The second section contends that Du Bois's account of race in the Jim Crow–era United States identifies a system of "signs" inherited from the property regime of chattel slavery that attempts to demarcate racialized (white) subjects from (Black) objects, casting the latter as both exploitable and expendable. The third section examines how racialized entitlement shapes global imperialist endeavors that treat nonwhite peoples and their lands as the a priori property of whites, available for use and disposal. Finally, the fourth section argues that the white entitlement Du Bois identifies is best understood as a pervasive, taken-for-granted interpretive schema, a religion of sorts, that fosters a stance of presumptive ownership toward the "darker world"—its people, land, and resources. The chapter's coda explores two recent phenomena—the dramatic Bundy standoffs in the American West and the everyday criminalization of "living while black"—that are enabled by an abiding faith in white dominion.

"Ownership of the Earth, Forever and Ever, Amen!"

The remarkable essay "The Souls of White Folk" in *Darkwater* opens with Du Bois's declaration that he is "clairvoyant."[2] Of white people he says, "I see in and through them . . . I see these souls undressed and from the back and side. I see the workings of their entrails."[3] As he shares what he finds there, he moves from a general description of the belief in white superiority to a more specific and startling formulation.

Du Bois describes the "sweeter souls of the dominant world," who make pleasant small talk with him. Yet "playing above their actual words" is another message:

"My poor un-white thing! Weep not nor rage. I know, too well, that the curse of God lies heavy on you. Why? That is not for me to say, but be brave! Do your work in your lowly sphere, praying the good Lord that into heaven above, where all is love, you may, one day, be born—white!"

I do not laugh. I am quite straight-faced as I ask soberly:

"But what on earth is whiteness that one should so desire it?'" Then always, somehow, some way, silently but clearly, I am given to understand that whiteness is the ownership of the earth, forever and ever, Amen![4]

This passage captures Du Bois's distinctive analysis of whiteness as a possessive stance, a mode of relationality that regards the world—and crucially, its nonwhite inhabitants and the places they live—as property, or potentially so. Whiteness entails a "passionate" belief in one's right to everything and anything. To be white is to feel that one holds a "title to the universe," according to Du Bois.[5]

On the one hand, this belief is utterly delusional. The essay labels the belief in total ownership "faulty" and an outright "lie." Du Bois stresses its falseness by redescribing the claim to ownership as the assertion of a "divine right to steal," exposing the legitimate-sounding right as a cover for the commission of crimes. But whiteness involves more than willful deception, Du Bois argues; it is a sort of madness. White folks imagine themselves to be "super-human"; they assume the posture of "world-mastering demi-gods." They are beholden to a mirage, one that may seem pleasant enough but that evokes in Du Bois only pity—pity for creatures who are "imprisoned and enthralled" by a "phantasy."[6]

However deeply white folks misapprehend the world and no matter how groundless the conviction that they hold a "title to the universe," its consequences are pernicious. After identifying this sense of "ownership" with the "white soul," the essay cites multiple forms of anti-Black oppression that seem to express this possessive outlook, from the "barbarism" of white mobs in US cities to the imperialist projects of white nations that "bleed and exploit the colonies of the world."[7] Thus, while the proprietary disposition Du Bois conceptualizes may be a hubristic delusion, it generates dire, tangible effects.

Moreover, as I show in the remainder of this section, the "phantasy" that defines whiteness for Du Bois, though sweeping in scope, is far from abstract or otherworldly. Rather, it originates in a specific, identifiable set of material practices. The "extraordinary dictum" that declares that white folks own the world is a vestige of the chattel slavery system that helped found racial capitalism.[8] Although Du Bois does not directly trace the problem of white entitlement to the institution of slavery in "The Souls of White Folk," once his argument there is read alongside his treatment of slavery in *Black Reconstruction,* the lineage of modern whiteness becomes clear. What Du Bois theorizes as whites' belief in their own total, almost ontological dominion is the unacknowledged inheritance of a system built upon "barter in human flesh."[9]

Black Reconstruction stresses the perverse form of ownership constitutive of American slavery. Du Bois illustrates this specific, definitive feature by citing slave codes that described slaves as "devisable like any other chattel" and "purely and absolutely property."[10] While *Black Reconstruction* famously casts the ex-slaves who helped win the Civil War as workers engaged in a "general strike," Du Bois also differentiates those held as slaves from even the most exploited workers. He pinpoints the specific, profound injustice of chattel slavery: "No matter how degraded the factory hand, he is not real estate."[11] He explains:

> In this vital respect, the slave laborer differed from all others of his day: he
> could be sold; he could, at the will of a single individual, be transferred for

life a thousand miles or more. His family, wife and children could be legally and absolutely taken from him. Free laborers today are compelled to wander in search for work and food; their families are deserted for want of wages; but in all this there is no such direct barter in human flesh.[12]

Du Bois directs attention to what Walter Johnson, drawing on the writings of James W. C. Pennington, a fugitive slave, called "the chattel principle."[13] This principle, which Pennington also referred to as the "property principle" and the "bill of sale principle," was enacted in dramatic fashion in the New Orleans slave showrooms Johnson studied, but it governed the slavery system as a whole, as Du Bois saw. The reduction of human beings to commodities with prices—fungible objects to be bought, sold, and traded—lay at the heart of American slavery. Du Bois finds *property relations* between owner and owned, and not only *exploitation relations* between boss and worker, to be constitutive of slavery in the United States.

The fugitive slave—a figure celebrated in *Black Reconstruction*—was subject to a complex legal construction that illustrates this "property principle."[14] Frederick Douglass (whom Du Bois frequently cites in the book) often dramatized this point by declaring to his audiences that he appeared before them as "a thief and a robber! This head, these limbs, this body, I have stolen from my master!"[15] The commodification that underwrote slavery perversely rendered Douglass a thief of his own person, guilty of a property crime against his white owner. Du Bois's discussion of fugitive slaves in *Black Reconstruction* also presents their actions as practical condemnations of the chattel principle. He suggests that fugitive slaves prompted intense vitriol from slaveholders in 1830–1860 because those who "sought freedom by running away from slavery" posed a double threat. First, they were an "important economic item"—every runaway slave was an "actual loss" for the masters. Even more critically, however, when these "black rebels" refused their own commodification and "ran away to freedom," they rejected the very premise of the regime: that persons could be *owned*.[16]

Black Reconstruction also contends that the property relations institutionalized in chattel slavery did not disappear with that regime's formal end. They were perpetuated by overt measures like the Black Codes that attempted to "make Negroes slaves in everything but name."[17] Running still deeper and animating those efforts at re-enslavement was, in the words of Carl Schurz, the Union general and future senator who reported on conditions in the South immediately following the Civil War and whom Du Bois quotes at length in *Black Reconstruction,* "an ingrained feeling that the blacks at large belong to the whites at large."[18] Schurz's contention—that "whites esteem the blacks as their property by natural right," regardless of the legality of slavery—is affirmed by Du Bois's analysis of the sense of totalizing ownership lodged in the very "souls" of white people.

Du Bois's reading of whiteness in "The Souls of White Folk" cites without explicitly naming the prior existence of a politico-legal order that "propertized human life."[19] When Du Bois speaks in the idiom of property relations ("ownership," "title") to characterize "modern" whiteness, his language evokes a specific historical precedent: a regime within which humans socially categorized as Black—and *only* those so categorized—could be held as "real estate," a fate from which all whites were shielded. By identifying whiteness as such with "ownership," Du Bois acknowledges that slavery's property regime was consequential for all white persons and not only for those who owned slaves.[20] When he refers to the "dominant world's" conviction that "whiteness is ownership of the earth, forever and ever, Amen!" the genealogy of this conceit is clear.

Yet Du Bois also believes there is something "new" about whiteness in the 20th century. "The Souls of White Folk" announces: "The discovery of personal whiteness among the world's peoples is a very modern thing—a nineteenth and twentieth century matter, indeed."[21] What can this mean? Although this claim is not rendered very precisely, it is possible to identify the historical dynamics that likely inform it. Broadly speaking, Du Bois seems to situate "the white man's title" in relation to revolutionary and emancipatory projects that preceded it. He references, for example, the lost aspirations of Enlightenment humanism. Just after specifying that the whiteness he analyzes is a "nineteenth and twentieth century matter," he notes, "even up into the eighteenth century we were hammering our national manikins into one, great, Universal Man, with fine frenzy which ignored color and race even more than birth. Today we have changed all that."[22] This formulation implies that he regards the "religion of whiteness" as partly new because it openly departs from the universalist ideals of the earlier age of the American, French, and Haitian revolutions. The promise to overturn social hierarchies has given way, he implies, to "virulent" racism, remarkable for its ascendance in the wake of political struggles that bore the mantle of universalism. Additionally, Du Bois's work is situated overtly *after* the "great age of emancipations," running from Britain in 1833 to Brazil in 1888.[23] Most obviously, *Black Reconstruction* tracks and laments the reinstitutionalization of white supremacy in the wake of the radical, broken promise of Reconstruction. Similarly, in "The Souls of White Folk," when Du Bois explains that a "the new religion of whiteness" is ascendant world-wide, he describes this shift as a "dampening" of the enthusiasm once felt for the pursuit of human freedom, and for the emancipation of slaves in partic-ular.[24] Part of what makes "whiteness" modern for Du Bois, then, is that it is constructed and asserted in contexts that once seemed headed in a very dif-ferent, egalitarian direction.

Ultimately, Du Bois's analysis of modern whiteness depicts it as a pow-erful force, both continuous and discontinuous with previous forms of racial oppression. The presumptive ownership Du Bois locates in white souls, as I argued above, is best understood as a revision of slavery's chattel principle. Linking his contemporaries' objectifying views of Black people to a "world campaign beginning with the slave trade," Du Bois criticizes the hold that the "shameful drama of the past" has on the present.[25] Yet Du Bois's argument is not simply that old ways of enforcing racial caste have been revived. Rather, both domestically and globally, Du Bois observes, inventive strategies redraw the color line in the 20th century. White dominion, then, is enacted in ways that are at once familiar and novel.

Du Bois's account of a racialized ethos of ownership resembles later work in critical race theory (CRT) that conceptualizes whiteness as property. Derrick Bell and Cheryl Harris, for example, each argue in their influential scholarship that there exists a "property right in whiteness." While there is no question that the idiom Du Bois deploys to characterize "modern white-ness"—ownership, title—resonates with these subsequent analyses, the approaches are not identical. While the later work foregrounds the way in which whiteness is held by persons as a form of valuable property, in the texts I examine here, Du Bois emphasizes the tendency of white subjects to look upon the world—and specifically those darker peoples and lands within it—as their property. In other words, the entity that is propertized in these ac-counts differs. In the CRT tradition, particularly in Harris's landmark essay, whiteness is property, according to US law and custom. Du Bois's insights into white dominion, however, target something else: a worldview that casts that-which-is-not-white (persons, lands, resources) as personal possessions that rightfully belong to those marked "white."

To clarify: Harris, building on Bell's formulation of whiteness as a "vested property interest" that delivers advantages to those who possess it, characterizes whiteness in her famous essay as "treasured property," "a valuable asset," and a "predicate for attaining a host of societal privileges."[26] While the precise meaning of whiteness as property has shifted in the 20th century, from a state-sanctioned legal status to a source of de facto privilege, Harris argues, "holders of whiteness" in the United States have for centuries enjoyed a form of "usable property."[27] While Harris provides a sophisticated analysis of the racialized advantage delivered to "possessors of whiteness," when Du Bois identifies the "silent but clear" belief that "whiteness is ownership of the earth, forever and ever, Amen!," he aims to capture something else.[28] The account of white dominion investigated here concerns less the unequal distribution of tangible and intangible goods along the color line (a topic Du Bois addressed in detail in much of his work) than the way in which "white souls" think and act in accordance with the conviction that racialized others are their property.

The understanding of proprietary whiteness advanced by Bell and Harris, then, is distinct from, though not incompatible with, Du Bois's thematization of the ethos of white entitlement. Indeed, that whiteness serves as "a highly valued and exclusive form of property" (Harris) in no way conflicts with Du Bois's claim that a "religion of whiteness" positions its faithful as the presumptive owners of the entire planet.[29] Moreover, the CRT tradition that conceives of whiteness as property is indebted to Du Bois's own formulation of whiteness as a "wage." For example, in one of the earliest explicit formulations of proprietary whiteness, Bell writes that slavery "provided mainly propertyless whites with a property in their whiteness," echoing Du Bois's argument in *Black Reconstruction* that maps how racial solidarity was achieved in the United States by way of the payment of a "public and psychological wage," to even the poorest whites.[30] Harris's essay makes this link explicit by citing Du Bois to explain "whiteness as racialized privilege" and stressing Du Bois's point that whiteness provided "real advantages" that were not only monetary.[31] Du Bois's insights into the wages of whiteness inform CRT's examinations of proprietary whiteness. Still, as I explained earlier, this chapter explores another, lesser-known dimension of Du Bois's thinking about white racial identity. This line of thinking asks: how does whiteness endure, not only as something akin to a valuable possession, but also as a comprehensive outlook that thingifies everything it sees?

To further examine Du Bois's distinctive reflections on this question, the next sections consider two primary and interconnected sites for the enactment of white dominion, drawn from his writings. The second section considers how the system of racial "signs" operative in the Jim Crow United

States updated yet largely sustained the owner/owned division definitive of slavery. In the third section, I probe Du Bois's treatment of the "new imperialism" of his age, which exposes a pattern of avarice expressive of white nations' intent to "own the world."

Dominion in America: Badges of Slavery in the Postemancipation United States

Du Bois's understanding of race transformed over the course of his long career, but by the 1930s he had arrived at his "mature concept," which prefigured later analyses of race as a social construction.[32] Several of the essays in *Dusk of Dawn* (1940) offer powerful refutations of biologistic accounts and provide a countertheory of race as an invented classification that enforces social hierarchies. Du Bois announces that a "scientific definition of race is impossible" and that the classification of humans by race is spurious. But while racial categorization has no basis in nature, the designations "white" and "black," Du Bois tells us, remain indispensable for the caste system he finds in the United States in 1940. He captures this paradox in an autobiographical description of his own life: "the difference in skin color was vastly overemphasized and intrinsically trivial."[33] How is this baseless yet all-important distinction made and remade, according to Du Bois? He presents three crucial claims: (1) race is a "badge" or a "sign," (2) the sign "black" functions to designate inferiority because it is associated with slavery and the historical fact of "propertized human life,"[34] and (3) the marks of race are enforced by both law and custom in the Jim Crow era.

First, to counter pseudo-scientific claims about race, Du Bois persistently refers to race as a kind of mark—he calls it both a "badge" and a "sign." In "The Concept of Race," for example, he declares that the "badge of color [is] relatively unimportant save as a badge."[35] In other words, skin color has little meaning in and of itself. It is one of many physical variations to be found among the species; however, it *is* important because it operates as a sign. And what does this sign communicate? *Black Reconstruction* makes the point plainly: "the Negro ... was compelled almost continuously to submit to various badges of inferiority."[36]

Du Bois traces the hierarchy-enforcing "badges" of his day directly to the institution of slavery.[37] The statement that skin color is "unimportant, save as a badge," is followed immediately by a reference to the "social heritage of slavery."[38] Here Du Bois suggests, albeit obliquely, that racial divisions persist because they signify *in accordance with* the foundational race-making institution in the United States. Du Bois makes this claim explicit in "The White World," after acknowledging that division by race is both "absurd" and highly consequential. He continues:

> If, as happened to a friend of mine, a lady in a Pullman car ordered me to bring her a glass of water, mistaking me for a porter, the incident in its essence was a joke to be chuckled over; but in its hard, cruel significance and its *unending inescapable sign of slavery,* it was something to drive a man mad.[39]

Du Bois's interpretation of this encounter clarifies how the badges of race function in the postemancipation United States. The designations "white" and "black" do not signify mere "difference" but instead reference a historically specific hierarchy dividing owner and owned. The classification "black" attached to the otherwise "unimportant" fact of skin color still signifies slavery, 75 years after emancipation.

Du Bois's analysis indicates that if race is a mark, it should be understood less as a noun than as a verb and that practices of marking are both de jure and de facto in character. A dialogue from "The White World" conveys this first point. Du Bois's "white friend, Roger Van Dieman," is deeply confused when confronted with Du Bois's claim that racial classification lacks scientific basis. He inquires whether Du Bois really means to say "there are no races" and asks, in disbelief, how then Du Bois can see himself as part of a Black community at all:

> [Van Dieman]: But what is this group; and how do you differentiate it; and how can you call it "black" when you admit it is not black?
> [Du Bois]: I recognize it quite easily and with full legal sanction; the black man is a person who must ride "Jim Crow" in Georgia.[40]

This exchange clarifies that race is (re)made by discriminatory conduct, and nothing else. "Black" is an invented category sustained by repetitive practices (such as the segregation of public transportation Du Bois cites) that effectively reinscribe the divisions of slavery. (Twenty years earlier, Du Bois noted that the mark "black" is uniquely durable: America has begrudgingly allowed "'new' white people" to acquire "place and power," while "against Negroes she can and does take an unflinching and immoveable stand . . . She trains her immigrants to the despising of 'n*****s' from the day of their landing."[41])

Du Bois maintains that discriminatory laws affix a degrading "badge"—specifically, the badge of slavery—onto some citizens, yet he does not think that caste is maintained by legal authority alone. Recall his anecdote concerning the white woman in the train car who ordered a Black male passenger to bring her a drink. Here the problem lies not with an overtly discriminatory law or policy but rather with a racialized schema that immediately and reflexively associates dark skin with servitude. (Du Bois captures this ready-to-hand association in an earlier *Darkwater* essay when he writes that the labor movement abandoned Blacks because like the rest of the "white world," they deeply believe "Negroes are servants; servants are Negroes."[42]) In the train example, the "inescapable sign of slavery" is enforced by default patterns of thought and everyday action, more so than by official "legal sanction." The ethos of dominion that Du Bois identified with whiteness in 1920's "The Souls of White Folk" is evident in this interaction too. Mistaking the Black passenger for a servant indicates that Blackness remains, in the words of Saidiya Hartman, "the mark of object status" in slavery's afterlife.[43] Such marks, Du Bois shows, are manufactured and sustained by habit no less than law.

"The Color Line Belts the World": Dominion as Colonial Aggrandizement

Du Bois's deft analyses of the US polity consistently place American racial dynamics within a global frame. As Lawrie Balfour points out, even the famous sentence that opens "Of the Dawn of Freedom" in the relatively early *The Souls of Black Folk* (1903) presents the "color-line" as a decidedly transnational phenomenon by connecting race-based hierarchies in the United States to those in "Asia and Africa."[44] Indeed, a "global orientation" is evident throughout Du Bois's long life and varied oeuvre.[45] This orientation grew into a more explicit set of politico-theoretical commitments with his important 1915 essay, "The African Roots of War," and gained fuller expression around 1919–1920, in the wake of World War I, when Du Bois created the Pan-African Congress (1919–1945) and published *Darkwater*.[46]

The essays in *Darkwater* address what Charles Mills has called "the idea of race as a global system."[47] More specifically, these writings depict the Jim Crow regime in the United States and aggressive Anglo-European imperialism as

mutually reinforcing programs of racial oppression. Connecting white nations' bloody quest for the "dark world's wealth and toil" to the subjugation
of Black people within the United States, as Du Bois does repeatedly, signals
that the project of colonization is not simply "external" and that freedom
struggles must traverse national boundaries.[48]

Du Bois's efforts to expose Euro-American domination of the "darker
races" as a global problem and to encourage the internationalization of resistance to racial capitalism are well recognized by most interpreters of his
middle- and late-period work.[49] Here I demonstrate that the concept of
white dominion in particular helps Du Bois forge the connection between
domestic and global forms of injustice in the early 20th century. The conviction that "whiteness is ownership of the earth forever and ever, Amen!"
underwrites both America's violently enforced system of racial marks and
brutal forms of empire building carried out around the globe. Just as Black
people in the post emancipation United States remain subject to laws and
norms that facilitate their treatment as possessions—whether as instruments
to be used for others' ends or as waste to be disposed of—there is a global pattern of "colonial aggrandizement," Du Bois charges, in which white nations
"divide up the darker world" to do with as they please.[50]

This section shows that the concept of white dominion is central to Du
Bois's analysis of colonialist expansion. Further, this concept—particularly
via the idiom of racialized enslavement—works in Du Bois's writings to
tether domestic and global forms of oppression together and to map relations between past and present. I also explain how this understanding of
"white title" connects the abuse and destruction of "darker peoples" to the
theft of "dark land."[51] Thus, white dominion entails a racialized, proprietary
relationship to both persons and places.

Du Bois's analysis of World War I in *Darkwater* treats it not as exceptional
but as consistent with prevailing patterns of colonization since the "later
nineteenth century"—patterns that express a racialized ethos of ownership.[52]
For example, his account of public reactions to the war among Allied countries reveals the workings of a proprietary worldview among white nations
and white citizens. He writes, "Behold little Belgium and her pitiable plight,
but has the world forgotten Congo? What Belgium now suffers is not half, not
even a tenth, of what she has done to black Congo . . ." He continues, noting
that as mass murder took place under King Leopold's regime, "Belgium
laughed, the cities were gay, art and science flourished," and other colonialist
powers, committing their own violent conquests elsewhere, did not object

to the slaughter.[53] Within the context of the essay, which opens with Du Bois's memorable formulation of the belief that "Whiteness is ownership of the earth, forever and ever, Amen!," the fact that Belgium has received widespread sympathy while the far greater death and destruction that Belgium wrought in "inmost Africa" remains unacknowledged and ungrieved can be seen as a manifestation of whites' presumptive title. The violence that shook Europe during the world war registered as remarkable and tragic precisely because white people suffered—those who believed that the world belonged to them and expected to be the agents, not the targets, of mass violence.

Divergent views of the conflict held by the "white world" and "dark world" are tied to these populations' differential exposure to the racialized ethos of ownership. Du Bois writes, "War is horrible! This the dark world knows to its awful cost. But has it just become horrible . . . ?" That Germany is condemned by the United States for its invasion of Belgium and that war as such is now lamented throughout Europe reveal to Du Bois only that whites were alarmed to discover they were not shielded from violence as they had been in so many recent colonial wars that devastated "darker peoples" ("in German Africa, in British Nigeria, in French and Spanish Morocco . . .").[54] The war was a cataclysm for "the white world," Du Bois avers, but others had long-standing, intimate knowledge of Europe's cruelty: "We darker men said: This is not Europe gone mad; this is not aberration nor insanity; this *is* Europe; this seeming Terrible is the real soul of white culture—back of all culture, — stripped and visible today."[55] The suffering wrought by the recent world war was nothing new, Du Bois says, for those "darker peoples of Asia and Africa" who were long subjected to "conquest and conquest." Much as Du Bois is able to see through white folk (announced in the essay's first lines), so too do darker people share a collective understanding of the "real soul of white culture." What lies there, "stripped and visible," is nothing but "rage for one's own nation to own the earth."[56]

This proprietary rage is not unique to the war. The *Darkwater* essays present World War I as the latest episode of a "new imperialism" dating to the late 19th century. Additionally, Du Bois sees the violent enactment of "white title" taking place simultaneously against nonwhites worldwide and against Black people in the United States. He writes:

Such is the silent revolution that has gripped modern European culture in the later nineteenth and twentieth centuries. Its zenith came in Boxer times: White supremacy was all but world-wide, Africa was dead, India conquered, Japan isolated, and China prostrate, while white America whetted her sword for mongrel Mexico and mulatto South America, lynching her own Negroes the while.[57]

This remarkable passage makes several important points. First, by dating this "silent revolution" the way he does, Du Bois connects it to the phenomenon of "modern whiteness," which he also locates in the "nineteenth and twentieth" centuries six pages prior. Thus, "the title to the universe claimed by White Folk" is coeval with the material practices of new imperialism. Next, by associating colonialist violence carried out in Africa, Asia, and the Americas with the lynching of Blacks in the United States, he depicts these international and domestic phenomena as mutually reinforcing forms of white entitlement. Additionally, key terms and points of reference amplify Du Bois's anti-colonial critique. When he references "mongrel Mexico" and "mulatto South America," he mockingly echoes the views of apologists for the Mexican-American War and proponents of US control of the Southern Hemisphere.[58] By identifying the "zenith" of the formation of new imperialism with "Boxer times," Du Bois does more than pinpoint the turn of the century (the Boxer Rebellion of 1899–1901) as a key historical juncture; significantly, he defines the epoch in relation to anti-colonial *resistance* that rejects the delusion that whites (ought to) own the world.[59]

As argued in the previous two sections, the concept of whiteness as dominion cannot be understood apart from the precedent of slavery and its defining property relations. The genealogy conveyed by Du Bois's account is complex, however, because he recognizes that racial orders of the early 20th century simultaneously reproduce the entrenched hierarchies of the past and innovate upon them. Thus, the racial signs operative in the Jim Crow South, we saw, were both an extension of slavery's "property principle" and an adaptation suited to the postemancipation era. Likewise, slavery figures prominently in Du Bois's critique of "new imperialism." He contends that the contemporary colonization of the "darker world" repeats and updates features of the legalized slave trade, an institution that was thoroughly global all along.

This argument, which Du Bois begins making in the late 1910s, lays the foundation for what Adom Getachew describes as the "empire as enslavement" thesis that rose to prominence among anti-colonial critics and nationalists following World War II.[60] Across his middle-period work

(1920–1940) and later, Du Bois analogizes the colonization of Africa, Asia, and South America in the late 19th and early 20th century to the prior legal slave trade, establishing historical repetition-with-a-difference. In "The Hands of Ethiopia," composed in 1918 and published in 1920's *Darkwater*, for example, he connects the "barbarous scramble" over Africa beginning in the late 1800s to the Atlantic slave trade that preceded it:

> For four hundred years white Europe was the chief support of that trade in human beings which first and last robbed black Africa of a hundred million human beings . . . Today instead of removing laborers from Africa to distant slavery, industry built on a new slavery approaches Africa to deprive the natives of their land, to force them to toil and to reap all the profit for the white world.[61]

Here white "ownership" is both sustained and revised for a new context. Quite simply: "If the slave cannot be taken from Africa, slavery can be taken to Africa."[62] This invocation of slavery highlights the global geography of "white title," both past and present, and the historical adaptations by which dominion endures.

Du Bois also cites the precedent of slavery to characterize the condition of colonized subjects beyond Africa. In *Black Reconstruction*, even as he argues for the distinctiveness of chattel slavery (the enslaved person was "real estate"), he observes that the "analogue today" to the American slave is the "yellow, brown and black laborer in China and India, in Africa, in the forests of the Amazon . . ."[63] This formulation positions the slave within the US regime not as anomalous but as precedent setting, modeling what would become a feature of global racial capitalism.[64] The "analogue" Du Bois advances, which links enslavement to colonialism, performs a "dual critique," in the words of Getachew. It positions empire as "a form of enslavement and international racial hierarchy."[65]

"New imperialism" is not simply a copy of anything that came before, however. Du Bois maintains that although economic domination is a recurrent practice of human societies, colonial powers operate with a "heaven-defying audacity" and on an unprecedented scale.[66] He also understands the colonial expansion undertaken by white nations in this period as a historically specific strategy that aimed to "solve" a particular problem—namely, the growing power of white organized labor within those countries. In 1920 Du Bois describes colonization as the "scheme of Europe," meant to provide "a way out of long-pressing difficulties." He clarifies what he means by noting that capitalist control of the white working classes has weakened and that greater economic equality is on the horizon in Europe. Colonization, then, is the "loophole" that allows for further capitalist accumulation—"no labor unions or votes or questioning onlookers or inconvenient consciences."[67] Europe's effort to "levy endless tribute on the darker world" is at least partially new, on Du Bois's rendering, because it is a historically specific attempt to stabilize capitalist rule against the gains of white labor.[68]

Du Bois's treatment of new imperialism likens the exploitation and degradation of the "darker peoples" it targets to slavery, yet also specifies that the proprietary "religion of whiteness" finds expression in the taking of "dark land" as well. The concept of "white dominion" I draw from Du Bois's work refers to a possessive orientation toward both people *and* land. It names a racialized ethos of ownership that simultaneously facilitates and is facilitated by practices of exploitation *and* dispossession.

The double valence of the "title to the universe" is most evident when Du Bois pairs the violent extraction of labor with the "stealing" of land.[69] He does so often. In one of many indictments of 20th-century empire building, he writes, "Colonies, we call them, these places where 'ni****s' are cheap and the earth is rich," bringing together the appropriation of both human labor and land. Likewise, what motivated the world war, he says, was competition for "the labor of yellow, brown, and black folks" *and* "the possession of land overseas."[70] "The Hands of Ethiopia" similarly condemns the expropriation of "both land and labor" in Africa.[71] Dispossession and exploitation are presented as complementary strategies of the new imperialism—strategies united by the worldview of white dominion.

Du Bois's approach foreshadows recent scholarship that draws on and reworks Marx's account of "primitive accumulation" to show that the dispossession of land is a constitutive and continuous feature of capitalism.[72] Rather than understanding what Marx called the "theft of land" as a temporal precursor to proletarianization, which is ultimately superseded by exploitation as the means of capital accumulation, political theorists including Robert Nichols and Onus Ulas Ince argue that "land grabs" are not a historical stage of capitalist development but rather, as Nichols puts it, "a distinct modality of its ongoing operation."[73] This insight builds upon Rosa Luxemburg's analysis in *The Accumulation of Capital,* which argues that capitalism's processes of accumulation do not rely on exploitation alone, but also on "colonial policy" and "war," that is, on accumulation via "imperialist expansion." "Force, fraud, oppression, looting" are the indispensable methods by which capital seizes land and raw materials, according to Luxemburg.[74]

Du Bois, like Luxemburg, places the violent dispossession of land and resources at the center of capitalism's global quest for profit.[75] Yet Du Bois's analysis stipulates that this form of accumulation, pursued aggressively through colonization, is a *racialized* practice. As Alberto Toscano explains, Du Bois was alert to the "racial coordinates of imperialism" in ways that Luxemburg was not.[76] Du Bois theorizes "colonial aggrandizement," and the "robbery" of land in particular, as techniques that inflict violence and coercion on *particular* peoples and places: the "darker world." Put slightly differently, Du Bois's theorization of white dominion invites consideration of what Siddhant Issar conceptualizes as "racial/colonial primitive accumulation."[77]

Indeed, Du Bois's emphasis on the theft of land and resources from "darker nations" suggests that the process of "development" within racial capitalism is historically inseparable from colonization.[78] Taking "possession of land" is a key feature of so-called "industrial development," Du Bois argues, and it follows a clear pattern: "the white world" has been engaged in "desperate competition for possession of colonies of darker peoples."[79] If Du Bois is now widely recognized as a theorist of what Cedric Robinson dubbed "racial capitalism," one might specify further that he was an important analyst of racial-colonial capitalism.

Du Bois's sustained attention to territorial dispossession as a key expression of white dominion is crucially important. As Aileen Moreton-Robinson argues, many analyses of whiteness that emerge out of African American studies focus exclusively on the constitutive role played by slavery and pay little or no attention to the theft of Indigenous lands. (Cheryl Harris's canonical essay is an exception, because she traces the rights and privileges that accrue to the "holders of whiteness" in the United States to the appropriation of native lands *and* the enslavement of Africans.[80]) Although Du Bois recognizes the theft of land as a recurring feature of racial-colonial capitalism, his treatment of colonialism, and settler colonialism specifically, is strikingly incomplete. On the one hand, Du Bois seems to recognize the specific characteristics of settlement in his analysis of 20th-century Africa. In the spirit of Patrick Wolfe's well-known formulation—"territoriality is settler colonialism's irreducible element"—Du Bois reports, "A recent law of the Union of South Africa assigns nearly two hundred and fifty million acres of the best of natives' land to a million and a half whites and leaves thirty-six million acres of swamp and marsh for four and a half-million blacks. In

Rhodesia over ninety million acres have been practically confiscated."[81] Du Bois describes violent territorial dispossession and displacement in African settler societies.[82] Yet consideration of settler colonialism in the United States is notably absent from his work. While the question of land is central to *Black Reconstruction*'s historical narrative, it appears only in relation to freed slaves' desire for land and the US government's refusal to provide it.

According to *Black Reconstruction*, following the Civil War, Negroes "wanted land to work."[83] Referencing the infamous promised 40 acres, Du Bois states that former slaves who actually received a small amount of land were ultimately "dispossessed" of it.[84] The planter South succeeded, via intimidation and violence, in their quest to "keep the bulk of Negroes as landless laborers."[85] The lengthy book makes no mention, however, of the prior dispossession that founded the country. There is no recognition of the fact that "slaves were brought to America as the property of white people to work the land that was appropriated from Native American tribes."[86] Du Bois's account doesn't simply neglect this reality; he actually feeds into settler colonial ideology by describing America's European settlers as the beneficiaries of "free land" and "endless land of the richest fertility."[87] He similarly refers to the "tremendous significance of free land in abundance" when describing the Western Migration of the 1800s.[88] Although Du Bois's powerful analytic of white dominion identifies a proprietary conceit at the heart of slavery and colonialism (and their historical reverberations), he never acknowledges or investigates the originary acts of dominion that founded the United States. To address Indigenous dispossession in that context, contra Du Bois, would require investigating how the racialized ethos of ownership in the United States is an inheritance of conquest and settlement no less than slavery.

So, can the imperialist expression of white dominion conceptualized by Du Bois be distinguished from the capitalist quest for surplus value? Du Bois affirms Marx and Engels's famous observation that the hunt for profits sends the bourgeoisie scurrying "over the entire surface of the globe," even as he critically alters it by specifying that planetary capitalism targets "the exploitation of darker peoples." "The Souls of White Folk" repeatedly describes the white world's relationship to "black and brown men" in terms of the former's use of the latter.[89] Such use involves many horrors—"slavery and rape," "disease and maiming"—all in the service of an identifiable end: "dividends" that are not only enjoyed by capitalists, Du Bois says, but also by white workers in Europe and the United States who profit from the exploitation and expropriation of the darker world.[90]

Although the sense of dominion that Du Bois associates with whiteness is on full display in the imperialist quest for profit, the presumption of ownership that Du Bois uncovers is not identical with the drive to exploit or dispossess racialized others for monetary gain. The "title to the universe" that resides within white souls surely informs the economic subordination of nonwhite people, but this "title" refers to something still vaster: an all-encompassing, lived faith.

A Religion of White Dominion?

In "The Souls of White Folk," Du Bois repeatedly likens whiteness as dominion to a religion, a gesture that indicates that the possessive orientation he conceptualizes is both comprehensive in scope and secured by deep conviction. The white interlocutor's belief that whiteness is "ownership of the world, forever and ever, Amen!" lays bare the religious dimensions of this "title." And Du Bois characterizes this "passionate" belief precisely as expressive of a "religion of whiteness." He also describes a "gospel" preached worldwide, consistent with the doctrine of white ownership that affirms that "a White Man is always right" and that nonwhite persons are "dogs of men."[91]

Du Bois twice describes the theft committed by colonizing white nations as "divine," creating a jarring juxtaposition that also implies whites believe their imperialist projects to be authorized by God.[92] Additionally, in a passage reiterating the claim that anti-Black racism in the United States resembles the practices of domination carried out by white nations worldwide, Du Bois writes: "For two or more centuries America has marched proudly in the van of human hatred,—making bonfires of human flesh and laughing at them hideously, and making the insulting of millions more than a matter of dislike,—rather a great religion, a world war-cry: Up white, down black . . ."[93] Whiteness, understood as a racialized "title to the universe" that authorizes the use, abuse, and destruction of those not marked as white, is itself a *global religion* that bonds the United States to its imperialist partners throughout the world.

To conceive of whiteness as a religion is distinct from claiming that Christian institutions have promoted white supremacy, although Du Bois did both.[94] He was a vocal critic across his writings of the corruption and hypocrisy of white Christian churches, exposing their active role in promoting a racist order (even as he also creatively reimagined Christianity for Black people in ways that anticipated Black liberation theology).[95] When Du Bois writes about a "religion of whiteness," he is not contending that organized religion is racist—though he believes that to be the case. Rather, he is urging his readers to recognize how whiteness is *lived as an existential faith*.[96]

I use "existential faith" purposely here, borrowing William Connolly's usage, to signify that whiteness as dominion serves as a worldview, one that may or may not be explicitly theistic.[97] This kind of lived faith elides any sharp distinction between the theological and the secular and encompasses explicit beliefs and tacit presuppositions, philosophical creeds and visceral sensibilities, knowing commitments and default intuitions. The existential faith that Du Bois brings to our attention might also be understood as a "horizon of white perception" helping to shape everything from foreign policy to routine social interactions.[98]

Indeed, by theorizing a modern "religion of whiteness," Du Bois anticipates later theories that address how racial hierarchies are reproduced in part by a hegemonic interpretive schema. This scholarship considers the power of a "white imaginary" or "racial imaginary" (Toni Morrison, George Yancy, Claudia Rankine), a "white racial frame" (Joe Feagin), and a white "optic" or "prism of perception and interpretation" (Charles Mills).[99] Though not identical to one another, these works converge on the idea that whiteness functions as a dominant, mostly unrecognized meaning-making apparatus, with far-reaching effects on thought, feeling, and action. This approach is influenced most directly by the signature analysis in Fanon's *Black Skin, White Masks* of the "white gaze," yet this reading reveals that Du Bois's account of whiteness as a comprehensive outlook on the world also foreshadows these later efforts.[100]

Du Bois not only investigates whiteness as an existential faith or horizon of perception but also ascribes to it a specific, consequential conviction: the presumption of totalizing ownership. That is, the perspectival and ethical regime Du Bois aligns with whiteness does not just ascribe inferiority to nonwhites; more precisely and more devastatingly, it is a vantage point that regards nonwhite persons, their lands, and their resources as properly *belonging to* whites, available for use and disposal.[101] Overt in the practices of slavery and colonization, the owning of darker persons and the taking of darker land, this powerful sense of "title" is not restricted to those manifestations, Du Bois suggests. It also operates subtly and insidiously, as a lived faith and a general orientation to existence, well into the 20th century.

Thus, whiteness as dominion is distinguishable from the "public and psychological wage" that Du Bois also identifies with whiteness (examined in

Chapter 2). It is not only that Du Bois understands white entitlement as a thoroughly global phenomenon in contrast to the wage, which is primarily presented as a mechanism of the US social order. Nor is it simply that whites' "title to the universe" appears less class specific (and therefore less obviously "compensatory") than the wage. Rather, what makes racialized dominion most distinctive is its expansive, religious quality—the way in which it serves as a broad and unquestioned schema for being-in-world. This sweeping, proprietary gospel of whiteness seems to outstrip the "wages of whiteness."

Perhaps we should think of the Du Boisean wage, then, as partly activated by this existential faith. Are the socialized goods and collective esteem enjoyed by whites partly enabled by an overarching interpretive framework that anoints those with "pale" skin as title bearers? I suggest that the horizon of perception sanctioning white dominion is not separate and apart from the compensatory dynamic Du Bois analyzed, even though they ought not to be collapsed together. The efficacy of the wage seems to depend in part on the conviction that the world belongs to white folk. Du Bois alludes to this possibility. He writes in "The Souls of White Folk" disappointingly of the "guild of laborers—the front of that very important movement for human justice" who did little to oppose the colonialist world war. However, he observes that this acquiescence to the war was unsurprising: it was "foreshadowed when in Germany and America 'international' Socialists had all but read yellow and black men out of the kingdom of industrial justice." He explains, "Subtly had they been bribed, but effectively: Were they not lordly whites and should they not share in the spoils of rape?"[102] This formulation suggests that the invocation of racialized entitlement—"were they not lordly whites?"—primed white workers to accept what Du Bois regards as a bribe. The transaction Du Bois recounts is conditioned by an expansive sense of dominion.

The question of how this existential faith or ethos of ownership is related to whiteness as pleasure is complicated. As we have seen, Du Bois pluralizes whiteness, exploring its multiple gratifications in ways that belie any neat, monadic account. Chapter 3, for example, showed that Du Bois probed the sadistic character of anti-Black violence and degradation without abandoning his political-economic critique of such brutality—suggesting that neither analysis on its own is sufficient. With regard to the "religion of whiteness" explored here, it may be that this faith, sanctifying white dominion, facilitates the disturbing forms of enjoyment that Du Bois encountered in his reflections on lynching and on Sam Hose in particular. An existential faith that believes the world to be the property of those marked white also positions nonwhite—what Du Bois calls "darker"—peoples and lands as available, usable, and disposable. And related acts of mistreatment and abuse may deliver to white "demi-gods" not only a vivifying sense of mastery but also felt pleasure in the suffering of racialized others. To make this connection is not to reduce white sadism to a mere effect or symptom of the existential faith explored here. Once again, we should follow Du Bois and resist the temptation to oversimplify the workings of whiteness. As wage, as pleasure, as dominion, its gratifications are plentiful and powerful.

Coda: Spectacular and Quotidian Acts of Faith

A racialized ethos of ownership lives on in our present, even under conditions of racial capitalism—post–civil rights and postindustrial—quite different from Du Bois's own. Consider, for example, the Bundy family standoffs that took place in the western United States in 2014 and 2016 and received wide media coverage. Both cases involved the armed occupation of federal lands by white ranchers and their supporters who vowed to "make war" on the Bureau of Land Management and the US government itself. As one reporter noted, "Throughout both occupations, the Bundys staged press conferences and carried their weapons openly. They did not hide the fact that they were illegally occupying federal government land."[103]

In April 2014, the bureau took steps to impound Nevada rancher Cliven Bundy's herd of cattle for the $1.1 million he owed in grazing fees and fines, which he had refused to pay for the past 20 years. Bundy, his two sons Ammon and Ryan Bundy, and friend and militia leader Ryan Payne called for support from far right groups and about 100 heavily armed supporters assembled in Nevada to confront the bureau. A tense, widely publicized standoff ensued. Militiamen bearings guns gathered on a highway overpass, while others on horses led a charge below to face off against federal agents. The bureau agents ultimately withdrew and abandoned their seizure of his cattle.

Two years later, Cliven Bundy's son, Ammon Bundy, who had participated in the Nevada standoff, drew national headlines when he led an armed group in seizing the headquarters of the 190,000-acre Malheur National Wildlife Refuge (MNWR) in rural Oregon. According to the younger Bundy, the occupation was a response to the imprisonment of the Hammond brothers, Oregon ranchers and anti-government activists who had recently been imprisoned for arson on public lands. Bundy declared that the massively armed

25 to 40 occupiers would stay until "they can use these lands as free men," perhaps even for "several years," though the occupation ended after 40 days (most participants surrendered to the FBI or left).[104]

Notably, neither the Bundys nor any of the other leaders and participants in these events were ever convicted of any crimes. Repeated delays in the Nevada case meant the Oregon occupation was tried first in federal court in Portland. It ended in "mass acquittals—of the Bundys themselves, of the militiamen who helped direct the takeover, and of their hangers-on"—on federal conspiracy and weapons charges.[105] Three different trials related to the Nevada standoff also resulted in no convictions for the Bundys or their accomplices. In January 2018, the last remaining case against Cliven Bundy, his two sons, and Ryan Payne was dismissed. As of 2021, Bundy continued to graze his cattle on federal land without paying or following any federal environmental laws.[106]

This impunity, along with the occupations themselves, reveals that the ethos of white dominion investigated by Du Bois continues to shape the present.[107] The Bundy saga is a stark illustration of the proprietary outlook Du Bois theorized in connection with both slavery and colonization. The stance of presumptive ownership toward the "darker world"—its people, land, and resources—that Du Bois identified with whiteness itself is on clear display in the Bundy cases. As Joshua F. J. Inwood and Anne Bonds have argued, rather than viewing these events simply as expressions of extremist anti-government ideology, we should recognize that they draw on and reinforce "configurations of race and property that obscure Indigenous geographies and reinforce hierarchies of race in the American West."[108]

The Bundy occupations (and their folk-heroic coverage by media outlets) are animated by a "settler imaginary," one that is both anti-Indigenous and anti-Black. The Bundys and their supporters draw directly on established discourses of race and property that rationalize "white possession."[109] For example, as the 2014 standoff was unfolding, Cliven Bundy told his supporters that he had a "preemptive" right to the land in Nevada, because his ancestors were there before the bureau was established (which is false).[110] His repeated references to his "ancestral rights" echo the 19th-century settler colonial doctrine of Manifest Destiny that cast "possession of the land" as a "right given by God to whites."[111] Bundy's comments, like the "settler imaginary" itself, engage in Indigenous erasure. Moreover, in press coverage of the Nevada standoff, there was almost no discussion of the legitimacy of his claim to the land in the first place. Bundy's assumption of a "natural right to the land" went largely unquestioned[112] even though his claim of "ancestral rights" blatantly ignores a prior act of dispossession: "Western Shoshone Nation's claim to the land predates his own."[113] Bonds and Inwood observe, "The unquestioned claims to land articulated by Bundy and his followers erase the Indigenous peoples who occupied Nevada for millennia prior to the arrival of white settlers and obscure Mormon histories in promoting slavery and in the colonization and genocide of the American West."[114]

A notorious 2014 *New York Times* interview with Cliven Bundy provides a crass reminder of the extent to which anti-Indigeneity and anti-Blackness remain "twin American ideologies," joined in the service of what Du Bois called a white "title to the universe."[115] (As discussed earlier in this chapter, Du Bois ignores the legacies of native dispossession in North America, even though he is attuned to settler colonialism in other parts of the world.) In the interview, Bundy offers an unsolicited, digressive commentary that begins with the comment, "I want to tell you one more thing I know about the Negro . . . " He continues, mobilizing familiar racist stereotypes before sharing, "I've often wondered, are they better off as slaves, picking cotton and having a family life and doing things, or are they better off under government subsidy? They didn't get no more freedom. They got less freedom."[116]

The dual rationalization of settler colonial dispossession and slavery, both integral to white supremacy as a foundational socio-spatial logic in the United States, is also evident in the Oregon case.[117] When Ammon Bundy explained the seizure of MNWR in Oregon, he said he was "driven" to respond to the imprisonment of the Hammond brothers because he felt his family, like theirs, was being targeted by the federal government: "Families like ours and Hammonds . . . are in the situation we're in where we're losing our heritage." The invocation of "heritage" aligns with the elder Bundy's incessant talk of "ancestral rights"; this shared vocabulary posits a racialized right to ownership (and a right to exclude) that completely overlooks the territorial rights and sovereignty of Indigenous peoples. Indeed, as the takeover of the MNWR was occurring, the chairwoman of the local Paiute Indians, Charlotte Rodrique, held a news conference. She stated, "This land belonged to Paiute people as wintering grounds long before the first settlers, ranchers and trappers ever arrived here. We haven't given up our rights to the land. We have protected sites there. We still use the land."[118]

The land on which the MNWR sits has a history that the Bundys' claims to property rights both overlook and presuppose. The wildlife refuge exists on land that was set aside in 1872 as the Malheur Reservation for the Paiute people. The Bannock War of 1878, a conflict between the federal government and the Bannock and Paiute people whose lands had been seized and appropriated by white settlers, ended with the defeat of the native people. "The survivors were sent to the Malheur Reservation in Oregon—land that was eventually turned into the Malheur National Wildlife Refuge."[119] This history was largely absent from discussions of the Bundys' occupation of the refuge.

Much as the history of Indigenous dispossession in Oregon was missing from the Bundys' self-presentation and mainstream media coverage, so too was the state's deep history of racial exclusion. The land violently appropriated from Indigenous peoples and transferred to white settlers was subject to explicitly racist policies. The Oregon Donation Land Act of 1850 offered 17% of the total lands in the state for free to white settlers only. When Oregon became a state in 1859, it was the only free state ever to join the union that had a constitution that barred Black people from living, working, or owning property in the state. As Inwood and Bonds show, "Oregon's historical development was formulated on a white settler project premised on the eradication of Native peoples *and* the exclusion of other racialized minorities."[120]

The actions of the Bundys and their supporters, openly celebrated in some media outlets and left unpunished by the US legal system, suggest that Du Bois's account of white entitlement still carries critical purchase here and now. A century after Du Bois identified the quasi-religious conviction according to which the world belongs to those who are white, the Bundys and their many supporters continue in the 21st century to mobilize "narratives of whiteness and land ownership that naturalize indigenous disappearance, black subordination, and white racial domination."[121]

The belief that "whiteness is ownership of the world, forever and ever, Amen!" is enacted not only in spectacular ways, as with the Bundy standoffs, but also in quotidian ones. Since 2018, social media hashtags, particularly #LivingWhileBlack, have helped to expose the frequency with which Black persons' very *presence* in everyday spaces is surveyed and criminalized. Such incidents, far from new but increasingly captured on cellphone video and widely circulated, have typically involved white people placing 911 calls to report that Black people "were occupying spaces that the callers believed they ought not occupy."[122] In recent years, cops have been called on Black people for things such as sitting in a Starbucks, playing golf, eating in a fast food restaurant, shopping in a store, staying at an Airbnb, and exercising in a gym.[123] In almost all of the documented cases, "the targeted men, women, and children were in places in which they had a legal right to be and engaging in activities in which they had a legal right to engage."[124]

"White caller crime," critic Michael Harriott's pithy description, refers to the "phenomenon of white people calling police on black people doing mundane things."[125] (Although most of the publicized cases dubbed "white caller crime" or #LivingWhileBlack involve white communication with police that does not result in arrest, data reveals a "longstanding pattern" of Blacks being arrested for "mundane actions," such as vandalism, vagrancy, curfew, loitering, and other nonviolent offenses at much higher rates than whites. Additionally, these racial disparities in arrests for minor offenses is strongly correlated with "White spaces."[126]) The practice of "racialized police communication" has been characterized as "panicked white people calling the police on people of color for doing perfectly legal things like grilling in a park, selling bottled water, swimming in a pool, moving into an apartment, sleeping on a common-room couch, and [insert any normal verb associated with human activity here]."[127] In these instances, of which there are many, white antagonists assume that certain spaces—shared private, public, and "third" spaces—*belong* to them such that they are entitled to regulate the presence of Black persons within them.[128] These acts mobilize racially biased law enforcement in their efforts to control or exclude Black persons and secure "white space."[129] Drawing upon tropes of Black criminality, these acts declare that Black people, engaged in ordinary life activities in common social spaces (where they are entitled to be), are "out of place." Such confrontations involve attempts to literally and figuratively "put blacks 'in their place.'"[130] They are contemporary expressions of white dominion.

In her account of "racial territoriality," Elise Boddie argues that places can "have a racial identity and meaning based on socially engrained racial biases regarding the people who inhabit, frequent, or are associated with particular places and racialized cultural norms of spatial belonging and exclusion."[131] This allows for a distinctive form of discrimination, Boddie argues, in which people of color continue to be excluded from certain spaces that are marked as socially and culturally white.[132] This ongoing practice has its roots in the United States' "spatial system" of slavery and Jim Crow segregation regimes in both the North and South—the domestic context that I previously showed was integral to understanding Du Bois's account of white dominion. Under slavery, Boddie shows, "the inability of slaves to choose any manner of space was fundamental"; plantations were spatially organized to maintain white power and the physical movement of enslaved persons was extraordinarily restricted.[133] The American slave regime was defined by "the complete authority of whites over blacks—including their corresponding power to exclude, marginalize, and confine slaves and even free blacks within prescribed spaces."[134] Of course, as Boddie argues, racial territoriality did not end with slavery but merely assumed an altered form—not only in the South's comprehensive system of "forced physical separation" but also in the North's de facto separation of whites and Blacks in housing, schools, and many other public and private spaces. Describing the conditions of the long Jim Crow era, Boddie writes:

> In both the South and the North, spatial separation extended far beyond neighborhoods and jurisdictional territories. Blacks and whites were required to remain separate across a seemingly limitless range of institutions—schools, buses, railways, parks, hospitals, private and public housing, bars and cocktail lounges, golf courses, boxing arenas, pools, restaurants, movie theaters, even snack bars, bathrooms, elevators, vending machines, telephone booths, and cemeteries.[135]

White-over-Black hierarchies in the United States have historically depended heavily upon the creation and maintenance of racially distinct territories and private and public institutional spaces. It is perhaps not surprising, then, to recognize a contemporary pattern of behavior in which white Americans treat certain areas as "off limits" to Black citizens and undertake to monitor, control, or exclude them entirely from these places. Given the extent of white supremacist spatial separation (captured in Boddie's statement above), it makes sense that many of the 21st-century incidents occur on sites "with long histories of racial exclusion and contestation"—such as universities, swimming pools, retail stores, and hotels.[136] Today's "antiblack spatial practices"—including but not limited to the "white caller crimes" addressed here—are tied to a long history of "spacism," the consolidation of white supremacy through territorialization.[137]

In a fascinating article, legal scholars Taja-Nia Y. Henderson and Jamila Jefferson-Jones show that when white people call 911 to report on Black people's mere presence—the "#LivingWhileBlack" phenomenon—they regularly rely upon "property law concepts, particularly trespass and nuisance," to elicit the response of law enforcement.[138] Although there are not actually competing property claims at stake in these incidents, Henderson and Jefferson-Jones's analysis of 911 calls shows that white antagonists "consistently leveraged property concepts of entitlement and belonging to advocate for the physical ouster of Black people from shared spaces."[139]

For example, in a notorious case that took place in Oakland, California, in 2018, a white woman named Jennifer Schulte (who became known as #BBQBecky on social media) called 911 to report that two Black males were "illegally using a charcoal grill in a non-designated area" of a public park.[140] In her 911 call, she demanded that the purported violation be "dealt with immediately so that coals don't burn more children and we have to pay more taxes." In casting the Black men as a dangerous nuisance, Schulte positioned herself as guardian of the public space of the park. When that proved unsuccessful (the 911 dispatcher did not send police to the park), Schulte shifted gears and "attempted to intimidate the group of barbecuers with claims that the park was her private property and that she, therefore, had the right to make them leave." These attempts to force the Black men from the park relied on "language of land use"—specifically the ideas of nuisance and trespass. In another widely publicized case, a white woman, Allison Ettel, also sought to exclude Black presence from a public space. She called 911 to report an eight-year-old Black girl for selling water on a public sidewalk (in front of the apartment building in which they both lived) near a San Francisco sports stadium. In the argument captured on video by the girl's mother, Erin Austin, a dispute over "property" ensues, with Ettel asserting, "It's not your property," denying any shared, equal interest in the sidewalk and flipping off Austin. These cases—occurring in the context of the large-scale displacement of Black people in the San Francisco Bay Area due to gentrification and massive cost-of-living increases in the region—involve the assertion of "property rights common to a white general public—rights that are exclusive of Black people and Black presence."[141]

Actions like these, in which whites act on behalf of an imagined and exclusive racialized public, are expressive of the faith Du Bois identified 100 years ago—that deep, unquestioned belief, launched in the souls of white folk, that they are the owners of the earth. The incidents exposed by #LivingWhileBlack are not really new, then, as Henderson and Jefferson-Jones also argue, apart from the technologies that allow for their easier documentation and publicity. There is an established tradition at work: the "casting of Blackness as a property harm," as an infringement upon what Du Bois calls "white title."[142]

For Du Bois, the gratifications of whiteness are plural. As we have seen, the "public and psychological wage," while important, should not be mistaken for an exhaustive account of the rewards that have attended social classification as "white," under shifting regimes of racial capitalism in the United States. The analysis of whiteness as pleasure revealed a mode of gratification that does not come in the form of status or belonging but in the form of enjoyment taken in the suffering of racialized others. This chapter has directed attention to another powerful source of gratification, derived from the quasi-religious belief in white "ownership of the world, forever and ever, Amen!" By theorizing a racialized "title to the universe," bound to slavery and colonization, Du Bois exposes whiteness as an existential faith that propertizes the world.

5

Resistances

Du Boisean Propaganda, World Building, and Black Lives Matter

If the gratifications of whiteness are many, what does this mean for anti-racist struggles? What strategies can interrupt the varied, plural forms of racialized reward that help sustain white supremacy? Du Bois incisively exposed the diverse gratifications attached to whiteness in the postemancipation United States—where it offered a sense of superior social standing, especially for the poor; served widely as a modality of sadistic pleasure; and provided a comprehensive, aggrandizing worldview. The preceding chapters also connected these insights to specific iterations of whiteness in the 21st century. I have mobilized Du Bois's analysis to suggest that contemporary American whiteness is not only a matter of unsought "privilege" or cognitive or moral lack (ignorance, indifference); rather, whiteness continues to serve as a potent source of deep and varied *gratification* for its bearers. If this is so—if whiteness endures as a polyvalent experience of public status, visceral enjoyment, and lived faith—how can these enduring patterns be undone?

This chapter takes up this important question. I first pursue a tantalizing suggestion found in 1940's *Dusk of Dawn*: that "propaganda" is vitally important for challenging the most pernicious forces that support white supremacy. "Propaganda" carries varied meanings throughout Du Bois's middle-period work, as I show, yet in *Dusk of Dawn*'s essays he uses the term to argue that typical methods of education and persuasion have proven inadequate for engaging the "habitual" and "irrational" dimensions of anti-Blackness; something else—"a persistent campaign of propaganda"—is called for. "Propaganda," though undertheorized by Du Bois, seems in this context to name creative and wide-ranging cultural-political interventions that are necessary because the gratifications of whiteness operate in ways that are not reachable by simple "appeal or argument." Building on Du Bois's suggestive invocation of "propaganda," I contend that insofar as whiteness, premised on the degradation of Blackness, continues to deliver multiple rewards

The Gratifications of Whiteness. Ella Myers, Oxford University Press. © Oxford University Press 2022.
DOI: 10.1093/oso/9780197556764.003.0005

to its bearers, its destabilization will also require multiple styles of resistance. The second half of this chapter explores this idea by way of the Black Lives Matter (BLM) movement in the United States, paying particular attention to the range of inventive protest tactics undertaken in its name. I argue that BLM's expansive repertoire affirms Du Bois's commitment to a protean politics that is creative, multidimensional, and unrelenting in its attempts to undo racial domination.

Propaganda's Layers

"Propaganda" at times appears in Du Bois's writings as an intriguing hint— a hint concerning how the gratifications of whiteness, parasitic upon anti-Black practices and beliefs, might be resisted and ultimately ended. Before exploring that possibility, however, it is worth considering some of the other, better-known ways that this charged term circulates in Du Bois's work: as a modality of white supremacy, as a countermodality of Black liberation, and (most notoriously) as a characteristic of "all art." These significations, I suggest, are not discrete or mutually exclusive, but rather serve as layers of meaning that can help us better discern what Du Bois is trying to do when he mobilizes this fraught term in *Dusk of Dawn*.

"Propaganda" in Du Bois's 1920–1940 writings most often refers to the centuries-old, pervasive mass communication of white supremacist ideology. This usage, which also stretches back to Du Bois's earliest published works, identifies a sweeping cultural project conveying that "everything great, good, efficient, fair, and honorable is 'white'; everything mean, bad, blundering, cheating, and dishonorable is 'yellow'; a bad taste is 'brown'; and the devil is 'black.'" Du Bois notes that such "propaganda" works through plural channels: it is "continually rung in picture and story, in newspaper heading and moving-picture, in sermon and school book."[1] Put plainly: "the modern world has been systematically taught to despise colored peoples."[2]

Black Reconstruction's unforgettable last chapter, "The Propaganda of History" details how scholars made "a deliberate attempt . . . to change the facts of history," disseminating an account of Reconstruction that portrayed it as a "hideous mistake."[3] As a result of the "propaganda" produced by leading historians and presented in textbooks, Du Bois argues, American children are taught that "1. All Negroes were ignorant"; "2. All Negroes were lazy, dishonest, and extravagant"; and "3. Negroes were responsible for bad government during Reconstruction."[4] Du Bois cites multiple studies in the chapter, most notably the work of the "Dunning School," and demonstrates that the academic field of history in the United States has advanced a white supremacist "myth" of Reconstruction that aims to legitimate racial caste. Historical research of Du Bois's era that depicted Reconstruction—the attempt to establish "abolition-democracy" in the United States—as an unmitigated disaster is part of an ambitious program to undermine the prospect of racial equality: "In propaganda against the Negro since emancipation in this land, we face one of the most stupendous efforts the world ever saw to discredit human beings, an effort involving universities, history, science, social life, and religion."[5] Across his middle-period writings, then, Du Bois condemns the wide-ranging "propaganda against the Negro" that reinforces white supremacy.

Significantly, however, he does not reject "propaganda" per se. A second, related usage of the term labels the National Association for the Advancement of Colored People (NAACP) (and Du Bois himself, in his organizational role there) as an agent of counter-"propaganda" meant to challenge the "training" that has convinced most Americans "that black folk are sub-human."[6] Du Bois identifies a Black political tradition of "organized opposition to the action and attitude of the dominant group"—a tradition that he says is exemplified by David Walker's *Appeal* and expressed in the work of the Niagara Movement and the NAACP. According to Du Bois, these political actors engage in "ceaseless agitation" in pursuit of equality, using "force of every sort: moral suasion, propaganda, and where possible even physical resistance."[7] When speaking of his own leadership role in the NAACP, Du Bois repeatedly characterizes it in terms of "propaganda": "My career as a scientist was to be swallowed up in my role as master of propaganda."[8] Reflecting on his position as editor of the NAACP's *The Crisis* and its wide circulation, he refers to the magazine as an "organ of propaganda" that played a key part in the organization's "assault" on white supremacy.[9]

Du Bois's commentary on anti-Black propaganda and the propaganda of the NAACP reveals something important. "Propaganda," for Du Bois, does not carry an exclusively sinister meaning. Rather, he uses the term in a neutral sense, as was common prior to World War I. Before it came to carry almost exclusively negative connotations due to the Allies' popularization of the term to characterize the actions of Germany, its neutral or "open-ended" meaning, derived from the Latin *propagare* (to propagate, to disseminate, to spread), was common.[10] It seems that Du Bois most often uses "propaganda" this way—to name a "mode of mass persuasion, neither good nor evil, that can be enlisted for a variety of purposes."[11]

Du Bois believes that "propaganda" may serve the interests of anti-Black domination or "propaganda" may serve the interests of Black liberation. In the writings cited above, "propaganda" is used to name *competing* attempts at mass persuasion.[12] There is no question, of course, that Du Bois saw white supremacist propaganda as dominant if not hegemonic—entrenched and resourced in unrivaled ways—but he also understood the creation and circulation of alternative propaganda to be desirable and necessary. "Propaganda" appears in Du Bois's writings above all as a tool of political struggle.

This understanding is important to keep in mind as we turn to Du Bois's infamous 1926 text, "Criteria of Negro Art." Most references to it center the memorable declaration, "All Art is propaganda," but focusing too myopically on this provocative claim leaves unexamined Du Bois's broader aims in the piece. Taking the essay as a whole, I argue, it is clear that its primary purpose is not to define what art is or what it should be, but rather to articulate a vision of *Black world building* that encompasses both those activities usually labeled "art" and those activities usually labeled "politics." "Propaganda" sutures the two.

In the opening paragraphs of "Criteria"—originally delivered as a speech at an NAACP annual conference in 1926 and published in *The Crisis* the same year—Du Bois indicates that he will present a perspective that mediates between two oversimplified understandings of art and politics. He identifies the first of these by imagining how some members of the audience might respond to learning of a lecture on the topic of "Negro Art": "How is it that an organization like this, a group of radicals trying to bring new things into the world, a fighting organization . . . how is it that an organization like this can turn aside to talk about Art?" But other listeners, he notes, may respond quite differently, expressing the second perspective. They may "feel a certain relief": "It is rather satisfactory after all this talk about rights and fighting to sit and dream of something which leaves a nice taste in the mouth."[13]

Du Bois continues, "Let me tell you that neither of these groups is right." Rather than directly explain why this is so, Du Bois makes a key move immediately following this statement—a move that opens up the wider horizon within which he intends to explore the relationship between art and politics. He states, "The thing we are talking about tonight is part of the great fight we are carrying on and it represents a forward and an upward look—a pushing onward." He continues, "There has been progress and we can see it day by day looking back along blood-filled paths." But, he says, it is not enough to simply keep "climbing": "It is time to know more precisely whither you are going and what you really want."

Du Bois then pointedly asks, "What do we want? What is the thing we are after?," inviting his audience to adopt a wide ethico-political perspective, one that stretches beyond any preconceptions they might bring to the topic of "Negro Art." Du Bois opens up this fundamental normative question— "what do we want?"—and suggests that Black Americans are in a unique position to think about this question boldly and creatively. He continues, "We want to be Americans, full-fledged Americans . . . But is that all? Do we want simply to be Americans? . . . We who are dark can see America in a way white Americans cannot. And seeing our country thus, are we satisfied with its present goals and ideals?" In this potent passage, Du Bois urges his audience to define their own collective aims and to work to build a society that realizes them, rather than accept the terms of the dominant social order.

Du Bois builds upon this provocation by asking his audience to imagine that they could actually have whatever they want:

> If you tonight suddenly should become full-fledged Americans; if your color faded, or the color line here in Chicago was miraculously forgotten; suppose, too, you became at the same time rich and powerful;—what is it that you would want? What would you immediately seek? Would you buy the most powerful of motor cars and outrace Cook County? Would you buy the most elaborate estate on the North Shore? Would you be a Rotarian or a Lion or a What-not of the very last degree? Would you wear the most striking clothes, give the richest dinners, and buy the longest press notices?[14]

Du Bois here urges his fellow Black Americans to ask themselves whether their only aspiration is to gain entry into a society preoccupied with wealth and status. Do they seek nothing more than admission into this superficial, competitive world?[15] Might there be something else worth fighting for?

Du Bois believes there is. He says, "Even as you visualize such ideals you know in your hearts that these are not the things you really want." He repeats his earlier claim that Black Americans have unique insight into the character of the country—those who have been "pushed aside" are not only better able to identify the wrongs that plague that society but also possess "a vision of what the world could be if it were really a beautiful world." That world would be one in which "we had, to be sure, not perfect happiness, but plenty of good hard work, the inevitable suffering that always comes with life; sacrifice and waiting, all that—but, nevertheless, lived in a world where men know, where men create, where they realize themselves and where they enjoy life. It is that sort of a world we want to create for ourselves and for all America."[16] Du Bois here speaks to the imaginative, world-building capacities of Black Americans and asks his audience to focus on a profound question—"what sort of world we want to create"—when reflecting on the topic of "Negro Art."

Shortly after the passage quoted above, in which Du Bois suggests that Black people might be uniquely capable of envisioning and striving for "a beautiful world," Du Bois turns to the question of beauty itself: "What is it?" Noting that its "variety is infinite" and offering examples, he next inquires, "What has this Beauty to do with the world? What has Beauty to do with Truth and Goodness—with the facts of the world and the right actions of men?" Artists, Du Bois says, will reply "Nothing," and they may even be correct. But as for Du Bois, he says that he "seeks with Beauty and for Beauty to set the world right. That somehow, somewhere eternal and perfect Beauty sits above Truth and Right I can conceive, but here and now and in the world in which I work they are for me unseparated and inseparable."[17] Du Bois refuses to define what Beauty *is*, but he specifies that under present conditions—"here and now"—he creates and engages with Beauty *for the sake of* the world. Art, he says, need not strive to transcend the ordinary world; it can instead endeavor to set that world "right." With this formulation, we can see Du Bois trying to mediate between the two seemingly opposed positions with which he started, positions that assumed the practice of politics and the practice of art to be separate and unrelated.

If the question for Black Americans is, as Du Bois has suggested, what "world we want to create," this points toward a vast collaborative project that entails not only overt political "fighting," in Du Bois's view, but also "the creation of Beauty." In the context of world building, "it is the bounden duty of black America to begin this great work of the creation of Beauty, of the realization of Beauty."[18] He grants to art a constructive role in the struggle for a freer, more just existence.

It is at this point in the essay that Du Bois declares, "All Art is propaganda and ever must be, despite the wailing of the purists." Du Bois crystallizes his "functional" account of art.[19] He explains:

> I stand in utter shamelessness and say that whatever art I have for writing has been used always for propaganda for gaining the right of black folk to love and enjoy. I do not care a damn for any art that is not used for propaganda. But I do care when propaganda is confined to one side while the other is stripped and silent.[20]

Du Bois declares that as a writer, he strives to make art that can be "used" to expand the possibilities for Black people to "love and enjoy." And he announces that he personally is uninterested in art that does not share this liberatory mission—that does not serve as propaganda for Black flourishing.

Du Bois also recognizes in this passage that any propaganda he or others make on behalf of a free Black existence is propaganda that will vie with the deep-seated propaganda that degrades that very existence.[21] As we saw earlier, when examining Du Bois's indictment of white supremacist propaganda alongside his affirmation of the NAACP's counterpropaganda, he depicts a social landscape inhabited by competing and incompatible forms of propaganda. In the passage above, he embraces "propaganda" but disputes its confinement to "one side."

Du Bois amplifies this point later in the essay, when he explains, "It is not the positive propaganda of people who believe white blood divine, infallible and holy to which I object. It is the denial of a similar right of propaganda to those who believe black blood human, lovable, and inspired with new ideals for the world."[22] This statement defends art that *propagates* belief in black humanity and lovability and participates in a world-building project animated by "new ideals."[23]

"Criteria of Negro Art," then, affirms the political import of artistic production. It makes an emphatic, uncompromising case for an *aestheticized politics* that Du Bois develops and affirms across his oeuvre.[24] As other readers have explored in detail, Du Bois consistently assigns to art a decisive role in social transformation, even across well-known shifts in his analysis of racial politics.[25] As Ross Posnock argues, "aesthetic experience" is integral to Du Bois's politics; Du Bois understands the aesthetic and the political as interrelated "experimental modes of conduct" that can work upon the settled beliefs and practices of white supremacist society.[26] As Melvin Rogers describes it, Du Bois "aestheticizes politics as an instrument of cultural transformation." He believes art can serve as "a vehicle for expanding the horizon" of those who encounter it.[27] Joseph Winters explains, "Art is, for Du Bois, one way for blacks to demonstrate their humanity in a world that questions or denies that attribute."[28]

Notably, Du Bois *enacts* this conviction himself, rather than just announcing it. His own writing style, which famously combines fiction, poetry, music, and scripture with historical, political, and sociological research, participates in an aestheticized politics that combats anti-Blackness. As Paul Gilroy argues, Du Bois's writings—especially the books *Souls of White Folk, Darkwater,* and *Dusk of Dawn,* which are internally multigeneric—demonstrate his creation of a "self-consciously polyphonic form." This "combination of modes and tones" is shaped by Du Bois's dissatisfaction with conventional scholarly styles and his desire to "convey an intensity of feeling" that no single register of address can achieve.[29]

In "Criteria of Negro Art," Du Bois explicitly defends his practice of the "art of assemblage"[30] by presenting the aesthetic as a "militant part of a political, economic, and cultural movement."[31] As Rogers writes, "Criteria" makes clear that Du Bois regards "art as a form of political action in a world of asymmetrical power relations that must stand alongside traditional modes of protest."[32] Put somewhat differently, and in terms of my reading above, Du Bois views art as one vital practice among many by which Black people can begin to build a different world.

In 1940's *Dusk of Dawn,* the term "propaganda" is used in ways that echo Du Bois's past reflections, but it also seems to have acquired a new charge. The essays in the book use the term in the first two senses outlined above—to characterize the multimedia communication of white supremacist ideology and to refer to the anti-racist counterprogramming pursued by groups such as the NAACP. But there is another usage evident in *Dusk* that deserves attention, one that builds on Du Bois's vision of aesthetic politics. "Propaganda," at key junctures in the text, seems to name a political practice that is at least in some important ways *new,* something that has not been tried before—or at least not to the extent that the situation requires. Moreover, these particular evocations are tied to Du Bois's recurrent concern throughout the book with the "irrational" dimensions of "race hate" and the possibility that racial caste is sustained by forces unresponsive to "reason or appeal" (a claim explored in detail in Chapter 3).[33] When commenting on this profound difficulty, Du Bois sometimes mobilizes "propaganda" to name an underspecified but vital activity—one that might be able to do battle with white supremacy in all its variety and tenacity.

In the essay "The White World," for example, Du Bois reports that "science today" has determined that many of the actions of the individual, or even *most* of them, "are not rational" and "arise from subconscious urges." While this fact raises pressing questions about the assignment of personal responsibility, he says, Du Bois's real interest lies elsewhere, with the implications of this discovery for anti-racist struggle:

> It is our duty to assess praise and blame for the rational and conscious acts of men, but to regard the vast area of the subconscious and the irrational and especially of habit and convention which also produce significant action, as an area where we must apply other remedies and judgements if we would get justice and right to prevail in the world.[34]

Du Bois declares that we must turn attention to a "vast area" that has been neglected—the domain of the subconscious and the habitual—which demands "other remedies" than the ones favored thus far in the battle against white supremacy. The hope of the NAACP had been, as Du Bois recounts throughout the book, that racial discrimination could be ended by education and reasoned argument—a hope he now regards as naive.

Before turning to the "other remedies" that Du Bois alludes to here, it is important to note that in 1940, Du Bois seems to characterize the efforts of the NAACP in a narrower, more rationalist way than is perhaps fair. In *Dusk of Dawn*, he characterizes it as an organization committed to the belief that "race prejudice is a matter of ignorance to be cured by information."[35] This was sometimes precisely how it represented itself. In the 1910 inaugural issue of *The Crisis*, for example, Du Bois wrote, "The object of this publication is to set forth the facts and arguments which show the danger of race prejudice."[36] Yet over the years of Du Bois's tenure (1910–1934), the NAACP was not exclusively concerned with disseminating "facts" and was actually engaged in a wide-ranging "cultural strategy."[37] This strategy included its early campaign against *Birth of a Nation* as well as the wide circulation of Black creative work over the years, especially in *The Crisis*, to contest stereotypes, encourage Black pride, and foster a sense of collective identity. (The journal was a major voice of the Harlem Renaissance.)[38] Its famous anti-lynching campaign is also significant in this regard. It included not only political lobbying and "quantitative and qualitative reporting" in *The Crisis* but also the publication of photos, political cartoons, plays, poems, and paintings therein, along with dramatic public protests that made use of the specific anti-lynching "visual vocabulary" established in *The Crisis*.[39]

Nonetheless, in *Dusk of Dawn* Du Bois appears newly alert to what he calls the "twilight zone," where race hate does not simply "melt" away when "the truth is presented"—a faulty assumption he sometimes associates with the NAACP.[40] So, what political methods can possibly reach the "unconscious wrongs which white folks are today inflicting on their victims"? Du Bois makes a notable suggestion:

> The present attitude and action of the white world is not based solely upon rational, deliberate intent. It is a matter of conditioned reflexes; of long followed habits, customs and folkways; of subconscious trains of reasoning and unconscious nervous reflexes. To attack and better all this calls for more than appeal and argument. It needs carefully planned and scientific propaganda; the vision of a world of intelligent men with sufficient income to live decently and with the will to build a beautiful world.[41]

Here Du Bois clearly positions "propaganda" as an alternative to "appeal and argument." "Propaganda" is cast as a method that could perhaps reach those "conditioned reflexes," seemingly impervious to more conventional forms of education and suasion. Of course, what Du Bois means by "carefully planned and scientific propaganda" is left unclear, but it is nonetheless evident that he uses the term to mark a horizon of creative political action that operates on important, overlooked registers.

Another essay, "The Colored World Within," clarifies that Du Bois uses "propaganda" at times to name a political practice that *differs from* the NAACP's strategy (which he labels "propaganda" in the second sense noted above). Writing of the NAACP's efforts in 1914–1924, he describes an unprecedented "united effort in the demand for Negro rights." Noting the organization's limited resources, he comments that even if they were better funded, there are "two assumptions usually made in such a campaign, which are not quite true; and that is the assumption on one hand that most race prejudice is a matter of ignorance to be cured by information and on the other hand that much discrimination is a matter of deliberate deviltry and unwillingness to be just." Du Bois continues, admitting that although "widespread ignorance" and "sheer malevolence" are at play, "the present attitude of the whites is much more the result of inherited customs and of those irrational and partly subconscious actions of men which control so large a proportion of their deeds." He explains that "attitudes and habits thus built up" cannot be changed by "sudden assault." They "call for a long, patient, well-planned, and persistent campaign of propaganda."[42]

Once again, Du Bois says very little about what exactly "propaganda" means in this context, but it is clear from the passage as a whole that he is referring to an undertaking *distinct from* that pursued by the NAACP (at least on this rendering), which sought to overcome "ignorance" with "information." He positions this alternative practice of "propaganda" as one that might, over time, be able to affect the forces—"unconscious cerebration and folkways"—that sustain white supremacy.

Years later, Du Bois again presents "propaganda" as an activity driven by the conviction that "telling people the truth" is an inadequate strategy for combatting anti-Blackness. "Propaganda," as before, refers to an underspecified but vital endeavor that aims to reach people in ways that the simple dissemination of information cannot. In a 1960 oral history interview, Du Bois uses "propaganda" to name an approach that strives to affect *action*—action that, as he specified previously, is "not based solely upon rational, deliberate intent." He explains:

> And I began to realize that I had overworked a theory—that the cause of the problem was the ignorance of people; that the cure wasn't simply telling people the truth, it was inducing them to act on the truth. If you showed the people that here the accusation of rape as cause of lynching was untrue . . . It wasn't enough, in other words, to simply study the Negro problem and put the truth before people. You've got to begin propaganda and tell the people: when you know something is wrong, you've got to do something about it.[43]

As in the *Dusk of Dawn* passages considered above, "propaganda" alludes to a style of political practice that stretches beyond "telling the truth" and strives to reach people in ways that are not strictly cognitive. Du Bois maintains that it is not enough to "study" the realities of American racism and present facts to the public. Referring to lynching, he suggests that debunking the myths around the practice, by showing them to be untrue, was of limited use. (In a 1916 issue of *The Crisis*, Du Bois described the NAACP's strategy in these terms: "We place frankly our greatest reliance in publicity. We propose to let the facts concerning lynching to be known."[44] As noted above, the NAACP's anti-lynching campaign was never quite this simple.) Reflecting on these

efforts years later, Du Bois notes that it is one thing to correct misinforma-
tion, but quite another to get people "to *act* on the truth." As before, Du Bois
provides little detail about what "propaganda" entails; he offers no examples
of propaganda in practice. Nonetheless, it seems that the term again stands
for a style of address that is not simply informational or argumentative, but
operates upon other registers—affective, visceral, somatic?—that might
begin to alter the "attitude and action of the white world."

To be sure, Du Bois does not provide a satisfying account of the activities
he associates with "propaganda." Rather, as I have suggested, in the instances
cited above, he uses the word to name a wide-ranging and multifaceted
political project, still to be defined, which might be able to do battle with
the equally wide-ranging and multifaceted reality of white supremacy. Du
Bois's layered commentary on "propaganda" remains suggestive rather than
definitive. As such, it presents an invitation that I take up in the next part
of this chapter, which considers the BLM movement and the range of creative protest practices undertaken in its name. I suggest that BLM's varied
repertoire—placed in the service of what Du Bois called "the right of black
folk to love and enjoy"—resonates with his vision of a protean politics of
Black liberation.

Making Black Lives Matter

Before exploring the specific and often innovative practices undertaken by
BLM activists, it is important to briefly address the genealogy, structure, and
aims of this political struggle. In less than a decade, BLM grew from a social
media hashtag crafted by three Black women activists in response to the 2013
acquittal of Trayvon Martin's killer to a massive movement by 2020.[45] After
community organizers Alicia Garza, Patrisse Cullors, and Opal Tometi created #BlackLivesMatter as a "call to action for Black people" following George
Zimmerman's acquittal, they continued collaborating with other organizers
to "move the hashtag from social media to the streets."[46] By 2014, large public
protests in response to the police killings of Eric Garner in Staten Island,
New York, and Michael Brown in Ferguson, Missouri, carried out largely
in the name of "Black Lives Matter," were capturing national and international attention. Many other demonstrations against police brutality—often
in response to the specific deaths of Black persons at the hands of police—
followed in subsequent years, in cities throughout the country.

In May 2020, bystander video depicting the Minneapolis police killing of George Floyd, an unarmed Black man alleged to have used a counterfeit dollar bill, was widely circulated. On the heels of the recent killings of Ahmaud Arbery (an unarmed Black jogger who was pursued and killed by two white men in Georgia) and Breonna Taylor (an unarmed Black woman killed in her bed by plainclothes police officers in Kentucky), film of George Floyd begging for this life while a police offer knelt on his neck until he died sparked demonstrations throughout the country and around the world. These actions, carried out largely under the heading of "Black Lives Matter," occurred on an unprecedented scale. In June 2020, multiple polls found that about 15 million to 26 million people in the United States participated in demonstrations over a period of several weeks, suggesting that BLM may be "the largest movement in the country's history."[47] In addition to the sheer numbers, this wave of political action was also notable because of its geographic reach: there were public protests in over 2,000 American cities and towns, in every single state.[48] The demonstrations not only took place in large cities but also "unfurled in rural, conservative and majority white communities," and in rich and poor areas.[49] Many of the participants were white, a shift from previous BLM actions (a point taken up in the Epilogue).[50] Public opinion also seemed to shift quickly in favor of the cause: support for the BLM movement grew in the first two weeks of protests almost as much as it had in the preceding two years (although white public opinion in particular has been "fickle").[51]

BLM is a notably decentralized grassroots movement. From the Ferguson, Missouri, uprising in 2014—which pushed "Black Lives Matter" into mainstream public discourse—to the movement's dramatic expansion in 2020, no single organization or leader has been at the helm. Instead, a "whole ecosystem" of organizations—national, regional, and local—have helped build BLM.[52] Even the Black Lives Global Network, founded by Garza, Tometi, and Cullors after the Ferguson uprising, was purposefully designed as a *network*, composed of multiple, semiautonomous chapters throughout the country.[53] Decentralization, Garza argues, is a politically savvy choice: it can help "level the playing field of power." It can allow "people who are often marginalized or blocked from exercising leadership to lead in public and out loud." Moreover, as BLM activists stress, a decentralized movement is not a leaderless movement; "decentralization means distributing leadership throughout the organization rather than concentrating it in one place or in one person or even a few people."[54] BLM can be seen, then, as a "leader-full organization"—a characteristic that might actually make it "smarter" than some traditional leadership structures. It may enable members and supporters to "fight more effectively." Garza writes, "Imagine if the Black Panther Party for Self Defense had functioned as a decentralized organization. Would it have been as easily decimated as it was under a centralized leadership framework?"[55]

BLM rose to prominence by condemning unjust (and often unpunished) killings of Black Americans by police.[56] Most large public demonstrations in the name of BLM have mobilized in response to particular incidents of police violence against Black persons. The declaration "Black Lives Matter" is also widely understood as a denunciation of police violence, albeit one that speaks in the affirmative, by asserting the value of Black humanity in a context of its routine devaluation and destruction.

Still, from its inception to its consolidation into a mass movement, the aims of BLM are also often defined by its participants in far broader ways. As Garza explained in 2014, "Black Lives Matter is a unique contribution that goes beyond extrajudicial killings of Black people by police and vigilantes." For Black lives to truly *matter* means not just that these killings end but that the wider conditions shaping Black life—including "Black poverty" and the fact that "1 million Black people are locked in cages"—are transformed.[57] As activist-scholar Barbara Ransby puts it, although police violence and the lack of accountability have been at the center of BLM protest activity, the "overall analysis" of most of the organizations involved is "far more expansive":

> Movement organizers have pointed out that the lack of affordable housing, low wages, the erosion of public services, the lack of jobs, and spiraling personal debt have all facilitated the slow death of tens of thousands of Black people deemed disposable to this labor-"light" economy of twenty-first-century racial capitalism, to which many are increasingly superfluous.[58]

The Movement for Black Lives (M4BL), an umbrella organization established in 2014 that includes most organizations associated with BLM, has likewise presented an ambitious, wide-ranging policy agenda, Vision for Black Lives, in 2016 and 2020. The coalition emphasizes that the Vision—a massive set of policy demands—is not limited to changes in policing. The six "planks" of the Vision make this clear: End the War on Black People; Reparations; Economic Justice; Invest/Divest; Community Control; and Political Power. Even the first platform, which targets "police and state-sanctioned violence" includes a sweeping set of policy demands that range from ending the use of past criminal history to restrict access to housing, education, employment, social programs and benefits, voting rights, parental rights, and other civil rights to a call for universal health care (under the heading "end the war on Black health and Black disabled people").[59]

As participants have noted, many BLM organizations and activists share a view of oppressions as "interlocking"; anti-Black racism, in other words, is understood to be bound up with capitalism, imperialism, ableism, and cisheteropatriarchy. Influenced by Black feminism and an intersectional analytic, BLM is a movement—founded by Black women—that simultaneously "centers, and is led by and rooted in, Black communities" *and* strives to ensure that "no one is left behind."[60] The latter commitment is sometimes expressed in the statement "All Black Lives Matter," underscoring that BLM aspires to dismantle every social system that impedes Black flourishing.[61] Garza explains what is at stake: "We need to ensure that the world that we fight for, the claim we lay to the future, is one that meets the needs of all those who have been marginalized."[62] Of course, not every person who has supported BLM's efforts is a proponent of all the policy demands enunciated by M4BL, nor are they necessarily committed to an intersectional, bottom-up model of social change. Nonetheless, it is important to recognize that for the organizations and individuals most responsible for building BLM's power, making "Black lives matter" means forging a world that not only is free of unjust police violence but also cares for Black people in a capacious sense, enabling them to thrive.

A Mosaic of Struggle

A widely circulated photo from a BLM protest, taken in Baton Rouge in 2016, shows a young Black woman in a flowing summer dress, standing firmly in the middle of a road, squarely facing a group of police in riot gear who are advancing on her.[63] One of the police appears to be grabbing her hand and zip tie handcuffs are visible; they are in the process of arresting her. The woman in the photo, Ieshia Evans, is still, while the armed officers are in motion. She appears both calm and resolute. Her feet are firmly planted on the ground, her posture strong, and her gaze back at the officers open and unflinching. The photo, taken by Reuters photographer Jonathan Bachman, is in many ways extraordinary.

One of the most striking elements of the image, however—the direct eye contact Evans delivers to the police lunging at her—is not unique to this particular moment. Rather, as Nicholas Mirzoeff and Nimalan Yoganathan have pointed out, a recurring practice of BLM protesters has been the "daring 'look back'" or "unflinching staring into the eyes of police."[64] An intentional "tactic," according to both Mirzoeff and Yoganathan, it also shows up frequently in news images of BLM, both before and after the iconic photo of Evans was published.[65]

This practice of "persistent looking" carries significant symbolic power. As Mirzoeff argues, the "look back," which is "foundational to BLM," implicitly references, and refuses, long-standing racialized norms governing who is authorized *to look* and who is expected to be *looked at*. As bell hooks explains, "An effective strategy of white supremacist terror and dehumanization during slavery centered around white control of the black gaze."[66]

Under chattel slavery in the United States, while near-constant surveillance of enslaved persons by overseers was standard, for an enslaved person to *look* at their owner or overseer was an act routinely met with punishment.[67] Later, the "unwritten rules" of the Jim Crow era dictated that "the mere act of making eye contact" was, for Black people, a violation that could readily result in insult, beating, or lynching.[68] "Reckless eyeballing"—looking by Black persons across the color line, most notably at white women—was often a pretext for allegations of assault and state or vigilante violence against Black men.[69] And the prohibition against Black looking, Mirzoeff contends, persists as an informal code even now. Consider, for example, that in 2015, "Freddie Gray's fateful encounter with Baltimore City police officers began, according to multiple police accounts, with eye contact," as Stacia L. Brown writes in "Looking While Black."[70] Mirzoeff puts it more starkly: "His only offence was that he met the look of a police officer in the eye, leading to an assumption of guilt for which he ended up dead."[71]

In his eulogy, Reverend Jamal Bryant, speaking to Freddie Gray's mother, emphasized the significance of her son's looking:

On April 12 at 8:39 in the morning, four officers on bicycles saw your son. And your son, in a subtlety of revolutionary stance, did something black men were trained to know not to do. He looked police in the eye. And when he looked the police in the eye, they knew that there was a threat, because they're used to black men with their head bowed down low, with their spirit broken. He was a threat simply because he was man enough to look some-body in authority in the eye.[72]

Bryant's suggestion that there was something "revolutionary" about a Black person looking police in the eye clarifies the power of BLM's "persistent looking" tactic. The "daring 'look back,'" as enacted by Black protesters facing heavily armed law enforcement, tacitly references and refutes the long-standing white supremacist norm that demands deference to white authority. And in the "afterlife of slavery," characterized in part by disproportionate carceral state violence targeting Black persons, the unflinching gaze of the BLM activist confronted by police is courageous and important.

This particular, powerful act of "persistent looking" should be understood as part of the "repertoire of contention" developed and used by the BLM movement since its inception in 2013.[73] BLM activists have created a rich and distinctive repertoire of protest tactics. Some are borrowed from previous social movements, and other signature practices—like "unrelenting staring"—are recent inventions. All are part of BLM's ambitious and potent effort—consisting of many different, sometimes experimental performances and claims—to expose white supremacy as the unacknowledged infrastructure and lived faith of American society.

Some of the most well-known and visible examples of BLM protest activity are those that bear a strong resemblance to direct action practices of other social movements: large public demonstrations—first in specific locations like Ferguson, Baltimore, and Minneapolis, and then expanding to every corner of the country by 2020. Although the scale of the protests that year was unprecedented, the central activity taking place—large numbers of people gathering, marching in the streets, chanting, holding signs, and demanding changes ranging from reform to revolution—would look familiar to any student of American politics. The sheer numbers present and the visibility of white participants were new, but the direct action on display was recognizable—part of the long lineage of antiracist struggle in the United States.

Other BLM tactics also draw on established practices of resistance that involve the disruptive occupation of public space—such as blockades of San Francisco's Bay Bridge in 2016, the 2020 closure of the 101 freeway in Los Angeles, and many other similar actions in multiple locations in the summer of 2020. In addition to roads and highways, BLM protesters have used their bodies to disrupt specific events, including the 2017 inauguration of President Trump and public transportation to the Super Bowl in 2018. As Randy Shaw points out, these actions embody the "No Business as Usual" ethos cultivated by ACT UP in the 1980s.[74] Another disruptive practice employed by BLM, the "die in," was also a key tactic of AIDS activism, as well as anti-war, anti-nuclear, and environmental movements.[75]

There are also several novel tactics BLM activists have crafted, which are now widely known and closely associated with the movement. One is the "unflinching stare" analyzed above. Two other important practices are the performance of "Hands Up, Don't Shoot" and the destruction/defacement/reclamation of white supremacist monuments. Each points to the creative, varied efforts undertaken by BLM advocates to contest the devaluation of Black life.

The "Hands Up, Don't Shoot" display is clearly recognizable; it has been enacted and documented countless times since 2014 and has become something of a "signature" of the movement. This complex and ambiguous act, usually consisting of both gesture and speech, emerged as a prominent feature of public protests in Ferguson in 2014. In this move, Black protesters raise their hands in the air while chanting, "Hands Up, Don't Shoot" in the presence of police, usually heavily armed. This embodied performance cited the testimony of Michael Brown's friend, who reported that Brown was shot by police with his hands up. Within days of Brown's killing, the statement "Hands Up, Don't Shoot," coupled with the action of hand raising, was a recurrent feature of the growing protests in Ferguson, often in the form of collective call-and-response sessions. This action, repeated many times since, is, of course, open to multiple interpretations, even among those allied with BLM. Dora Apel's reading of "Hands Up, Don't Shoot," for example, criticizes the maneuver for signaling Black "defenselessness and submission" vis-à-vis state power. It figures Black Americans as "respectful" and law-abiding, Apel argues, and the perception of Blacks as "non-threatening" and "non-resistant" is soothing to moderates; it "does not fundamentally threaten white racial power."[76] Yet other commentators question this formulation. Juliet Hooker suggests it is too simplistic; the "Hands Up, Don't Shoot" political actors are not presenting themselves as passive but likely intend the gesture to register "not as deference but as defiance."[77] (Hooker makes this point in relation to dominant accounts of the civil rights movement as well: those who "subscribe to the romantic narrative of the civil rights movement" also tend to see the Black activists of the 1960s as "passive victims," while the protesters actually "viewed themselves as engaged in defiant resistance."[78]) Mirzoeff also regards the gesture as defiant in the sense that it proclaims a "right to exist." And it does so in part by performatively dwelling in the moment *before* Michael Brown and other similar victims of police violence were killed. By citing this "vital moment" in which the dead are still alive, the "Hands Up, Don't Shoot" gesture rejects closure; it refuses to "move on" from the brutal, unnecessary loss of life.[79]

BLM activists have also undertaken direct action to dismantle racist statues and monuments, especially those commemorating the Confederacy. (Du Bois wrote in 1931 of the great "ingenuity" evident in Confederate monuments' inscriptions to "liberty." A truthful inscription, he writes, would read: "Sacred to the Memory of Those Who Fought to Perpetuate Human Slavery!"[80]) Understanding that the presence of such objects in public space serves to "re-circulate white supremacy through the social body," BLM protesters have toppled, beheaded, painted, and otherwise disturbed these "ideological powerhouses" in myriad creative ways.[81] In many instances, the statue or monument has been literally destroyed by activists; in others it has been reclaimed while legal battles over official removal continued. For example, in May 2020, BLM protesters in Birmingham, Alabama, top-pled a bronze statue of a Confederate navy captain, Charles Linn; activists in Nashville brought down a statue of pro-lynching politician Edward Carmack; and in Richmond, Virginia, Confederate icons Jefferson Davis, Robert E. Lee, Stonewall Jackson, and J. E. B. Stuart were covered in protest graffiti.[82] These acts are part of BLM's growing tactical repertoire, animated by the insight that it is impossible to "divorce Confederate iconography from the treatment of African-Americans as second-class citizens of this country during Jim Crow and now."[83] Moreover, while it is commonplace to think and talk about these objects as "symbols," we might interpret BLM's direct action a bit differently. Wrecking these public things "is not *symbolic* of a dis-mantling; it *is* a dismantling, bit by physical bit, of anti-Black racism and hi-erarchical racial ordering."[84]

Although Confederate iconography has long been a target of Black re-sistance, the actions of BLM have helped generate widespread, vocal op-position to such monumental public art.[85] In 2015, following large BLM protests in Ferguson and Baltimore, and on the heels of the white suprem-acist Charleston church massacre, the activist Bree Newsome Bass climbed to the top of the South Carolina State Capitol flagpole and removed the Confederate flag, amid growing calls to abandon symbols of the Confederacy, and was arrested. (The flag Newsome Bass took was replaced within hours. The state legislature passed a bill just weeks later, however, that permanently removed the flag from the statehouse.) Over the next four years, at least 114 Confederate symbols were removed throughout the United States, despite President Trump's defense of their "beauty" in 2017, following violent white supremacist riots in Charlottesville.[86]

In the spring and summer of 2020, however, as BLM was re-energized in response to George Floyd's death, Confederate statues and monuments increasingly became the target of direct action, reminiscent of Newsome Bass's maneuver five years earlier. In cities throughout the United States, protesters engaged in "creative destruction" to remove or remake these objects. According to art historian Verity Platt, the "wave of statue-felling" that swept the United States in 2020 made it clear that "we are living in a time of iconoclasm." As in other epochal moments, "image breaking has served as a powerful demonstration of a break with the old order." Importantly, "these are not simply acts of destruction" but practices that "generate new images that can be powerful agents of social change."[87] These "defacements" are also "refacements," to borrow the vocabulary of Bruno Latour.[88]

Creative destruction of monuments and statues certainly "generates new images," as Platt notes, but it sometimes does even more—constituting a communal space where there once was none, forging new relationships and common practices. A particularly striking example of such a trans-formation took place in Richmond, Virginia, in the spring and summer of 2020 at the site of a large, 60-foot-high monument to Robert E. Lee. The physical structure remained architecturally intact throughout 2020, but it was thoroughly transformed by BLM activists: covered in colorful paint and graffiti with messages reading "stop killing us" and "defund the police."[89] It was also dramatically lit at night, with large images of George Floyd and other major figures including Harriet Tubman, Frederick Douglass, Du Bois, Malcolm X, and John Lewis projected upon the edi-fice at different times. The altered monument also became the focal point for public gatherings—first, for the BLM protests that peaked in late May and early June, and then for something more like a "block party," with music, dancing, voter registration booths, food trucks, a lending library, and portable basketball hoops. At least for a time, the small park with the transformed Lee statue at its center became a "round-the-clock commu-nity space."[90]

BLM's Propaganda?

What if we read BLM's tactics—both familiar and innovative—as examples of a Du Boisean aesthetic-political practice of world building? Put slightly differently, these recent creative, varied undertakings seem to embody the "propaganda" Du Bois gestured toward when using the term in *Dusk of Dawn*. There it signaled multidimensional, expansive efforts aiming not only to educate or persuade but also to reshape the "subconscious" and the unspoken perceptions and feelings helping to hold white supremacy intact. BLM's wide-ranging and inventive methods resonate with Du Bois's unusual conception of propaganda and the account of aesthetic-political struggle in which it is embedded.

A more conventional interpretation of BLM's practices might focus on *framing*, the signifying work that is a staple of social movements. A frame is an interpretive schema that (1) "punctuates" or points out a specific injustice; (2) makes diagnostic and prognostic attributions; and (3) articulates or "packages" events and experiences so that they "hang together in a relatively unified and meaningful way," providing a reusable map for meaning making.[91] Importantly, framing is not only about the *words* used by movement actors. Actions also signify. Doug McAdam argues that in order to understand framing—the "principal weapon" of emergent movements—it is important to pay attention to the "tactical choices" at play.[92] So when we consider BLM's engagement in framing, or signifying work, we are interested not only in what BLM activists *say* but also in what they *do*.

While all social movements are arguably engaged in framing, according to David Snow and Robert Benford, only occasionally does a movement succeed in establishing a "master frame"—a "generic" schema that "provides a grammar" that is widely used to interpret the social world and is capable of sustaining a "cycle of protest."[93] (A classic example is the US civil rights movement and the "master frame" associated with Martin Luther King Jr.[94]) Has BLM generated its own master frame? In important respects, this seems indisputable. Master frames capable of sustaining a cycle of protest share certain features: they are "elaborated" rather than "restricted." A "flexible," as opposed to "rigid," mode of interpretation allows for "extensive ideational amplification and extension."[95] Additionally, a master frame's *resonance* will depend on how central its "ideas and meanings" are to "the ideology of the targets of mobilization." A resonant master frame draws on a "larger belief system" to "strike a responsive chord"; the more it activates "extant beliefs, myths, folktales, and the like," the more salient it will be.[96]

To the extent that BLM is involved in "framing," they have succeeded on both fronts. Their words and actions have produced a legible, widely used, and *flexible* frame. The very openness of the declaration "Black Lives Matter" allows the articulation of plural claims to be made in its name.[97] As we saw above, these range from calls for police reform to demands for massive economic redistribution. "Black Lives Matter" allows for extensive elaboration of the many ways that American society fails to show care and regard for Black people. As activists have emphasized, for Black lives to truly matter would require not only drastic changes to policing but also other major transformations: living wages, robust social protections including universal health care and free quality higher education, along with debt forgiveness, reparations, and more. That all of these claims have been made with reference to "Black Lives Matter" demonstrates the existence of a flexible master frame.

A master frame's potency is due not only to its elaborativeness but also to its *resonance*—its ability to tap into its audience's "larger belief system" and place it in relation to credible empirical evidence in a way that sparks response. BLM seems to do this by drawing on a powerful American political ideology that promises equality and juxtaposing that axiomatic faith with evidence of routine, disparate harm targeting Black citizens. "Black Lives Matter" gains salience, particularly in the context of police killings, from the way it tacitly cites the professed norm of equal treatment while telling a story about the fatally unequal treatment of Black Americans. Resonance here is not achieved simply by pointing out a contradiction (between ideal and reality); it is, crucially, an artistic achievement. A resonant master frame that can galvanize cycles of protest, as BLM has, is less a logical argument than a compelling *narrative* that weaves together ideational and empirical elements in a way that "rings true."[98]

If we tend to the artistic elements of BLM's framing practices—the "strategic dramaturgy" in which activists are engaged—as well as the movement's impressively varied range of tactics, we might say that BLM is engaged in a vast "propaganda" campaign, in Du Bois's final sense of the term.[99] BLM's creative elaboration of a master frame, both flexible and resonant, can be understood as a key part of this campaign. Yet as BLM strives for the kind of deep cultural transformation—simultaneously political, aesthetic, and economic—that Du Bois signaled with his call for "propaganda," they may not only be constructing a "master frame" but also attempting to *insert a counterworld* into the world of their opponents.

Glenn Mackin develops such a reading of BLM in conversation with Jacques Rancière's political theory. Rancière's work famously emphasizes the co-constitution of the political and the aesthetic, specifically by understanding political action as a reconfiguration of the "sensory order." According to this view, politics is fundamentally about transforming "the order of the visible and sayable."[100] This occurs, Rancière contends, when the "uncounted" within a given society act together in ways that contest the reigning "configuration of the perceptible."[101] This move, if successful, is two-fold: it involves making present previously unseen/unheard subjectivities *and* previously unseen/unheard matters of dispute, simultaneously.[102]

In conversation with Rancière and BLM activism, Mackin offers an account of "political-aesthetic transformation" that occurs through "actions that invoke a comprehensible counterworld." In contrast to readers of Rancière who regard aesthetic refiguration as a break with "reason and communicability" and unlike those commentators who regard BLM as abandoning persuasion altogether, Mackin argues that BLM attempts to present a counterworld through a mixture of cognitive, communicable, and aesthetic elements.[103] Moreover, this attempt, like those of other dissident political actors, is always *imbricated* in the dominant sensory order; it is not radically outside that order, but instead "reorganizes its resources" to present an alternative interpretation of existence that is *both* legible and disruptive.

BLM activists "expose and challenge dominant patterns of perception and interpretation. They inaugurate the 'world of competing worlds' that Rancière identifies with politics."[104] How? For one, Mackin points out, many participants in BLM believe that American society is "founded on something like what Charles Mills calls a racial contract." Yet this structure of white domination remains unacknowledged by many white people (and some nonwhite people), who either do not recognize the existence of "racialized patterns of wealth, poverty, education, contact with the criminal justice system, and access to economic opportunities" or do not see those patterns as resulting from a long-standing system of racial domination. For example, many white people perceive police violence against Black Americans as either the fair enforcement of neutral laws or exceptional abuses that can be readily corrected. In this context, BLM activists try to demonstrate that this violence is no such thing; it is "but one manifestation of a regime that treats nonwhite lives as less valuable." In Rancièrean terms, BLM is engaged in a "clash over sense"—a struggle between a dominant order of sense that does not allow for the perception of white supremacy as such and a "counterworld" in which white supremacy is both real and contested.

The "Hands Up, Don't Shoot" gesture (discussed above) can also be understood in these terms. Mackin says it is possible that the move functions in the way Dora Apel alleges, positioning Black people as submissive victims of exceptional police violence and thereby soothing white observers. He continues, "Yet something else is also going on. The protesters are inserting their counterworld into the world of their opponents."[105] They do so through "complex mimicry." They mime the "'reasonable person's response to the police" to demonstrate that those who view Black persons as violent or irrational are wrong. They also mime the gesture that Michael Brown, by some accounts, was engaged in when he was shot. Performing the "Hands Up, Don't Shoot" gesture and speech en masse in public confrontations with police, BLM protesters both identify themselves with Brown and associate the (usually heavily armed) police present with the police who killed Brown. This gesture, then, does not just position Black citizens as passive but also "restages the conflict between the protesters and the police and between the police and Michael Brown in a way that offers proof of the protesters' claims about the existence of white supremacy." "Proof" here is not strictly logical, of course; it comes by way of a "political-aesthetic declaration."

"Black Lives Matter" as a (written and verbal) statement also works to summon a counterworld. Mackin explains:

> The remarkable feature of this declaration is that it raises a claim that almost no one explicitly denies. There is no overt debate about whether black lives matter. The disagreement is about whether the world the claim refers to—*a world in which it is necessary to state that black lives do in fact matter*—exists. Asserting that black lives matter therefore invokes a counterworld; the assertion declares that the world we currently inhabit is one in which black lives do not matter or at least do not matter equally.[106]

The invocation of a counterworld is always a multidimensional endeavor. It cannot be accomplished solely through rational argument or the dissemination of information. In the case of BLM, their efforts involve the presentation of facts showing that Black Americans are subjected to "group-differentiated vulnerability to premature death"; the articulation of determinate policy proposals; and a range of performative, creative acts.[107] These elements constitute an ambitious, aesthetic-political effort to disturb settled perceptions and contest the prevailing racial order—a wide-ranging enterprise not unlike the "propaganda" Du Bois called for nearly a century ago.

Conclusion

The various ways that "propaganda" appears in Du Bois's work—though partially distinct—are connected by an abiding concern with how to transform modes of seeing, feeling, and thinking so that Black freedom can be realized. As we saw, Du Bois harshly condemns the "propaganda" of white supremacy—the wide-ranging media by which Blackness is degraded and whiteness exalted. Yet Du Bois is also committed to the development and circulation of counterpropaganda that can dispute dominant representations of the so-called "races." This was the intent of *The Crisis*: to produce and share "propaganda" on behalf of Black humanity. Du Bois's most infamous statement about "propaganda" is the declaration that "all Art is propaganda." Yet the purpose of the text in which that famous line appears is not to advance a dogmatic definition of art. Rather, it is to bring the political and the aesthetic together, and to celebrate the world-building capacity of Black persons, which persists even under profound constraint. The final, fascinating version of "propaganda," appearing in *Dusk of Dawn*, names an undertheorized but vitally important form of political action that strives to work upon the "irrational" dimensions of "race hatred." For Du Bois, reshaping the "unconscious" and "subconscious" beliefs and habits of white Americans is a key aspect of the struggle against white supremacist capitalism.

Indeed, all of his uses of "propaganda" convey Du Bois's belief that human emancipation depends not only on fact finding and argument or changes to law and policy but also on creative cultural endeavors that unsettle "race hate" and prepare the ground for a multiracial revolution against capitalism.

Prior chapters showed that the gratifications that attach to whiteness in the United States are complex and plural. So too must be the politics that resist it. This is, above all, what Du Bois seems to be getting at when he invokes "propaganda" in this last sense. He is calling for practices of polyvalent resistance, born of the understanding that sensorial and aesthetic transformations are integral to revolutionizing the political economy and finally establishing abolition-democracy. BLM's tactics—especially when linked to radical rather than reformist claims about what it would mean to materially affirm

that Black lives matter—reflect this Du Boisean understanding. It is imperative to reshape dominant modes of perception and feeling, and this requires
enacting an array of political-aesthetic interventions.

BLM is not primarily focused on white people or white identity, though
it includes the dominant racial group among its addressees. (The rightwing
rejoinder, "All Lives Matter," clearly illustrates just how jolting many whites
found the explicit reference to—and defense of—Black existence by name.)
The defining principle of this diffuse yet formidable political front is the dignity and value of Black persons, rather than any claim about whiteness per
se. Yet BLM is a determined, robust effort—consisting of many different,
sometimes novel actions—to expose white supremacy as the disavowed
framework and civic religion of American society. Understood in these
terms, white supremacy enables the routine disregard for Black lives *and* the
patterns of racialized gratification investigated in this book. So while BLM
remains rightly focused on Black persons and their vulnerability within the
current order, the tenacious, repeated insistence that "Black Lives Matter"
has the potential to disturb the familiar circuits by which whiteness delivers
material, psychological, emotional, and spiritual rewards.

Epilogue

Abolitionist Possibilities

There isn't any Negro problem; there is only a white problem.
—Richard Wright (1946)

Saying "I have privilege" doesn't *do* anything.
—Lauren Michele Jackson (2019)

Whiteness has long served as a potent source of gratification for its bearers. Although its rewards—wage, pleasure, dominion—assume different forms today than at the time of Du Bois's writing, they persist nonetheless. Whiteness continues to *gratify* in ways that contemporary discourses of privilege or ignorance miss; those who travel under its sign are not only passive, accidental recipients of racialized goods, nor do they simply suffer from a profound lack of understanding about the racial order in which they live (though these things may also be true). As this project has suggested, most, if not all, persons classified as white are (also) positively attached to that mark, in ways that are uncomfortable to admit. This attachment is not wholly surprising, however, once we acknowledge the specific racialized gratifications Du Bois's thinking has brought into view—a sense of belonging and value, feelings of enjoyment and safety, and a fortifying faith, all connected to one's experiences living in the world as "white."

If this account is at all convincing, what does it imply about the role that white people can or should play in political struggles targeting white supremacy (including but not limited to Black Lives Matter [BLM], discussed in Chapter 5)? If many white people, even those who might identify themselves as "anti-racist," are practiced in receiving valuable rewards by way of their racial position and are therefore more deeply connected to their whiteness than is often recognized, what does this mean for thinking about

The Gratifications of Whiteness. Ella Myers, Oxford University Press. © Oxford University Press 2022.
DOI: 10.1093/oso/9780197556764.003.0006

political change? More specifically, what does it suggest about whites' ability to assume and enact responsibility for ending racial domination?

In his middle-period work, Du Bois struggled with the question of white agency. Facing the seeming intractability of US racial hierarchy, Du Bois spoke often of how difficult it was to mobilize white citizens to join Black citizens in the fight against an unjust society and polity. As we have seen in this book, the widespread inaction of white Americans in the first half of the 20th century prompted Du Bois to wonder about the very nature of "race hate." Could white people be reached? How? What would it take to spur them to act in support of Black freedom? By 1934, when he resigned from the National Association for the Advancement of Colored People (NAACP), Du Bois sounded pessimistic about the very prospect (a pessimism that only grew over the rest of his life, culminating in his self-exile to Ghana in 1961).[1] Upon the occasion of his departure from the NAACP, he explained that Black leaders had long supposed that "white America did not know or realize the continuing plight of the Negro." Accordingly, for more than two decades, the strategy of organizations like the NAACP had been to "put the essential facts before the American people"—"by book and periodical, by speech and appeal, by various dramatic methods of agitation." These efforts, however, culminated in a troubling impasse, according to Du Bois: "Today there can be no doubt that Americans know the facts; and yet they remain for the most part indifferent and unmoved."[2]

The portrait this book offers of racialized gratification, developed through Du Bois's middle-period writings, may shed some light on the predicament he outlined above. If facts and information about racial oppression are often insufficient motivators for action, not only in Du Bois's context but also in our own, this may have something to do with the extent to which whites have been acculturated to receive—and to expect—an array of rewards, in the form of standing, enjoyment, and entitlement, which are bound up with their lived identity as "white." Reluctance to relinquish these reliable forms of gratification may help explain the frustrating dilemma Du Bois identified.

Still, what shall we make of recent signs that some white Americans are not entirely "indifferent and unmoved"? For example, white racial attitudes have shifted significantly since 2014, with more white people now acknowledging that anti-Black discrimination is a problem that should be addressed.[3] And surprising numbers of white people showed up in cities around the country, and the world, to participate in BLM protests in 2020. There is also a pronounced popular-cultural interest in learning about racism, white supremacy, and white identity. To be sure, there are plenty of well-documented reasons to be skeptical about these phenomena. Might the shifts in public opinion or the presence of white protesters in the streets be fleeting? Perhaps the BLM demonstrations in the summer of 2020, which were majority white nationally, were truly novel—prompted by a "perfect storm" that arose out of a nightmarish global pandemic, the resurgence of white nationalism in the United States and abroad, and the Trump presidency—and therefore unlikely to be repeated. Moreover, isn't it the case that many of the white people who express their opposition to white supremacy do so in seemingly easy and trite ways—by posting on social media or by reading now-bestselling books on race?[4] Where is the evidence of a lasting commitment to engage in the work of sustained organizing to create a more egalitarian society? Should we expect that white people in this country will, in meaningful numbers, not simply push for reforms to the existing order but agitate for the kind of radical change Du Bois understood was necessary for abolition-democracy to be realized?

We should not expect this. But neither should we too quickly discount the political openings the contemporary scene may offer. It seems clear that there has been a shift in consciousness among some whites since BLM first appeared in 2014—increased recognition of the institutionalized mistreatment of Black people (not only by the carceral system) and a new willingness to examine how whites have been advantaged by de jure and de facto white supremacy in the United States. Right-wing attacks on everything from "wokeness" to "critical race theory" (construed as any curriculum that truthfully addresses how racism has shaped US institutions) can be seen as defensive responses to these signs of flux. It remains to be seen whether the country will undergo a meaningful "reckoning" or not.[5] But it does little good to overlook the fact that at least some white Americans, in greater numbers than before, have—in Du Bois's terms—been "induced to act." Even when they have done so imperfectly, the very fact that they are no longer simply "indifferent and unmoved" is an opportunity for radicalization.

Moreover, some of the conditions that supposedly made 2020's surge of white protest activity anomalous are also potentially focal points for building a broader progressive movement. For example, the COVID crisis that by some accounts made Americans more "emotional" and therefore inclined to participate in street protests also laid bare the miseries exacted by global capitalism in general and by the United States' especially punitive regime in particular.[6] Were people in the streets in the summer of 2020 aggrieved not only by the senseless murder of George Floyd but also by a government that quite obviously cared very little about its citizens' lives? The immiseration of low-wage workers, disproportionately people of color and women, whose labor enriches a thriving billionaire class and the uncounted and uncompensated carework performed mostly by women, for example, were long-standing features of American life made more obvious in the pandemic. The rise of white nationalism (targeting not only Blacks but also other racialized minorities, especially Asian Americans and Jews) and its endorsement—by President Trump and most members of the Republican Party, even in the wake of the January 2021 siege on the Capitol—is a continuing, pernicious reality that can perhaps serve as a site for ambitious multiracial organizing. Of course, there are no guarantees that the needless suffering wrought by today's capitalist order or the resurgence of violent white nationalism will in fact serve as targets of sustained action by whites who identify as anti-racist or as supporters of BLM.[7] But rather than foreclose the possibilities of the present—where a meaningful number of white Americans are at least willing to say that white supremacy is real and wrong—it might make sense to treat this as a crack to be pried open. Can these initial signs of attention and concern be pushed in a politicizing direction, toward bold collective action?

In that spirit, what principles and practices might guide such an effort? What examples might be built upon? Taking as a starting point Du Bois's incisive critique of racial capitalism and his arresting vision of a transformed, socialist, and democratic society conducive to human flourishing, I offer three tentative reflections on expanding and deepening white participation in emancipatory struggles.[8]

First, it is worth reflecting on the fraught question of whites' role in political projects focused on combatting and ending racism. As previous chapters explored, in the middle of his long career, Du Bois moved away from trying to marshal white Americans to actively support the NAACP agenda, expressing profound doubt about the likelihood of such mobilization while simultaneously advocating for separate consumer cooperatives as a way of building collective power among Blacks.[9] But although Du Bois had largely given up on whites' interest in or ability to fight for a racially just "industrial and cultural democracy" by the time he left the NAACP in 1934, just a few decades later, both civil rights and Black Power leaders urged sympathetic whites to take on specific roles and tasks in relation to their respective movement goals. Here I want to briefly consider the approach taken by Black Power actors in the late 1960s, who counseled white Americans to use community organizing strategies to build political capacity with other white people, with the aim of eventually working in coalition with Black groups. This model was presented by the Student Nonviolent Coordinating Committee (SNCC) beginning in 1966 and laid out in Kwame Ture and Charles V. Hamilton's *Black Power: The Politics of Liberation* in 1967. Ture and Hamilton write in their book that the philosophy and praxis of Black Power welcomes "white people of good will." Indeed, "there is a definite, much-needed role whites can play"—a role that has "educative, organizational, and supportive" components.[10] The educative function, they explain, is rooted in the fact that white people have special "access" to other whites. Although whites have been "reluctant to go into their own communities—which is where the racism exists," this is precisely what "whites who see the need for basic change" should do. In addition, the organizational task is linked to a long-term goal of building "a coalition of poor blacks and poor whites."[11] But whites first need to "mobilize and organize" other whites in ways that make effective coalition with Black liberationists possible. Lastly, while Black organizations must be Black led, Ture and Hamilton argue that white people "can and do play very important supportive roles in these organizations." Provided that white people do not come into Black spaces hoping to "'come alive through the black community,'" pushing a "color-blind" ideology, or attempting to "lead or set policy," they can lend valuable practical support.[12]

This approach, outlined by Ture and Hamilton, which emphasizes "autonomous" and "affiliate" organizing, informs some white anti-racist activism today, including the work of Showing Up for Racial Justice (SURJ), a national network founded in 2009 that seeks to "move white people to act as part of a multi-racial majority for justice."[13] SURJ says that their role is to "undermine white support for white supremacy and to help build a racially just society."[14] The practices of one of SURJ's most active member groups, the Alliance of White Anti-Racists Everywhere—Los Angeles (AWARE-LA), are shaped by the white-on-white community organizing and multiracial coalitional model developed by Black Power proponents, as well as the white anti-racist activist Anne Braden, in the 1960s.[15] To pursue the goal of white people educating themselves and each other about racism, rather than expecting Black people and other people of color to teach them, AWARE-LA holds monthly "Saturday Dialogue" meetings. These gatherings are "for white anti-racists who want to discuss issues of identity, community, privilege and racism in our lives with the intention to strengthen our practice as anti-racists in alliances, relationships, and interactions with people of color." This educational practice is connected to more overtly political action as well. AWARE-LA includes the White People 4 Black Lives (WP4BL) collective—an "activist project" that endeavors to "act in solidarity" with organizations led by people of color on behalf of "the abolition of the white supremacist system." This approach is intended to avoid the common pitfall whereby white progressives try to "take over" groups that are by and for people of color. AWARE-LA's emphasis on "supporting" and "amplifying" political projects that are defined and led by people of color is consistent with the model advanced by earlier Black radicals.

Neither Ture and Hamilton's conceptions of white participation nor SURJ's and AWARE-LA's philosophies and activities are presented here as unassailable ideals. Instead, they are invitations to think more about how white anti-racist political agency can be forged in ways that push beyond today's popular practices of therapeutic white "consciousness raising," the stuff of workshops and book clubs. Both the Black Power framework and SURJ's practical efforts center on community organizing and coalitional politics— on building collective power. Although there is clearly an "educative" dimension to this work, it is distinguishable from projects whose primary intent is for white people to acknowledge that they themselves are privileged. (Robin D'Angelo's wildly popular workshops, for example, have as their stated goal that white attendees "identify personal complicity."[16]) The point of the model sketched above is not to "confess" one's whiteness or to acknowledge, with words, one's complicity, but to build shared political capacity that can be used to engage in solidaristic action with other groups seeking to end white supremacy.[17] This vision is a valuable counter to models of whites' "awakening to race" that are mostly individualized and self-confessional. As sociologist Jeb Aram Middlebrook writes:

> Without readily available models of white antiracist organizing, however, white antiracist work often ends at writings, lectures, workshops, conferences, or networks. These approaches are necessary components to any social movement but would never be characterized by scholars or organizers as THE movement. Believing that education is the beginning and end of all antiracism efforts assumes . . . that ending white racism is simply a matter of consciousness-raising—as if structural and institutional white supremacy is not also an impediment to racial justice; as if the question of white supremacist capitalism is not also a question of power and consent; as if white supremacists aren't *always* organizing.[18]

Surely some form of "consciousness-raising" has a part to play in the politicizing strategies laid out by Black radicals and experimented with by SURJ. The crucial difference, however, is the decisive move toward collective organizing and action.

Second, I suggest that the most hopeful—and the most serious—challenges to racial inequality in the United States at present are those that are boldly visionary in their aims, most notably contemporary abolitionism, which unapologetically seeks, in the words of Ruth Wilson Gilmore, to "change everything." As abolitionists regularly underscore, the "destructive" project of abolishing police and prisons is paired with a "constructive" project of building a society that materially affirms that "life is precious."[19] Mariame Kaba clarifies: "It is a movement *for* different ways of living together."[20]

This movement draws directly on Du Bois's thought, particularly his conceptualization of "abolition-democracy" in *Black Reconstruction*.[21] In particular, contemporary abolitionists draw on Du Bois's insights into the importance of institution building to create the material conditions of freedom. Angela Davis explains, "When I refer to prison abolitionism, I like to draw from the DuBoisian [sic] notion of abolition democracy. That is to say, it is not only, or not even primarily, about abolition as a negative process of tearing down, but it is also about building up, about creating new institutions."[22] Following Du Bois's insight that "You could remove the chains, but if you did not develop the institutions that would allow for the incorporation of previously enslaved people into democratic society, then slavery would not be abolished," Davis positions today's abolition movement as part of a continuing struggle to establish the abolition-democracy Du Bois envisioned.[23]

As we have seen, in much of Du Bois's middle-period work, he advanced a radical-utopian vision of a world in which the "color line" no longer governed life chances and a socialist economy "distribute[d] the world's goods to satisfy the necessary wants of all."[24] Alongside scathing indictments of the harms wrought by the reigning regime of racial capitalism, Du Bois regularly invoked a future society and polity that would support the well-being of all people.

Du Bois also believed that the "darker world" was uniquely capable of engaging in visionary politics.[25] In the 1926 speech and essay "The Criteria of Negro Art" (discussed in Chapter 5), Du Bois tells his mostly Black audience, "We who are dark can see America in ways that white Americans cannot." He means not only that they can perceive its inequality, cruelty, and hypocrisy but also that they are able to imagine more freely, to craft "a political vision that exceeds the limits set by the white imagination," in the words of Joel Olson.[26] After stipulating in the "Criteria" speech that "we who are dark" have a special understanding of the United States, he continues: "Seeing our country thus, are we satisfied with its present goals and ideals?" Du Bois suggests that those who have been "pushed aside" should not be content with the reigning values of American society. Indeed, he indicates that Black people may already be in possession of a "vision of what the world could be if it were really a beautiful world."[27] This world is "a world where men know, where men create, where men realize themselves and where they enjoy life." Du Bois believes that there is a form of radical thought specific to Black Americans, tied to their particular struggles in this country, which offers a vision of a better life for all citizens: "It is this sort of a world we want to create for ourselves and *for all America*."[28]

The radical-utopian ethos of today's abolitionists resonates with important elements of Du Bois's thinking, even as it also pushes beyond the parameters of his political thought. Like Du Bois before them, today's abolitionists seek a full-blown alternative to racial capitalism. The specific goal of abolishing police and prisons is situated within an audacious political program that addresses itself to "the entire ecology of precarious existence."[29] Abolitionist organizers draw on and expand upon the utopianism of earlier Black radical theorizing, including Du Bois's. "Racial capitalism," for example, is the named target of contemporary abolitionist political work, yet their "bottom-up" approach to sociopolitical change addresses itself to the many cross-cutting vulnerabilities produced by entrenched sexism, xenophobia, ableism, transphobia, and more.

As many abolitionists point out, it is not a coincidence that the movement is being led by Black women (including Davis, Gilmore, and Kaba, among others).[30] One of today's most radical political projects, one that doggedly insists another world is possible, has been defined and advanced by Americans who are subject to the interlocking forces of anti-Black racism and sexism. Perhaps this affirms Du Bois's belief that experiences of exclusion and marginalization nurture not only a critical perspective on the current order but also a creative, radical imagination that can see beyond it.[31] And just as Du Bois affirmed Black Americans' ability to envision and build a better world "for ourselves and for all America," so too do today's abolitionists put forth an ideal of a "world where we have everything we need: food, shelter, education, health, art, beauty, clean water, and more things that are foundational to our personal and community safety," in the words of Kaba.[32] That it is Black women leading this radical-utopian movement is not surprising, according to Angela Davis: "Historically, black feminists have had visions to change the structure of society in ways that would benefit not just black women but everyone."[33]

The entry of abolitionist demands—most prominently, "defund the police"—into mainstream political conversation in the United States is a heartening, albeit uncertain, development. What was once considered a fringe discourse came to circulate much more widely, in a relatively short amount of time, thanks to the work of abolitionist organizers. Abolitionists, often aligned with BLM, have emphasized that divesting in police means investing in social supports, as the Movement for Black Lives (M4BL) platform specifies.[34] Keeanga-Yamahtta Taylor suggests that as a result of the abolitionist movement, people are better able to "generalize from police violence to the ways that public funding for police comes at the expense of other public institutions."[35] The imperative "defund the police" is now available as a common (and contested) political object around which coalitional actors can direct their energies.[36] It presents an opportunity for white Americans to act as agitators, not reformers, in Olson's words, and to practice a politics of identification in which "defund the police" acts as third term, a shared objective, linking together multiple constituencies.[37]

Finally, when considering the possibilities for white progressive political agency today, Du Bois's theoretical and practical target—racial capitalism—remains a crucial orienting concept. Dual temptations—an anti-racist politics that leaves capitalism untouched and a race-blind "class first" politics—are as ever-present as they were in Du Bois's day. The writings that form the heart of this book expose the inadequacy of both.

Today's "black neoliberal politics" imagines Black freedom in terms of access to, and success within, reigning capitalist culture.[38] Yet in the writings examined in this book, Du Bois consistently took aim at this aspiration, questioning those who would confine "Black struggle within an established economic form, one that puts and holds market actors in competitive relation and effectively guarantees unequal outcomes," in the words of Andrew J. Douglas.[39] Du Bois's writings push us to confront the possibility that capitalism itself must be overturned—for the sake of Black liberation in particular and human emancipation in general. There is no reason, Du Bois thinks, to accept a political-economic system that requires deep inequality and "relies on fictions of differing capacities, historically, race," to explain away those inequalities.[40] On the other hand, the fantasy of a raceless class politics still captivates some on the left, 100 years after Du Bois tried to dispel it. Du Bois explained why this purported shortcut to economic transformation would not work. He wrote in *Darkwater*, "Do we want the wants of American Negroes satisfied? Most certainly not, and that negative is the greatest hindrance today to the reorganization of work and redistribution of wealth, not only in America, but in the world."[41] Isn't it still the case that this "negative" impedes the building of a mass movement against capitalism?

This would seem to be corroborated by the recurring hostility white Americans have shown toward even modest efforts at redistribution. For example, in recent US history and up to the present, a vast array of public goods—goods that would benefit most Americans, but which are perceived as serving primarily people of color—have been resisted, opposed, and sometimes even destroyed. Why? As Heather McGhee's excellent book, *The Sum of Us: What Racism Costs Everyone and How We Can Prosper Together*, shows, a powerful "zero-sum paradigm" has long governed the thinking of many white Americans. This framework produces a "false sense of competition" among racialized groups, leading white people to believe that any government action delivering benefits to nonwhites, and Blacks in particular, amounts to a loss for whites. This view holds even when the public goods in question serve or would serve many whites.[42] The central parable in McGhee's book makes this point tragically clear. In the 1950s, fights over the integration of public swimming pools—often large, beautiful pools that were prized by their towns and cities—were common. In many cases, whites were so unwilling to share these community goods with Black people that they either privatized them as "clubs" admitting only whites or, shockingly, drained or filled in the pools, depriving everyone of a valuable public resource. The destruction of these particular public goods is emblematic, McGhee shows. The "impulse to exclude" today is directed at a "pool of resources rather than a literal one."[43] When it comes to the defunding of public higher education and the refusal to provide universal health care, for example, "racism is the unnamed actor."[44] McGhee provides compelling social scientific and historical evidence to demonstrate that white people often "resist policies that could benefit *them*, just because they might also benefit people of color."[45] Du Bois identified this habit of thought repeatedly in his writings, as discussed in Chapter 2. He claimed that people had been taught to regard any improvement in the lives of Black people—even a change that would also benefit whites, such as growing union membership—as a "degradation of [their] own status." Like McGhee, Du Bois believes this "zero-sum" thinking is not natural or inevitable; he emphasizes that it is the product of "long cultural training."[46] Crucially, this training will have to be worked upon directly. That is, there is no possibility of achieving the downward economic redistribution that would benefit most Americans without going "through race." Whether the goal is a massive, sustained investment in public goods within a capitalist economy (McGhee) or the more radical aim of creating a truly socialist system (Du Bois, for many years), it is obvious that sweeping economic transformation cannot bypass the politics of race.[47]

Du Bois warned that the development of "class consciousness"—all-important in the struggle for a socialist future—could not be achieved without "the abolition of race prejudice."[48] What might it mean to affirm Du Bois's conviction that it is necessary to "pass through a politics of race" in the fight for a more egalitarian economic order?[49] The call to "defund the police," noted above, is an interesting example for reflecting on this question. The demand, though not overtly race specific, was advanced in a political context that linked it to Black existence from the start. Proponents enunciated "defund the police" specifically in response to the harms policing has disproportionately caused to Black communities (including but not limited to killings at the hands of cops). At the same time, as public discussion of this idea grew, its advocates frequently underscored that this call for divestment carried with it a claim for investment in other social institutions, such as those that provide housing, food, education, rehabilitation, health care, and other basic needs. Thus, the claim that the police should be defunded in order to save Black lives also posed questions about the basic economic ordering of our society—about how public money is spent and how it might be spent differently, in support of a society that fosters widespread well-being. The call to "defund the police" does not lead in any straight line toward a socialist movement, or even toward robust public supports, of course. Yet the demand, articulated with the race-conscious principle that "Black lives matter," also made the allocation of collective resources for everyone a central object of public debate in a new way.

These three reflections on the prospects for anti-racist action by whites in the United States are offered up somewhat hesitantly, in light of this book's larger argument about the many ways whiteness continues to gratify its bearers. I have shown that Du Bois's middle-period writings contain a compelling, pluralistic theory of the multiple rewards—material, psychic, affective, existential—that have accompanied classification as "white" within the

US racial order, even across dramatic political, social, and economic changes. These powerful gratifications, dependent upon the devaluation of Blackness, have helped sustain white supremacy over time. If this is correct, then white people—likely even those who strive to be "anti-racist"—are more positively attached to their racialized identity than anyone cares to admit. These attachments impede, without foreclosing, a broad push for a more equal and free way of living together.

Is it possible to undo the entrenched routes by which racial identification delivers psychological, emotional, and spiritual goods to white people? Can we become less attached to these familiar, harmful, sources of satisfaction? In closing, I want to propose that challenging the way that whiteness gratifies its bearers requires something more than criticism; it calls for creating and enacting other modes of fulfillment. That is, we need forms of standing, pleasure, and belonging that reject, rather than reify, racial hierarchy.

Could such gratifications be found in the kind of organizational and coalitional work considered above? In other words, could white people, at least those who are already partly disposed toward something called "anti-racism," potentially find meaningful rewards in sustained collaborative political activity targeting the injustices of racial capitalism? Maybe. While movement building is notoriously demanding and uncertain, it may also be the case, as Hannah Arendt puts it, that "acting is fun." In a 1970 interview, expressing admiration for the leftist student movements of the time, Arendt interprets their efforts as exemplary of the "action in concert" she thought was constitutive of politics itself. And she claims that their organizing was also enjoyable: "It turned out that acting is fun. This generation discovered what the eighteenth century had called 'public happiness,' which means that when a man takes part in public life he opens up for himself a dimension of human experience that otherwise remains closed to him and that in some way constitutes a part of complete 'happiness.'"[50] A provocative twist on this idea is articulated by Wendy Brown: "Anyone who has ever been part of a movement not to dominate but to liberate, not to seize power, but to challenge prevailing systems of power, may have had the experience of the sexual rush that arises in making things happen in the world, awakening the hidden, denied, sleeping, or frightened element in people and bringing forth the power of that element. The thrill of defiance, of assertion of right, of standing up for life or home or justice against those who care little for these things—there is indeed something sexual about this thrill."[51]

The idea that a particular kind of happiness and even erotically charged joy can be found in collective political action has been affirmed by some anti-racist activists. For white participants in racial justice movements, fulfillment comes from "acting in concert" with other people to challenge white supremacy and in the process learning to do whiteness otherwise. Anne Braden, a celebrated white Southern radical (1924–2006) whose life and philosophy remains a touchstone for white anti-racist activists today, including AWARE-LA's membership, described in a 2006 interview an important realization she had in 1951. Braden was several years into full-time civil rights organizing when she met with William Patterson, then chair of the Civil Rights Congress: "He said, you know you do have a choice. You don't have to be part of the world of the lynchers. You can join the other America—the people who struggled against slavery, the people who railed against slavery, the white people who supported them, the people who all through Reconstruction struggled. He came on down through history of the people who have struggled against injustice—the Other America."[52] Braden regards this moment as pivotal because it allowed her to place herself within an admirable transgressive tradition, without disavowing the fact of her whiteness. Braden came to see herself as inhabiting and practicing what is sometimes called a "radical white identity." This concept is central to AWARE-LA's philosophy and practice. An organizational document titled "Toward a Radical White Identity" explains its significance, which is cultural rather than strictly individual: the goal is to create a "community of white anti-racist people who represent a subculture of whiteness." Cultivating this subculture means rejecting the fantasy of post-racialism or colorblindness while making room for a "different way of being white"—one that is forged practically, through "collective learning" among white people and "community organizing and social justice campaigns" in alliance with groups led by people of color. The purpose of developing this subculture is to contribute practically to ending white supremacy, of course, but it may also yield gratifications for its participants—a sense of "dignity" and a "positive" identity defined by political commitment.[53] Mark R. Warren's study of long-term white racial justice activists also suggests that such engagement can be deeply rewarding, despite its frustrations. Seasoned activists reported that building relationships, including interracial relationships, as they organized against white supremacy, offered valuable experiences of belonging and community. Working together on shared projects, animated by a vision of a "racially just future," provided activists with a sense of purpose. As one of them explains, "I'm contributing to the world that I want to live in."[54]

In Warren's analysis these rewards appear as happy side effects of dedication to a righteous cause, but is it possible to prioritize and seek pleasure within a radical politics targeting racial capitalism? Abolitionist writer and activist adrienne maree brown, taking inspiration from Audre Lorde's work on the "uses of the erotic," explores this possibility with the concept of "pleasure activism." This term brings together ideas usually viewed as distinct—pleasure, or "a feeling of happy satisfaction and enjoyment," with activism, or "efforts to promote, impede, or direct social, political, economic, or environmental reform or stasis with the desire to make improvements in society." Brown's conceptualization understands "pleasure" to be both an object of collective political action and an experience generated in and through such action. So, pleasure activism takes as a starting point the conviction that "we all need and deserve pleasure and that our social structures must reflect this" but also affirms that "organizing work" itself can be practiced in ways that "actually feel good." Brown argues that contemporary abolitionist politics need not be oriented around "suffering" even as it seeks to alter "long-term oppressive conditions." Is it possible to "center pleasure and joy as resistance" in political struggle? What if we could learn "to make justice and liberation the most pleasurable experiences we can have on this planet"?[55]

Even sustained participation in efforts to combat white supremacy cannot simply extinguish the modalities of racialized gratification at the heart of this book—wage, pleasure, dominion. These patterns are long-standing and socially reinforced, as my reading of Du Bois has made clear. Still, their hold may lessen as experiences of esteem, enjoyment, and purpose accrue that are tied to egalitarian aspirations rather than bound to anti-Black customs.

In the memorable 1940 essay "The Concept of Race," Du Bois presents an arresting allegory that reveals the stakes of this predicament.[56] Writing about the dynamics of racial domination, Du Bois borrows from Plato's *Republic* to conjure a scene of imprisonment. Du Bois explains the experience of the dominated:

It is as though one, looking out from a dark cave in a side of an impending mountain, sees the world passing and speaks to it; speaks courteously and persuasively, showing them how these entombed souls are hindered in their natural movement, expression, and development; and how their loosening from prison would be a matter not simply of courtesy, sympathy, and help to them, but aid to all the world.[57]

The text goes on to describe the futility of this plea. Even if "one talks on evenly and logically," the people passing by "do not hear at all, or hear but dimly, and even what they hear, they do not understand." The people trapped inside, Du Bois says, may even become "hysterical" over this nonresponse and start yelling and making a scene, to no avail. They are only "screaming into a vacuum unheard."

The remainder of this rich and layered passage emphasizes the profound effects of this drama upon the ignored and discounted "prisoners." Yet Du Bois has already made a striking point about those "people passing by." In the quote above, he specifies that as the people trapped in the cave struggle to gain the attention of those outside, they try to "show" passersby not only how restricted their "entombed souls" are but also that "their loosening from prison would be a matter not simply of courtesy, sympathy, and help to them, but *aid to all the world*." This last clause registers Du Bois's conviction that the fate of Black people is inseparable from the fate of all peoples. The story of the cave captures the agony of those locked within, but the "tragedy" of the situation is not limited to the incarcerated. "All the world" suffers so long as the possibilities of "bottom-up" liberation remain unrealized.

Notes

Chapter 1

1. In this book, I use "America" and "American" to refer to the United States, as is conventional there, although I understand the position of critics who find this shorthand to be imperialist.

2. Immediately after the election, Mike Davis argued that contrary to the "revolt" narrative, "the pro-Republican blue-collar realignment in presidential politics" was already the status quo. Mike Davis, "Not a Revolution—Yet," *Verso Books Blog,* Nov. 15, 2016. http://www.versobooks.com/blogs/2948-not-a-revolution-yet.

   Later, more developed analyses of the election results confirmed this view. Nicholas Carnes and Noam Lupu, drawing on all available academic survey data concerning the 2016 election, find that the following claims, frequently made about the 2016 presidential election, are simply "false": (1) that most Trump voters were white working-class Americans, (2) that large numbers of white working-class voters who had cast ballots for Obama in 2012 switched to Trump in 2016, and (3) that white working-class voters were pivotal in several key swing states. They find that a fourth, often heard claim—that most white working-class voters supported Trump—is accurate but misleading absent a wider historical context. There is nothing particularly unique or unprecedented about Trump's popularity among this group: "white working-class Americans have been gradually supporting Republican presidential candidates at higher and higher rates for the past two and a half decades." Nicholas Carnes and Noam Lupu, "The White Working Class and the 2016 Election," *Perspectives on Politics* 19, no. 1 (March 2021): 57.

3. John Hudak, "A Reality Check on 2016's Economically Marginalized," *Brookings,* Nov. 16, 2016. https://www.brookings.edu/blog/fixgov/2016/11/16/economic-marg inalization-reality-check/?utm_campaign=Brookings+Brief&utm_source=hs_em ail&utm_medium=email&utm_content=37763319. Writing just after the election, Hudak notes, "The conversation around the 'economically marginalized' has focused almost exclusively on white working class voters, and that is a travesty. There are many other Americans who are not traditionally grouped under the heading 'white working class voters' who remain economically marginalized—and most of them voted for someone other than Donald Trump." Gurminder K. Bhambra points out that the dominant narrative about the "white working class" that emerged prominently in postelection discourse emphasized this group's feelings of having been "left behind," yet any "empirical category of the 'left behind' understood in terms of socio-economic disadvantage contains within it significant proportions of the Black and minority ethnic population." Gurminder K. Bhambra, "Brexit, Trump and

Methodological Whiteness: On the Misrecognition of Race and Class," *British Journal of Sociology* 68, no. S1 (2018): S216.

4. Nicholas Carnes and Noam Lupu, "It's Time to Bust the Myth: Most Trump Voters Were Not Working Class," *Washington Post,* June 5, 2017. See also David Roediger, "Who's Afraid of the White Working Class," *Los Angeles Review of Books,* May 17, 2017, which argues that the group of voters who are problematically identified as "white working class" voted more like whites as a whole than other working-class races; racial identity predicted voting for Trump far better than income level did.

5. Nicholas A. Valentino, Fabian G. Neuner, and L. Matthew Vandenbroek, "The Changing Norms of Racial Political Rhetoric and the End of Racial Priming," *Journal of Politics* 80, no. 3 (July 2018): 757–71 argue that the "public acceptability of racially hostile rhetoric in mainstream American politics" has increased significantly since the 2008 election of Obama.

6. This framing was already taking shape even before Trump was elected. During the 2016 presidential campaign, Bernie Sanders and President Obama both suggested that Trump supporters were primarily economically struggling whites who were vulnerable to Trump's promises to "Make America Great Again." Commentators including Jamelle Bouie and Matt Yglesias rejected this claim at the time, arguing that Trump's racism and bigotry were precisely what attracted white voters. A revealing *Washington Post* article published during the primaries—Max Ehrenfreund and Scott Clement's "Economic and Racial Anxiety: Two Separate Forces Driving Support for Donald Trump," March 22, 2016—did not so much contest the terms of this debate as ratify them.

7. In "The White Working Class and the 2016 Election," Carnes and Lupu criticize the "haphazard definitions of *the working class*" used by journalists covering 2016 election results (56). The term has most often been used to refer to whites without a college education, but this omits information about profession, income, and wealth (it cannot distinguish between a construction worker and a CEO, for example). This is particularly problematic for understanding Trump's win. See also Christine J. Walley, "Trump's Election and the 'White Working Class': What We Missed," *American Ethnologist* 44, no. 2 (2017): 231–36 on the misunderstandings that result from defining "working class" as those without a college degree, which "lumps together an extraordinarily broad range of groups" and contributes to "confusing media discussion around class" (231).

8. Daniel Cox, Rachel Lienesch, and Robert P. Jones, "Beyond Economics: Fears of Cultural Displacement Pushed the White Working Class to Trump," *Public Religion Research Institute*, May 9, 2017. https://www.prri.org/research/white-working-class-attitudes-economy-trade-immigration-election-donald-trump/.

9. Carnes and Lupu, "It's Time to Bust the Myth."

10. Carnes and Lupu, "The White Working Class and the 2016 Election," 58.

11. Brian N. Schaffner, Matthew MacWilliams, and Tatishe Nneta, "Understanding White Polarization in the 2016 Vote for President: The Sobering Role of Racism and Sexism," *Political Science Quarterly* 133, no. 1 (2018): 9–34 argue that "the gap between college-educated and non-college-educated whites was possibly the single

most important divide documented in 2016, and it was the culmination of an increasing divide in party identification among college-educated and non-college-educated whites following Obama's election in 2008." They find that racist and sexist attitudes were strongly related to support for Trump and estimate that these attitudes "explain at least two-thirds of the education gap among white voters in the 2016 presidential election" (11).

12. Most exit polls found each of these figures to be higher, but here I cite data drawn from a postelection survey study of validated voters. Pew Research Center, "An Examination of the 2016 Electorate, Based on Validated Voters," Aug. 9, 2018. https://www.pewresearch.org/politics/2018/08/09/an-examination-of-the-2016-electorate-based-on-validated-voters/.

13. Cox et al., "Beyond Economics"; Niraj Chokshi, "Trump Voters Driven by Fear of Losing Status, Not Economic Anxiety, Study Finds," *New York Times,* April 24, 2018. https://www.nytimes.com/2018/04/24/us/politics/trump-economic-anxiety.html; Emma Green, "It Was Cultural Anxiety That Drove White Working Class Voters to Trump," *The Atlantic,* May 9, 2017. https://www.theatlantic.com/politics/archive/2017/05/white-working-class-trump-cultural-anxiety/525771/; Diana C. Mutz, "Status Threat, Not Economic Hardship, Explains the 2016 Presidential Vote," *Proceedings of the National Academy of Sciences* 115, no. 19 (March 2018): E4330–E4339. https://www.pnas.org/content/115/19/E4330

14. Ryan Lizza, "What We Learned About Trump Supporters This Week," *New Yorker,* Aug. 13, 2016. https://www.newyorker.com/news/daily-comment/what-we-learned-about-trumps-supporters-this-week. Lizza cites Jonathan T. Rothwell and Pablo Diego-Rosell's Gallup study, "Explaining Nationalist Political Views: The Case of Donald Trump," August 2016. http://papers.ssrn.com/sol3/papers.cfm?abstract_id=2822059. See also Nate Silver, "The Mythology of Trump's 'Working Class Support,'" *FiveThirtyEight,* May 3, 2016. https://fivethirtyeight.com/features/the-mythology-of-trumps-working-class-support/.

15. Carol Anderson, *White Rage: The Unspoken Truth of Our Racial Divide* (New York: Bloomsbury Publishing, 2016), Ch. 5.

16. Green, "It Was Cultural Anxiety." These findings aligned with experimental studies that find that perceived shifts in long-standing features of the US racial order prompt defensiveness by some whites. In experiments, whites' political views generally shift rightward if they are reminded of macro-level developments such as Obama's presidency or the future majority-minority makeup of the US population. A sense of imperiled "symbolic group status" seems to be activated in these cases. Maureen A. Craig and Jennifer A. Richeson, "On the Precipice of Majority-Minority America: Perceived Status Threat from the Racial Demographic Shift Affects White Americans' Political Ideology," *Psychological Science* 25, no. 6 (June 2014): 1189–97; Maureen A. Craig and Jennifer A. Richeson, "More Diverse Yet Less Tolerant? How the Increasingly Diverse Racial Landscape Affects White Americans' Racial Attitudes," *Personality and Social Psychology Bulletin* 40, no. 6 (2014): 750–61; Robb Willer, Matthew Feinberg, and Rachel Wetts, "Threats to Racial Status Promote Tea Party Support Among White Americans," May 4, 2016. http://ssrn.com/abstract=

2770186. See also Brenda Major, Alison Blodorn, and Gregory Major Blaskovich, "The Threat of Increasing Diversity: Why Many White Americans Support Trump in the 2016 Presidential Election," *Group Processes & Intergroup Relations* 21, no. 6 (2018): 931–40, which finds that when white Americans high in racial/ethnic identification were reminded that nonwhite racial groups will outnumber whites in the United States by 2042, they experienced "group status threat" and reported increased support for Trump.

17. Herbert Blumer, "Race Prejudice as a Sense of Group Position," *Pacific Sociological Review* 1, no. 1 (Spring 1958): 4.

18. Anne Case and Angus Deaton's 2015 working paper documenting increased mortality among middle-aged white Americans since the turn of the 21st century (in contrast to declining mortality rates among middle-aged Black and Hispanic Americans) was the subject of extensive reporting and commentary as soon as it appeared. Their interpretation of the increased mortality rates, due primarily to drug and alcohol deaths and suicide, as "deaths of despair" born of a "sense of hopelessness" was at the center of public discussion. Anne Case and Angus Deaton, "Rising Morbidity and Mortality in Midlife Among White Non-Hispanic Americans in the 21st Century," *PNAS* 112, no. 49 (November 2015): 15078–83. https://doi.org/10.1073/pnas.151 8393112; Lenny Bernstein and Joel Achenbach, "A Group of Middle-Aged Whites Is Dying at a Startling Rate," *Washington Post*, Nov. 2, 2015. https://www.washing tonpost.com/national/health-science/a-group-of-middle-aged-american-whites-is-dying-at-a-startling-rate/2015/11/02/47a63098-8172-11e5-8ba6-cec48b74b2a7_st ory.html; Olga Khazan, "Middle-Aged White Americans Are Dying of Despair," *The Atlantic*, Nov. 4, 2015. https://www.theatlantic.com/health/archive/2015/11/boom ers-deaths-pnas/413971/; Ross Douhat, "The Dying of the Whites," *New York Times*, Nov. 7, 2015. https://www.nytimes.com/2015/11/08/opinion/sunday/the-dying-of-the-whites.html; Paul Krugman, "Despair, American Style," *New York Times,* Nov. 9, 2015. https://www.nytimes.com/2015/11/09/opinion/despair-american-style.html.

I think this widely circulated story of racialized suffering depends for its force on the unspoken belief that whites ought to be faring better—not just better than they currently are, but *better than* nonwhites. See Nikhil Pal Singh and Thuy Linh Tu's excellent article, "Morbid Capitalism," *N + 1*, no. 30 (Winter 2018): 101–15, which characterizes the public narrative of white morbidity as one of "racial declension" (103).

19. Ashley Jardina, *White Identity Politics* (Cambridge: Cambridge University Press, 2019), 2. See also Mutz, "Status Threat, Not Economic Hardship."

20. John Sides, Michael Tesler, and Lynne Vavreck, *Identity Crisis: The 2016 Presidential Campaign and the Battle for the Meaning of America* (Princeton, NJ: Princeton University Press, 2018), 177. See also Schaffner et al., "Understanding White Polarization."

21. Arlie Russell Hochschild, *Strangers in Their Own Land: Anger and Mourning on the American Right* (New York: New Press, 2016). The book details Hochschild's efforts to grapple with the "Great Paradox" of American politics—the fact that many people who are harmed by conservative policies are likely to vote for them. In her in-depth

ethnographic study of Tea Party supporters in southwest Louisiana, who are all white and mostly older, Christian, male, and non–college educated, Hochschild seeks to uncover the "deep story"—the "feels as if" story—that motivates their support for conservative politicians and policies (135). According to Hochschild, we can best understand how things feel for her "Tea Party friends" by way of a metaphor: waiting in line. The condensed version is: "you" are waiting "patiently" in a line leading up a hill. Hochschild continues, "You are situated in the middle of this line." Just over the hill is the American Dream, where everyone in the line is headed. You've waited a long time and worked hard, but the line is barely moving. "In fact, is it moving backward? . . . Look! You see people cutting in line ahead of you! You're following the rules. They aren't. As they cut in, it feels like you are being moved back. How can they just do that? Who are they? Some are black" (137–39). Hochschild does not exactly ignore the racial dynamics that characterize her deep story, but even as she notes that those perceived as "line-cutters" are first and foremost Black, she does not, in her further reflections, ask why Blacks appear in the emotional lives of her subjects solely as cheats who ought to be *behind and beneath* them in line and whose perceived mobility elicits irritation and resentment. (It is hard not to be reminded of Du Bois's remark, "In Central Park I have seen the upper lip of a quiet peaceful man curl back in a tigerish snarl of rage because black folk rode by in a motor car. He was a white man." W. E. B. Du Bois, "The Souls of White Folk," in *Darkwater: Voices from Within the Veil* [Oxford: Oxford University Press, 2007 (1920)], 17.)

Paul Pierson, "Listening to Louisiana: What 'Climbing the Empathy Wall' Can (and Can't) Tell Us About the Populist Right," *British Journal of Sociology* 68, no. 1 (2017): 133–37 convincingly argues that Hochschild downplays the salience of racial hierarchy in the lives of her subjects. Gurminder K. Bhambra, "Brexit, Trump, and 'Methodological Whiteness'" provides an excellent analysis of Hochschild and argues that "there is little in the book that addresses the history of the United States as structurally organized around race as the primary category of differentiation" (225).

22. Nell Irvin Painter, "What Whiteness Means in the Trump Era," *New York Times*, November 12, 2016. https://www.nytimes.com/2016/11/13/opinion/what-whiteness-means-in-the-trump-era.html. See also Ben Zimmer, "Talk of Whitelash Revives 1960s Term," *Wall Street Journal*, November 16, 2016. https://www.wsj.com/articles/talk-of-a-whitelash-revives-a-1960s-term-1479479174.

23. W. E. B. Du Bois, *Black Reconstruction in America: An Essay Toward a History of the Part Which Black Folk Played in the Attempt to Reconstruct Democracy in America, 1860–1880* (Oxford: Oxford University Press, 2007 [1935]), 573. Du Bois uses the language of "caste" in *The Souls of Black Folk* (Oxford: Oxford University Press, 2007 [1903]) and *Darkwater*. "Color caste" appears regularly in *Black Reconstruction* and thereafter. The significance of this term is twofold. First, by persistently describing the postemancipation United States as a caste society, Du Bois confronts and rejects the romanticized view that "there is no caste here," enshrined in *Plessy v. Ferguson* (1896). Additionally—and unlike Isabelle Wilkerson's recent use of the term to describe the contemporary United States—when Du Bois speaks of "caste," he is naming an oppressive structure of racial capitalism (see Chapter 2). "Caste" for Du Bois refers not

simply to racial domination but also to its imbrication with class domination. For example, he writes in *Black Reconstruction* of the establishment of "caste" in the United States following Reconstruction and specifies that the domination of Blacks as a "servile caste" was also a matter of economic exploitation and material deprivation: their assignment to inferior schools and transportation, confinement to "ghettoes," and denial of basic infrastructure like lighting, sewage, and paved streets. On the other hand, as readers of Wilkerson's bestselling book have pointed out, her account of "caste" in the United States pays almost no attention to the distribution of material resources or to the co-constitution of racism and capitalism. In fact, the paradigmatic examples of contemporary caste enforcement in the United States for Wilkerson involve well-off, professional Black people facing personal hostility from whites who perceive them as having stepped out of their assigned place. Isabelle Wilkerson, *Caste: The Origins of Our Discontents* (New York: Random House, 2020); Hazel V. Carby, "The Limits of Caste," *London Review of Books,* August 2020. https://www.lrb.co.uk/the-paper/v43/n02/hazel-v.-carby/the-limits-of-caste; .

24. Du Bois, *Black Reconstruction,* 573–74.

25. In this book, I capitalize Black when talking about individuals or groups. As Lori L. Tharps explains, "Black with a capital B refers to people of the African diaspora." Lori L. Tharps, "The Case for Black with a Capital B," *New York Times,* November 18, 2014. https://www.nytimes.com/2014/11/19/opinion/the-case-for-black-with-a-capital-b.html. See also Nancy Coleman, "Why We're Capitalizing 'Black,'" *New York Times,* July 5, 2020. https://www.nytimes.com/2020/07/05/insider/capitalized-black.html.

Only in 2020 did this become a mainstream practice in the United States, but racial justice activists had pushed for this change for decades, echoing Du Bois's 1920s campaign to push major media outlets to capitalize the word "negro." Du Bois wrote that "the use of a small letter for the name of twelve million Americans and two hundred million human beings [is] a personal insult." (The *New York Times* refused to do so in 1926 but made the change in 1930.) However, I do not capitalize "white" in this book, although I have reservations about that choice. It remains in lowercase here both to avoid establishing a false equivalency with "Black" and because the capitalized "White" has been a purposeful tactic of white nationalists for years and I do not want to lend legitimacy to that usage. I think the best argument for capitalizing "white," however, is that it might help make whiteness more visible *as* a racialized identity—unmasking "Whiteness" as an American racial identity as historically important as "Blackness." Nell Irvin Painter, "Why 'White' Should Be Capitalized," *Washington Post,* July 22, 2020. https://www.washingtonpost.com/opinions/2020/07/22/why-white-should-be-capitalized/. See also "Explaining AP Style on Black and white," https://apnews.com/article/archive-race-and-ethnicity-9105661462.

In the text of this book, I adopt these practices when writing in my own voice but retain the original capitalization style in all direct quotes.

26. Du Bois, *Black Reconstruction,* 8, 24, 106.

27. Du Bois, *Black Reconstruction,* 573.

28. Du Bois, *Black Reconstruction,* 24.

29. Joshua Zietz, "Does the White Working Class Really Vote Against Its Own Interests?," *Politico,* Dec. 31, 2017. https://www.politico.com/magazine/story/2017/12/31/trump-white-working-class-history-216200/.

30. Joan C. Williams, "The Democrats' White People Problem," *The Atlantic,* December 2018. https://www.theatlantic.com/magazine/archive/2018/12/the-democrats-white-people-problem/573901/.

31. Jamelle Bouie, "The Joy of Hatred," *New York Times,* July 19, 2019. https://www.nytimes.com/2019/07/19/opinion/trump-rally.html.

32. On Trump's coalition, see Hugh Gusterson, "From Brexit to Trump: Anthropology and the Rise of Nationalist Populism," *American Ethnologist* 44, no. 2 (2017): 209–14 on the US media's "dominant 'blue collar narrative,'" which effectively conceals "the role of the petty bourgeoisie and the wealthy in Trump's coalition" (209).

33. Adam Serwer, "The Nationalist's Delusion," *The Atlantic,* Nov. 20, 2017. https://www.theatlantic.com/politics/archive/2017/11/the-nationalists-delusion/546356/.

34. Charles Blow, "'The Lowest White Man,'" *New York Times,* Jan. 11, 2018. https://www.nytimes.com/2018/01/11/opinion/trump-immigration-white-supremacy.html.

35. David Roediger, *The Wages of Whiteness: Race and the Making of the American Working Class* (London and New York: Verso, 2007 [1991]).

36. For the classic statement of the idea of white privilege, see Peggy McIntosh, "White Privilege and Male Privilege: A Personal Account of Coming to See Correspondences Through Work in Women's Studies," *Peace and Freedom,* July/August 1988. More recently, Robin DiAngelo's language of "white fragility" has been adopted in some circles (especially the corporate world, where DiAngelo is a highly paid consultant) to describe how whites guard this privilege. Although DiAngelo argues that the enactment of "white fragility" serves to leave "white supremacy"—"an overarching political, economic, and social system of domination"—intact, her account is primarily about whites' feelings in the context of interpersonal dynamics. Focused on "white fragility" as a problem of emotional self-regulation, DiAngelo's remedies are therapeutic rather than political: white people—particularly "white progressives," DiAngelo's main audience—are told to "Breathe. Listen. Reflect." when "white fragility surfaces" (147). The near-exclusive focus on one-on-one interactions (particularly in the workplace) is presupposed to lead to structural change: if "our interpersonal relations" were to change, "so would our institutions" (144). On the problems with the assumption that more ethical relations between selves and others would result in political transformation, see Ella Myers, *Worldly Ethics: Democratic Politics and Care for the World* (Durham, NC: Duke University Press, 2013).

37. I use "white supremacy" and "white supremacist" in this book in roughly the same way as Charles Mills, to name "a political system, a particular power structure of formal or informal rule, socioeconomic privilege, and norms for the differential distribution of material wealth and opportunities, benefits and burdens, rights and duties," in which that differential distribution generally advantages those classified as "white" while disadvantaging those who are not. Charles Mills, *The Racial Contract* (Ithaca, NY: Cornell University Press, 1997), 3. I also use the term "racism" more or less interchangeably, despite the limitations of this practice. Lastly, "anti-Blackness"

here refers to a specific modality of racism—one that is indispensable to the construction of "whiteness" in the United States. Although "anti-Blackness" has been popularized relatively recently, I use this language when referring to Du Bois's views or other features of his political context if I believe it expresses the spirit, albeit not the letter, of the historical reference.

38. Charles Mills, "Global White Ignorance," in *Routledge International Handbook of Ignorance Studies*, ed. Matthias Gross and Linsey McGoey (New York: Routledge, 2015), 217. Although Mills includes in the category of ignorance "perception, conception, memory, testimony, and motivational group interest," all are understood as deficits, limitations, or "cognitive distortions." Charles Mills, "White Ignorance," in *Race and Epistemologies of Ignorance,* ed. Shannon Sullivan and Nancy Tuana (Albany: State University of New York Press, 2007), 23, 35. See also Jennifer Mueller, "Racial Ideology or Racial Ignorance? An Alternative Theory of Racial Cognition," *Sociological Theory* 38, no. 2 (2020): 142–69 for a developed theory of racial ignorance (TRI) that builds on Mills's work. Popular commentary such as Nicholas Kristof's seven-part "When Whites Just Don't Get It" series in the *New York Times* (2014–2016) presents a simplified version of a "racial ignorance" argument: "smug white delusion" prevents widespread recognition of the problem of anti-Black racism.

39. Michelle Alexander, *The New Jim Crow* (New York: New Press, 2010), 234. See also 203–4 on "racial indifference."

40. Mills, "Global White Ignorance," 217.

41. Toni Morrison, *Playing in the Dark: Whiteness and the Literary Imagination* (New York: Vintage Books, 1992), 11, 90.

42. bell hooks, "Representing Whiteness in the Black Imagination," in *Displacing Whiteness: Essays in Social and Cultural Criticism*, ed. Ruth Frankenberg (Durham, NC, and London: Duke University Press, 1997), 339.

43. bell hooks, "Representing Whiteness," 339. On this point, see also George Yancy, "Introduction: Flipping the Script" to *Look, A White! Philosophical Essays on Whiteness* (Philadelphia: Temple University Press, 2012), 1–16.

44. Peter Erickson, "Seeing White," *Transition* 67 (1995): 174. Erickson is referring here to the absence of Black voices in work by Theodore Allen, David Roediger, and Alexander Saxton, major contributors to "whiteness studies."

45. Eric Arnesen, "Whiteness and the Historians' Imagination," *International Labor and Working Class History* 60 (Fall 2001): 3–32; Andrew Hartman, "The Rise and Fall of Whiteness Studies," *Race Class* 46, no. 2 (2004): 22–38; and John Munro, "Roots of 'Whiteness,'" *Labour/La Travail* 54 (Fall 2004): 175–92 all cite Du Bois's *Black Reconstruction* as a formative text for the development of "whiteness studies" in the United States in the 1990s and 2000s.

46. Peter Erickson, "Seeing White"; Daniel Martinez HoSang, "'We Have No Master Race': Racial Liberalism and Political Whiteness," in *Racial Propositions: Ballot Initiatives and the Making of Postwar California* (Berkeley: University of California Press, 2010), 13–23.

47. It is worth noting that much of that criticism came from scholars committed to a "class-first" perspective that regards race strictly as an ideological tool of capitalist

domination. See, for example, Arneson, "Whiteness and the Historians' Imagination," and Hartman, "The Rise and Fall of Whiteness Studies." Cedric Johnson likewise critiques the concept of "whiteness" on the grounds that "it does not help us to advance the intellectual and political project of anti-capitalism." Cedric Johnson, "The Wages of Roediger: Why Three Decades of Whiteness Studies Has Not Produced the Left We Need," *Nonsite.org*, no. 29. https://nonsite.org/the-wages-of-roediger-why-three-decades-of-whiteness-studies-has-not-produced-the-left-we-need/. On the actual diversity of scholarship within the "whiteness tent," see Munro, "Roots of 'Whiteness.'"

48. Grace Elizabeth Hale, *Making Whiteness: The Culture of Segregation in the South, 1890–1940* (New York: Pantheon Books, 1998); Mills, *The Racial Contract*; Joel Olson, *The Abolition of White Democracy* (Minneapolis: University of Minnesota Press, 2004); Alexander Saxton, *The Rise and Fall of the White Republic: Class Politics and Mass Culture in Nineteenth Century America* (London: Verso, 1990); Shannon Sullivan, *Revealing Whiteness: The Unconscious Habits of Racial Privilege* (Bloomington: Indiana University Press, 2006).

49. This rough periodization is shared even by scholars who otherwise analyze the emergence of a "white" racial category quite differently. For example, see Theodore W. Allen, *The Invention of the White Race*, Vols. 1 and 2 (London: Verso Books, 2012 [1994; 1997]), which provides a materialist account of the white race as a "social control formation," and alternately, Nell Irvin Painter, *The History of White People* (New York: W. W. Norton & Company, 2011), which emphasizes the role that Enlightenment science and philosophy played in establishing racial classifications linked to skin color. Charles Mills, "W. E. B. Du Bois: Black Radical Liberal," in *The Political Companion to W. E. B. Du Bois*, ed. Nick Bromwell (Lexington: University Press of Kentucky, 2018) briefly explores two schools of thought—short vs. long periodization—that address the question "When does race enter the world?" The "short periodization" view, articulated in divergent ways by Allen and Painter, argues that "race and racism are products of modernity," while the long periodization view may posit either that there were (non-color-coded) forms of "racial" classification in antiquity or that there were forms of specifically anti-Black racism before modernity. Mills aligns Du Bois's with the short periodization view but suggests that it might be productively questioned by the long periodization view: "Du Bois and others who locate racism and anti-Black sentiment solely in modernity may have too sanguine and abbreviated a view of its longevity in the West and may be failing to appreciate how profoundly it was formed by Greco-Roman thought and the inherited iconography of Christian eschatology" (22–25).

50. As Daniel Martinez HoSang argues, the challenge is to take "the violence and power of these 'traditions' of racism seriously without regarding them as primordial and thus inevitable." HoSang, *Racial Propositions*, 18.

51. Cheryl Harris, "Whitewashing Race, Scapegoating Culture," *California Law Review* 94, no. 3 (2006): 916.

52. Manning Marable's *W. E. B. Du Bois: Black Radical Democrat*, 2nd ed. (New York: Routledge, 2016) argues that Du Bois's vast polyphonic oeuvre is more

consistent than usually supposed, because Du Bois offered a "black radical and democratic analysis of US and global society" across his long career.

53. Du Bois, *Black Reconstruction,* 11.

54. Du Bois uses the language of "dark people," "darker people," "dark world," and "darker
world" in both *Darkwater* and *Dusk of Dawn: An Essay Toward an Autobiography of a
Race Concept* (Oxford: Oxford University Press, 2007 [1940]). The description of empire is from Du Bois, "Science and Empire," in *Dusk of Dawn,* 48.

55. "Hispanic or Latino" is the terminology used in the US census. Sabrina Tavernese,
"Why the Announcement of a Looming White Minority Makes Demographers
Nervous," *New York Times,* Nov. 22, 2018. https://www.nytimes.com/2018/11/
22/us/white-americans-minority-population.html; William H. Frey, "US White
Population Declines and Generation 'Z-Plus' Is Minority White, Census Shows,"
Brookings, June 22, 2018. https://www.brookings.edu/blog/the-avenue/2018/06/21/
us-white-population-declines-and-generation-z-plus-is-minority-white-census-
shows/.

56. Olson, *The Abolition of White Democracy,* xxii.

57. Evelyn Brooks Higginbotham, "African-American Women's History and the
Metalanguage of Race," *Signs* 17, no. 2 (Winter 1992): 256.

58. Du Bois, "The White World," in *Dusk of Dawn,* 69; Du Bois, "The Concept of Race," in
Dusk of Dawn, 59.

59. Harris, "Whitewashing Race," 916.

60. Lewis Gordon, "Critical 'Mixed Race'?," *Social Identities* 1, no. 2 (August 1995): n.p.

61. Lani Guinier and Gerald Torres, *The Miner's Canary: Enlisting Race, Resisting Power,
Transforming Democracy* (Cambridge, MA: Harvard University Press, 2003), 224.

62. Nikhil Pal Singh, *Black Is a Country: Race and the Unfinished Struggle for Democracy*
(Cambridge, MA: Harvard University Press, 2004), 32.

Chapter 2

1. W. E. B. Du Bois, *Black Reconstruction in America: An Essay Toward a History of the
Part Which Black Folk Played in the Attempt to Reconstruct Democracy in America,
1860–1880* (Oxford: Oxford University Press, 2007 [1935]), 573–74.

2. Cedric J. Robinson, *Black Marxism: The Making of the Black Radical Tradition* (Chapel
Hill: University of North Carolina Press, 2000 [1983]) introduced the term "racial
capitalism" to denote, contra orthodox Marxism, that the historical developments of
capitalism and racism were inseparable. Robinson credits Du Bois with making foundational contributions to the development of this concept. He notes that Du Bois's
middle- and late-period work, according to which capitalism is inextricably bound to
slavery and imperialism, influenced the later work of Eric Williams and Oliver Cox
(*Black Marxism,* Ch. 9). In recent years, the idea of "racial capitalism" articulated by
these thinkers has re-emerged in critical-theoretical scholarship on contemporary
political economy. See Chris Chen, "The Limits of Capitalist Equality: Notes Toward

an Abolitionist Antiracism," *Endnotes* 3 (September 2013). https://endnotes.org.uk/issues/3/en/chris-chen-the-limit-point-of-capitalist-equality; Michael C. Dawson and Megan Ming Francis, "Black Politics and the Neoliberal Racial Order," *Public Culture* 28, no. 1 (2015): 23–62; Robin D. G. Kelley, "What Did Cedric Robinson Mean by Racial Capitalism?," *Boston Review,* Jan. 12, 2017. https://bostonreview.net/articles/robin-d-g-kelley-introduction-race-capitalism-justice/.

3. Jodi Melamed, "Racial Capitalism," *Critical Ethnic Studies* 1, no. 1 (2015): 77.

4. Du Bois, *Black Reconstruction,* 24. See Chapter 4 in this book on why "racial-colonial capitalism" might be a more precise and useful concept than "racial capitalism."

5. See Chapter 4 on how Du Bois's conceptualization of whiteness as dominion exposes racial capitalism's dependence on both exploitation and expropriation.

6. Ruth Wilson Gilmore, "Abolition Geography and the Problem of Innocence," in *Futures of Black Radicalism,* ed. Gaye Theresa Johnson and Alex Lubin (New York: Verso, 2017), 225.

7. On Du Bois's relationship to Marxism and to the Communist Party USA (CPUSA), see Robinson, *Black Marxism,* Ch. 9. Nikhil Pal Singh, *Black Is a Country: Race and the Unfinished Struggle for Democracy* (Cambridge, MA: Harvard University Press, 2004), Ch. 2, offers a fascinating account of Du Bois's contributions to Black radical thought in the 1930s. Singh shows how Du Bois's thinking, which increasingly "entailed a risky defense of black particularity," was met with resistance by the American Black intelligentsia he had earlier helped found (75).

8. Ibram X. Kendi, *How to Be an Antiracist* (New York: One World Books, 2019), 160.

9. Du Bois, *Black Reconstruction,* 484–85.

10. W. E. B. Du Bois, "The Negro and Social Reconstruction," in *Against Racism: Unpublished Essays, Papers, Addresses,* ed. Herbert Aptheker (Amherst: University of Massachusetts Press, 1985), 112.

11. Du Bois, "The Negro and Social Reconstruction," 137.

12. Du Bois, *Black Reconstruction,* 520.

13. The outbreak of bloody anti-Black violence in East St. Louis in 1917 was precipitated by rapidly growing numbers of Black workers in local factories (the Black population in the city had doubled in seven years) and, more specifically, according to some accounts, by the hiring of Black workers (along with white) to replace striking white workers in an aluminum plant in May. Tim O'Neil, "Look Back: Race Hatred, Workforce Tensions Explode in East St. Louis in 1917," *St. Louis Post Dispatch,* July 2, 2021. https://www.stltoday.com/news/local/history/race-hatred-workforce-tensions-explode-in-east-st-louis-in-1917/article_9bfa1b5d-c627-5dc7-b1da-6d589 93f3ecb.html; Alex Park, "The St. Louis Area Has a Long History of Shameful Racial Violence," *Mother Jones,* Aug. 18, 2014. https://www.motherjones.com/politics/2014/08/riot-east-st-louis-ferguson-history-race/.

14. W. E. B. Du Bois, "Of Work and Wealth," in *Darkwater: Voices from Within the Veil* (Oxford: Oxford University Press, 2007 [1920]), 48.

15. Du Bois, *Black Reconstruction,* 352.

16. Edmund Morgan's groundbreaking *American Slavery, American Freedom* (New York: W. W. Norton & Co., 1975) argued, via the documentary history of colonial Virginia,

that racism emerged in America only around 1660, and hence was more a consequence of the growing slave trade than its antecedent. His core finding was that the institutionalization of white supremacy occurred after the switch from servant to slave labor, and that the new laws constructed "a screen of racial contempt" meant to discipline the workforce and prevent uprisings by the poor. Morgan's work, which directly challenged the idea of "innate" racism proffered by influential historians such as Winthrop Jordan, inspired a generation of scholars who sought to examine "race" as a constructed, rather than given, classification. See for example Theodore W. Allen, *The Invention of the White Race*, Vols. 1 and 2 (London: Verso Books, 2012 [1994; 1997]), which argues that "the 'white race' [was] invented as a social control formation." Allen stresses that the codification of white supremacy in the late 17th and early 18th centuries was spurred by Bacon's Rebellion and the perceived threat of uprisings by the poor. Institutionalizing white advantage in legislation such as the 1705 Virginia Act Concerning Servants and Slaves, according to Allen, was a "deliberate decision" by economic elites seeking to foreclose class solidarity. See also David Roediger, *How Race Survived US History* (New York: Verso Books, 2010), Ch. 1, which draws on Morgan's work to conceptualize race as a way of creating "ersatz unity" through a social and legal category—"white"—that weakened the power of the poor. For an excellent analysis of the vexing questions surrounding debates over the "origins" of white supremacy, see Alexander Saxton, Introduction to *The Rise and Fall of the White Republic: Class Politics and Mass Culture in Nineteenth-Century America* (London: Verso Books, 1990).

17. W. E. B. Du Bois, "The Concept of Race," in *Dusk of Dawn: An Essay Toward an Autobiography of the Race Concept* (Oxford: Oxford University Press, 2007 [1940]), 65.

18. Du Bois, *Black Reconstruction*, Ch. 1.

19. Saxton, *Rise and Fall*, 15.

20. Du Bois, "Concept of Race," 52.

21. Robinson, *Black Marxism*, 26.

22. Michael C. Dawson, "Hidden in Plain Sight: A Note on Legitimation Crises and the Racial Order," *Critical Historical Studies* 3, no. 1 (Spring 2016): 147.

23. Melamed, "Racial Capitalism," 77. See also Jackie Wang, *Carceral Capitalism* (South Pasadena, CA: Semiotexte, 2018) for a reading of contemporary neoliberal racial capitalism that interprets it as simultaneously homogenizing and differentiating.

24. Nikhil Singh, "On Race, Violence, and So-Called Primitive Accumulation," *Social Text* 34, no. 3 (September 2016): 34. Michael C. Dawson conceptualizes the division between free and less-than-free labor as follows: "This racial separation is manifested in the division between full humans who possess the right to sell their labor and compete within markets and those that are disposable, discriminated against, and ultimately either eliminated or superexploited." Dawson, "Hidden in Plain Sight," 147–48.

25. W. E. B. Du Bois, "Marxism and the Negro Problem," *The Crisis* 40 (May 1933): 104.

26. Du Bois, *Black Reconstruction*, 19. "Super-exploitation" was a key concept in the work of James Boggs, who argued, "Economic development has been the reason for the super-exploitation of blacks at every stage, and the super-exploitation of blacks has in

turn accelerated economic development. Thus the American way of life has been created, a life of expanding comfort and social mobility for whites, based upon servitude
and lack of freedom for blacks." James Boggs, *Racism and the Class Struggle: Further
Pages from a Black Worker's Notebook* (New York: Monthly Review Press, 1970),
167. See also Edna Bonacich, "Class Approaches to Race and Ethnicity," *Insurgent
Sociologist* 10, no. 2 (Fall 1980): 9–23, which explores different accounts of "super-
exploitation." Boggs can be placed within the tradition Bonacich identifies with Oliver
Cox, for whom "super-exploitation of dark-skinned workers is rooted in the imperi-
alistic expansion of Western European capitalism" (13) (Cox did not use the precise
term "super-exploitation," however). Boggs connects Europe's treatment of racialized
labor in external colonies to the treatment of Black labor in the United States, which
houses a "colony inside its own border" (Boggs, *Racism and Class Struggle,* 156).

27. Du Bois, "Marxism and the Negro Problem," 104. Other theorists of racial capitalism
emphasize that in the United States, disposability—not only super-exploitation—
characterizes the experiences of Black people, especially since the end of Jim Crow
and the ascendance of neoliberalism. On shifting "epochs" of racial capitalism, see
Dawson, "Hidden in Plain Sight." For a compelling analysis of the "dialectic of disposability and super-exploitation" that characterizes the condition of Black people
within contemporary US capitalism, see Siddhant Issar, "Theorising 'Racial/Colonial
Primitive Accumulation': Settler Colonialism, Slavery, and Racial Capitalism," *Race &
Class* 63, no. 1 (2021): 23–50.

28. Saidiya Hartman, *Scenes of Subjection: Terror, Slavery, and Self-Making in 19th
Century America* (Oxford University Press, 1997), 120.

29. Du Bois, *Black Reconstruction,* 11.

30. See Hartman, *Scenes of Subjection,* Ch. 4, on the "refiguration of subjection" after the
abolition of slavery.

31. W. E. B. Du Bois, "The Right to Work," in *Du Bois: Writings,* ed. Nathan Huggins
(New York: Library of America, 1986), 1236. Essay originally published in *The Crisis,*
April 1933. For later challenges to the naiveté of the "unite and fight" edict that echo
Du Bois's, see Boggs, *Racism and the Class Struggle* , especially the essay "Meaning of
the Black Revolt in the USA," and Stuart Hall's 1980 essay, "Race, Articulation, and
Societies Structured in Dominance," in *Black British Cultural Studies: A Reader,* ed.
Houston A. Baker, Jr., Manthia Diawara, and Ruth H. Lindeborg (Chicago: University
of Chicago Press, 1996): 16–60.

32. Du Bois writes, "There is no automatic power in socialism to overrise and sup-
press race prejudice. This has been proven in America" in "Social Planning for the
Negro, Past and Present," *Journal for Negro Education* 5, no. 1 (January 1936): 123.
Elsewhere he writes that the Socialist Party wrongly "assumes that the uplift of the
white worker will automatically emancipate yellow, brown, and black." Du Bois, "The
Negro and Communism" in *W. E. B. Du Bois: A Reader,* ed. David Levering Lewis
(New York: Henry Holt and Co., 1995), 585.

33. W. E. B. Du Bois, "The Class Struggle," in *The Emerging Thought of W. E. B. Du
Bois: Essays and Editorials from the Crisis,* ed. Henry Lee Moon (New York: Simon and
Schuster, 1972), 269. Essay originally published in *The Crisis,* August 1921. Writing

70 years later, Derrick Bell affirms that white supremacy is "a principal stabilizer" of American capitalism, which sustains "wage slavery" for both whites and Blacks. Yet Bell claims that even a total economic revolution would not "erase—and might intensify—the need of whites to measure their self-worth by maintaining blacks in a subordinate status." Derrick Bell, "The Final Civil Rights Act," *California Law Review* 79, no. 3 (May 1991): 607–8.

34. Du Bois, "The Negro and Social Reconstruction," 141.

35. Du Bois, "Marxism and the Negro Problem," 104.

36. Du Bois, "Marxism and the Negro Problem," 104. In "The Class Struggle," Du Bois writes, "Theoretically we are a part of the world proletariat . . . but practically we are not a part of the white proletariat" (269). See also W. E. B. Du Bois, "The Position of the Negro in the American Social Order: Where Do We Go from Here?," *Journal of Negro Education* 8, no. 3 (July 1939), where Du Bois rejects the "economic philosophy" that supposes "the white laborer . . . is forced by his necessities, to emphasize class interests rather than racial antagonisms" (555).

37. Du Bois, "Marxism and the Negro Problem," 104.

38. W. E. B. Du Bois, "The Negro and Radical Thought," in *Emerging Thought*, 268. Essay originally published in *The Crisis*, July 1921.

39. This is Roediger's description of an insight he found in the work of C. L. R. James, which also captures a key feature of Du Bois's work after about 1920. See David Roediger, "Accounting for the Wages of Whiteness: US Marxism and the Critical History of Race," in *Wages of Whiteness and Racist Symbolic Capital*, ed. Wulf D. Hund, Jeremy Krikler, and David Roediger (Munster: LIT Verlag, 2010), 21. Du Bois's point also partially anticipates the Combahee River Collective's famous 1977 statement on "interlocking" oppressions. They write, "We are socialists because we believe that work must be organized for the collective benefit of those who do the work and create the products, and not for the profit of the bosses. Material resources must be equally distributed among those who create these resources. We are not convinced, however, that a socialist revolution that is not also a feminist and anti-racist revolution will guarantee our liberation." The Combahee River Collective, "The Combahee River Collective Statement," 1977. https://www.blackpast.org/african-american-history/combahee-river-collective-statement-1977/.

40. W. E. B. Du Bois, "The Colored World Within," in *Dusk of Dawn*, 103. See also W. E. B. Du Bois, "The Right to Work," in *Du Bois: Writings*, ed. Nathan Huggins (New York: Library of America, 1986), 1236.

41. Allen, *The Invention of the White Race*, 2 vols.; Theodore W. Allen, "Summary of the Argument of the Invention of the White Race by Its Author," (1998). http://www.elegantbrain.com/edu4/classes/readings/race-allen.html.

42. David Roediger, *The Wages of Whiteness: Race and the Making of the American Working Class*, rev. ed. (London: Verso, 2007), 7.

43. Roediger, *The Wages of Whiteness*, 11. Roediger says no body of thought rivals Du Bois's in its attention to the "dialectics of race and class."

44. This is sometimes framed as a question of whether anti-Black racism is an "ideology" in the limited sense of operating exclusively as a tool of class oppression.

This is the argument advanced by Allen, *The Invention of the White Race,* Vols. 1 and 2, and Barbara Jeanne Fields, "Slavery, Race, and Ideology in the United States of America," *New Left Review* 181 (May–June 1990). Roediger's work including *The Wages of Whiteness* rejects Fields's view that race "is entirely socially and historically constructed as an ideology in a way that class is not" (7).

45. Du Bois, "Colored World," 103. Roediger cites this passage in *Wages of Whiteness,* 14.

46. Roediger, *Wages of Whiteness,* 8. Peter Kolchin, "Whiteness Studies: The New History of Race in America," *Journal of American History* 89, no. 1 (June 2002): 154–73 offers some helpful comparisons of Allen's and Roediger's respective approaches to the study of the historical construction of "whiteness," though he is too dismissive of both.

47. Du Bois, "Of Work and Wealth," 49.

48. Du Bois, "Of Work and Wealth," 49.

49. Du Bois, "Of Work and Wealth," 50.

50. Du Bois, "Social Planning," 125.

51. Du Bois, "Colored World," 103.

52. Du Bois, "Concept of Race," 52.

53. As Roediger emphasizes, Du Bois's formulation of a wage that is "public and psychological" does not imply that whites did not also enjoy material advantages on the basis of their racial classification. David Roediger, "Accounting for the Wages of Whiteness," 24–25. Today racialized material benefits are evident in white/Black wealth and income gaps in the United States. On the persistent wealth (total assets and debts) inequality between white and Black American households, see Melvin Oliver and Thomas Shapiro, *Black Wealth/White Wealth: A New Perspective on Racial Inequality,* 2nd ed. (New York: Routledge, 2006) and Kriston McIntosh, Emily Moss, Ryan Nunn, and Jay Shambaugh, "Examining the Black-White Wealth Gap," Brookings Institute, Feb. 27, 2020, which finds that the wealth gap between white and Black families has worsened in recent decades. https://www.brookings.edu/blog/up-front/2020/02/27/examining-the-black-white-wealth-gap/. Data from 1979–2016 shows that a Black-white wage gap persists in the United States that is not explainable by differences in age, education, job type, or location. See Mary C. Daly, Bart Hobijn, and Joseph H. Pedtke, "Disappointing Facts About the Black-White Wage Gap," *FRBSF Economic Letter,* September 2017. https://www.frbsf.org/economic-research/publications/economic-letter/2017/september/disappointing-facts-about-black-white-wage-gap/. Additionally, Black-white wage gaps worsened between 2000 and 2020. Elise Gould, "Black-White Wage Gaps Are Worse Today Than in 2000," Economic Policy Institute, Feb. 27, 2020. https://www.epi.org/blog/black-white-wage-gaps-are-worse-today-than-in-2000/.

54. Du Bois, *Black Reconstruction,* 573.

55. Du Bois, *Black Reconstruction,* 8–9. In an 1861 essay, Karl Marx described poor whites in the South, who greatly outnumbered the white slaveholders, as having entered into an alliance with them. Like Du Bois later, Marx identified cross-class white solidarity as integral to the maintenance of the slave system and focused on how such poor whites were "tamed" by the hope that they would someday become property holders (of land and slaves) themselves. See Karl Marx, "The North American

Civil War," in Karl Marx and Friedrich Engels, *The Civil War in the United States,* ed. Andrew Zimmerman (New York: International Publishers, 2016), 39–48. Du Bois makes a similar claim in *Black Reconstruction,* regarding what he calls "the American assumption" or "the assumption that any American could be rich if he wanted to" (493), which he says helped thwart truly significant economic redistribution following the Civil War. Du Bois departs from Marx's view by arguing that the alliance between propertied and propertyless whites, though fueled partly by the dream of social mobility in the future, is also sustained by the esteem that poor whites enjoy in the present.

56. Du Bois refers to "pale, white faces" in "The Souls of White Folk," in *Darkwater,* 16. See also David Roediger, who argues that the identity of the "freeman"—"propertied if only in his whiteness"—was constituted in contrast to the African American "anticitizen" in *How Race Survived,* 13.

57. Du Bois, *Black Reconstruction,* 8–9, 21.

58. Du Bois, *Black Reconstruction,* 16, 17, 21.

59. Du Bois, *Black Reconstruction,* 22. "Abolition-democracy" stands for a political-economic order that briefly seemed possible during Reconstruction but was not realized, on Du Bois's telling. The hyphenate names a society that has taken the material steps required to abolish slavery (including slavery "by another name") and to incorporate Black people into an expansive multiracial polity that has also socialized industry. Establishing abolition-democracy, according to Du Bois, required more than the "mere legalistic freeing of the slaves" and the extension of the franchise (*Black Reconstruction,* 168). It required the use of "confiscated and redistributed wealth" in the South to ensure that freedmen would experience "real economic emancipation," so that a "real democracy of industry for the masses of men" might be built (*Black Reconstruction,* 476, 168). Du Bois's understanding of abolition-democracy informs contemporary abolitionist politics. For example, Angela Davis explains that today's "prison abolitionist struggle follows the anti-slavery abolitionist struggle of the nineteenth century; the struggle for an abolitionist democracy is aspiring to create the institutions that will truly allow for a democratic society." Angela Davis, *Freedom Is a Constant Struggle: Ferguson, Palestine, and the Foundations of a Movement* (Chicago: Haymarket Books, 2016), 25. On Du Bois's relationship to contemporary abolitionism, see the Epilogue.

60. Du Bois, "Of Work and Wealth," 45–46.

61. Roediger, *Wages of Whiteness,* 11. Roediger explains the meaning of belonging to the dominant racial category under the conditions of 19th-century industrial capitalism: "one might lose everything but not whiteness" (60).

62. Du Bois, *Black Reconstruction,* 680.

63. Du Bois, *Black Reconstruction,* 680, 700, 557.

64. Cheryl Harris, "Whiteness as Property," *Harvard Law Review* 106, no. 8 (June 1993): 1759.

65. Du Bois, *Black Reconstruction,* 8, 106.

66. Du Bois, *Black Reconstruction,* 106.

67. Joel Olson, *The Abolition of White Democracy* (Minneapolis: University of Minnesota Press, 2004), 14.

68. Robinson, *Black Marxism*, 201.

69. Herbert Blumer, "Race Prejudice as a Sense of Group Position," *Pacific Sociological Review* 1, no. 1 (Spring 1958): 5.

70. Erica K. Wilson, "Monopolizing Whiteness," *Harvard Law Review* 134 (May 2021): 2382–448 uses the "social closure" theory developed by Raymond Murphy, by way of Max Weber, to analyze "white-student segregation" in racially diverse metropolitan areas in the United States. Wilson argues that in these contexts segregation is the result of practices of social closure, "a process of subordination whereby one group monopolizes advantages by closing off opportunities to other groups" (2383).

71. Du Bois, *Black Reconstruction*, 530.

72. W. E. B. Du Bois, "My Evolving Program for Negro Freedom," in *What the Negro Wants*, ed. Rayford W. Logan (Chapel Hill: University of North Carolina Press, 1944), 27–57.

73. Du Bois wrote often of "social equality" in his work. As Jill Locke notes, "social equality" was a "loaded term" in the Jim Crow era—"officially understood to mean the ability for blacks and whites to enjoy the same social institutions but fraught with anxieties about 'race mixing' and the end of whiteness as a distinctive color and racial marker." Jill Locke, "Little Rock's Social Question: Reading Arendt on School Desegregation and Social Climbing," *Political Theory* 41, no. 4 (Aug. 2013): 535. Over many years, Du Bois made the case for "social equality" in the institutional sense noted above, and also explicitly defended the right to interracial marriage. See, for example, "Social Equality and Racial Intermarriage," *World Tomorrow* (March 1922): 83–84, as well as 1944's "My Evolving Program." Du Bois is also reported to have quipped in 1930 that Black people who do not desire social equality with white people are "either asses or liars." See T. D. Hawkins, Letter from T. D. Hawkins to W. E. B. Du Bois, Nov. 15, 1930, W. E. B. Du Bois Papers (MS 312), Special Collections and University Archives, University of Massachusetts Amherst Libraries. https://credo.library.umass.edu/view/full/mums312-b054-i107.

74. Du Bois, "My Evolving Program," 53. "Public services" is one of three categories Du Bois discusses in relation to "social equality." The other two are "private social intercourse" and "social uplift (education, religion, science, and art)."

75. Du Bois, "My Evolving Program," 54.

76. Du Bois, "My Evolving Program," 55. Du Bois refers to "just sharing of public conveniences with all citizens."

77. On the tragic quality of American racial caste, see especially Du Bois, "Of Work and Wealth," 41, and *Black Reconstruction*, 264.

78. Du Bois, *Black Reconstruction*, 106.

79. Du Bois, *Black Reconstruction*, 290.

80. This question persists well into the 20th century. See Bonacich, "Class Approaches to Ethnicity and Race" on scholarly disagreement over whether white workers' oppression of nonwhite workers is "rational," that is, yields overall gains for them, or if

white workers' oppression of nonwhite workers is only a product of manipulation by capitalists and ultimately a loss for them.

81. Karl Marx, "Marx to Sigfrid Meyer and August Vogt in New York, April 9, 1870," in Marx and Engels, *Civil War in the United States*, 204.

82. W.E.B. Du Bois, "The Black Man and the Unions," in *Emerging Thought*, 158. Essay originally published in *The Crisis*, March 1918.

83. Du Bois, *Black Reconstruction*, 437.

84. Du Bois, *Black Reconstruction*, 557.

85. On the "Masters of Industry" as breeders of mobs and lynchings, akin to ringmasters "cracking their whips," see "Dives, Mob and Scab, Limited," in *Emerging Thought*, 161. Essay originally published in *The Crisis*, March 1920. On how employers play workers off each other, see "Black Man and Unions," 158.

86. Du Bois, "Black Man and Unions," 158.

87. Du Bois, "Of Work and Wealth," 47. He also describes white workers as "distracted by race hatred" in "Of the Ruling of Men," in *Darkwater*, 66.

88. Du Bois, "The Negro and Social Reconstruction," 140. In "Marxism and the Negro Problem," addressing the expansion of a "world market," Du Bois writes, "capitalists have consolidated their economic power . . . and bribed the white workers by high wages, visions of wealth, and the opportunity to drive 'n*****s' " (104).

89. W. E. B. Du Bois, "Black and White Workers," in *Emerging Thought*, 275. Essay originally published in *The Crisis*, March 1928.

90. Noel Ignatin, "Black Worker, White Worker: Understanding and Fighting White Supremacy" (1972) characterizes white skin privilege as "poison bait" for white workers. http://www.sojournertruth.net/bwww.html. In a later speech and essay, Ignatiev (née Ignatin) writes of his contemporary United States, "The problem is that many of the slaves think they are parts of the master class because they partake of the privileges of the white skin. We cannot say it too often: whiteness does not exempt people from exploitation, it reconciles them to it." Noel Ignatiev, "The Point Is Not to Interpret Whiteness but to Abolish It," (1997). https://blog. pmpress.org/2019/09/16/the-point-is-not-to-interpret-whiteness-but-to-abolish-it/.

91. Derrick Bell, *Faces at the Bottom of the Well: The Permanence of Racism* (New York: Basic Books, 1992), 8–9.

92. Noel Ignatin, "Letter to Progressive Labor," 157. See also Ted Allen's "Letter of Support" in response to Ignatin, which states, "While history has shown that the white-skin privilege does not serve the real interests of the white workers, it also shows that the concomitant racist ideology has blinded them to the fact" (180). Both pieces were originally published together by Students for a Democratic Society (SDS) in 1967. Reprinted as "White Blindspot: The Original Essays on Combatting White Supremacy and White-Skin Privilege," in *Revolutionary Youth and the New Working Class: The Praxis Papers, the Port Authority Statement, the RYM Documents and Other Lost Writings of SDS*, ed. Carl Davidson (Pittsburgh, PA: Changemaker Publications, 2011), 148–81.

93. Allen, *Invention of the White Race,* Vol. 1, 19, 23. Some arguments citing Du Bois stress short- vs. long-term interests rather than false vs. real interests, which is more consistent with Du Bois's own claims. See, for example, Olson, *Abolition of White Democracy,* 142, as well as some (but not all) of Ignatiev and Allen's early formulations in "White Blindspot." In a 1929 speech, Du Bois clarified that Black workers were not appealing for charity from whites by explaining, "It is an appeal to white workmen to stop cutting off their own noses to spite their face." Du Bois, "The Denial of Economic Justice to Negroes," in *W. E. B. Du Bois Speaks: Speeches and Addresses 1890–1919,* ed. Philip S. Foner (New York: Pathfinder Press, 1971), 44.

94. Du Bois, *Black Reconstruction,* 290.

95. Harris, "Whiteness as Property."

96. Du Bois, "Negro and Communism," 589.

97. Du Bois, "Negro and Communism," 589. Here he specifies the form this oppression takes: "Mobs, riots, and the discrimination of trade unions have been used to kill, threaten, and starve black men."

98. Du Bois, "Marxism and the Negro Problem," *The Crisis* 40 (May 1933): 104.

99. Du Bois, *Black Reconstruction,* 106.

100. Du Bois, *Black Reconstruction,* 549.

101. Cedric Robinson notes that Du Bois's writings present a long view of white-over-Black domination in the United States, one that emphasizes enduring patterns, as when Du Bois traces the racial violence of the American labor movement in the 20th century to its "roots" in 19th-century white mobs active before and during the Civil War. Robinson, *Black Marxism,* 202.

102. Du Bois, *Black Reconstruction,* 549.

103. Karl Marx, "Marx, on behalf of the International Working Men's Association, Letter to President Abraham Lincoln, Nov. 22, 1864," Marx and Engels, *Civil War in the United States,* 154–55. This sentiment is echoed in a famous passage from *Capital,* Vol. 1, Ch. 10, in which Marx writes, "In the United States of North America, every independent movement of the workers was paralyzed so long as slavery disfigured a part of the Republic. Labor cannot emancipate itself in the white skin where in the black it is branded. But out of the death of slavery a new life at once arose," excerpted in Marx and Engels, *Civil War,* 194.

104. Marx, "Marx to Meyer and Vogt, 1870," in Marx and Engels, *Civil War in the United States,* 204.

105. For a discussion of the "whitelash" narrative, sometimes associated with Du Bois, which circulated in the wake of the 2016 presidential election, see Chapter 1.

106. Du Bois, *Black Reconstruction,* 66.

107. Du Bois, *Black Reconstruction,* 287.

108. Du Bois, "The Position of the Negro in the American Social Order," 564. See also Du Bois, "Colored World," 104.

109. Du Bois, *Black Reconstruction,* 9.

110. Du Bois, *Black Reconstruction,* 83.

111. W. E. B. Du Bois, "The Hands of Ethiopia," in *Darkwater,* 35.

112. Du Bois, "Hands of Ethiopia," 35. Du Bois also refers here to the "passionate, deep-seated heritage" that instills the belief that "black folks are sub-human." He notes that such training "can be moved by neither argument nor fact."

113. On "guerilla warfare," see Du Bois, *Black Reconstruction,* 106, 552.

114. Du Bois, *Black Reconstruction,* 555.

115. Du Bois, *Black Reconstruction,* 555. See also W. E. B. Du Bois's 1926 essay, "The Shape of Fear," *The North American Review* 223, no. 831 (June-Aug. 1926): 291–304, which also traces "the mob spirit" in America to an "inner nucleus of fear" (295).

116. David Roediger examines how anti-Black violence helped constitute white unity during Reconstruction in *How Race Survived,* 110–19.

117. Du Bois, "Of Work and Wealth," 46.

118. Du Bois, "Of Work and Wealth," 46.

119. Du Bois, "My Evolving Program," 55.

120. "Segregation" and "resegregation" here refer not simply to patterns of physical separation, but more crucially to "separation for the purposes of securing *subordination*." Sharon Stanley, "The Enduring Challenge of Racial Integration," *Du Bois Review* 12, no. 1 (2015): 9. Likewise, while the terms "segregation," "desegregation," and "integration" are all contested, I use the latter term not as a measure of "proximity to whiteness" but rather as a way of naming the "incorporation of Black Americans on terms of full equality into the polity." As Stanley points out, even proponents of "aggressive" desegregation measures, such as Justice Breyer, rely on an understanding of segregation that is too "numerical" and "White-centric"; it defines an integrated society as "one in which Blacks share all their spaces and institutions with substantial numbers of Whites" (11).

121. Though it is beyond the scope of this discussion, "white flight"—the movement of white Americans from urban areas with large racial minority populations to suburban areas—marks another way that white Americans resisted desegregation and sought to secure the most valuable public educational resources for themselves in the post-*Brown* era.

122. Mark Golub, "Remembering Massive Resistance to School Desegregation," *Law and History Review* 31, no. 3 (August 2013): 504.

123. George Lewis, *Massive Resistance: The White Response to the Civil Rights Movement* (London: Hodder Arnold, 2006), 17.

124. Lewis, *Massive Resistance,* 8.

125. Golub, "Remembering Massive Resistance," 494. Lewis, *Massive Resistance,* 8.

126. Their efforts were quite successful. By 1965, a full decade after the historic *Brown* decision, "less than 3 percent of the South's African Americans attended school with whites, and in Alabama, Arkansas, Georgia, Mississippi, and South Carolina that number remained substantially below 1 per cent" (Lewis, *Massive Resistance,* 114).

127. The Democratic primary debates in the race for the 2020 US presidency revealed that "busing" still serves as the commonsense way of talking about the history of desegregation in this country. Matt Stevens, "When Kamala Harris and Joe Biden Clashed on Busing and Segregation," *New York Times,* July 31, 2019. https://www.nytimes.com/2019/07/31/us/politics/kamala-harris-biden-busing.html.

Nikole Hannah-Jones says of this default language: "That we even use the word 'busing' to describe what was in fact court-ordered school desegregation, and that Americans of all stripes believe that the brief period in which we actually tried to desegregate our schools was a failure, speaks to one of the most successful propaganda campaigns of the last half century." Nikole Hannah-Jones, "It Was Never About Busing," *New York Times,* July 12, 2019. https://www.nytimes.com/2019/07/12/opin ion/sunday/it-was-never-about-busing.html.

128. Matthew F. Delmont, *Why Busing Failed: Race, Media, and the National Resistance to School Desegregation* (Berkeley: University of California Press, 2016), 6, 21.

129. Richard Rothstein, "The Racial Achievement Gap, Segregated Schools, and Segregated Neighborhoods—A Constitutional Insult," *Race and Social Problems* 7, no. 1 (March 2015): 21–30. Rothstein argues that the long-term effects of discriminatory housing policies are so vast and enduring that it may make sense to talk about the *contemporary* residential segregation of low-income Black children as de jure.

130. Alex Nazaryan, "School Segregation in America Is as Bad Today as It Was in the 1960s," *Newsweek,* March 22, 2018. https://www.newsweek.com/2018/03/30/sch ool-segregation-america-today-bad-1960-855256.html.

131. Hannah-Jones, "Never About Busing."

132. See Delmont, *Why Busing Failed,* 2–3. Delmont explains that from 1920 to 1970, the number of American students riding publicly funded buses grew from 600,000 to 20 million. In fact, transportation by school bus in this era was often an educational privilege provided only for whites, while Black students were left to walk long distances to school. Additionally, school buses were often used to transport students long distances in order to *maintain* segregation; Linda Brown, the plaintiff in *Brown v. Board of Education,* rode a bus over 20 miles to attend a Black school when the white school was only four blocks from her home. And in Boston, which became a central site in the battle over "busing" in the 1970s, majorities of middle and high school students were already bused prior to court-ordered busing, with little fanfare. In sum, the use of school buses was not a problem until it was linked to desegregation.

133. Delmont, *Why Busing Failed,* 4.

134. Delmont, *Why Busing Failed,* 4–5. Title IV, section 401b included the provision: " 'desegregation' shall not mean the assignment of students to public schools to overcome racial imbalance." In subsequent years white politicians and parents cited the Civil Rights Act to support the maintenance of white schools in the North.

135. Alexander Nazaryan, "Whites Only: School Segregation Is Back, from Birmingham to San Francisco," *Newsweek,* May 2, 2017. https://www.newsweek.com/2017/05/19/ race-schools-592637.html.

136. Emma Brown, "On the Anniversary of Brown v. Board, New Evidence That US schools Are Resegregating," *Washington Post,* May 17, 2016. https://www.washing tonpost.com/news/education/wp/2016/05/17/on-the-anniversary-of-brown-v-board-new-evidence-that-u-s-schools-are-resegregating/.

137. Nikole Hannah-Jones, "Segregation Now," *Pro Publica*, April 16, 2014. https://www. propublica.org/article/segregation-now-full-text.

　　In the 21st century, the proportion of schools segregated by race and class has grown. A 2016 Government Accountability Report found that "the proportion of schools segregated by race and class—where more than 75 percent of children receive free or reduced-price lunch, and more than 75 percent are black or Hispanic— climbed from 9 percent to 16 percent of schools between 2001 and 2014. The number of the most intensively segregated schools—with more than 90 percent of low-income students and students of color—more than doubled over that period." See Emma Brown, "On the Anniversary of Brown v. Board."

138. Stanley, "The Enduring Challenge of Racial Integration," 9.

139. Emma Brown, "On the Anniversary of Brown v. Board." Additionally, on average, teachers in schools serving primarily nonwhite students are less experienced, lower paid, and less likely to be certified than peers at majority-white schools. See Lindsey Cook, "U.S. Education: Still Separate and Unequal," *US News and World Report*, Jan. 28, 2015. https://www.usnews.com/news/blogs/data-mine/2015/01/28/us-educat ion-still-separate-and-unequal.

140. Hannah-Jones, "Segregation Now."

141. Sarah Mervosh, "How Much Wealthier Are White School Districts Than Nonwhite Ones? $23 Billion, Report Says," *New York Times*, Feb. 27, 2019. https://www.nyti mes.com/2019/02/27/education/school-districts-funding-white-minorities.html.

142. Hannah-Jones, "It Was Never About Busing."

143. Hannah-Jones, "Segregation Now."

144. Delmont, *Why Busing Failed*, 21.

145. These shifts included the Southern Strategy, the passage of bipartisan anti-busing legislation, Nixon-appointed Supreme Court judges, and the *Milliken v. Bradley* decision (1974), which barred desegregation measures across district lines.

146. The first proponents of the school choice paradigm were Southern segregationists in the 1950s who sought to evade the consequences of *Brown* by arguing for "freedom of choice" and the use of vouchers in order to maintain segregated schools. Later, however, following the Civil Rights Act of 1964, some civil rights activists saw school choice programs such as magnet schools and voluntary transfers as tools in the battle for integrated public schools. Allison Roda and Amy Stuart Wells, "School Choice Policies and Racial Segregation: Where White Parents' Good Intentions, Anxiety, and Privilege Collide," *American Journal of Education* 119, no. 2 (February 2013): 261–93.

147. Roda and Wells, "School Choice Policies and Racial Segregation," 262. Even modest efforts to link school choice policies to desegregation goals have been successfully challenged in court. In the 2006 case *Parents Involved in Community Schools vs. Seattle School District*, the Supreme Court sided with the plaintiff, a group of white parents who alleged that the school district's policy of using race as one of several "tiebreakers" in admission decisions (in order to maintain schools with populations roughly proportional to the racial makeup of public school students at large) was a violation of the 14th Amendment's equal protection clause. See Cara Sandberg,

"The Story of *Parents Involved in Community Schools*" (Student paper, UC Berkeley School of Law, 2011) on Seattle's discriminatory history. https://www.law.berkeley.edu/files/The_Story_of_Parents_Involved_Sandberg.pdf.

Chief Justice John Roberts Jr. wrote in the majority opinion, "The way to stop discrimination on the basis of race is to stop discriminating on the basis of race." Alexander Nazaryan notes, "By conflating integration with discrimination, Roberts effectively reversed *Brown v. Board*" (Nazaryan, "Whites Only").

148. Roda and Wells, "School Choice Policies," 264.

149. Dana Goldstein, "One Reason School Segregation Persists: White Parents Want It That Way," *Slate,* July 15, 2016. https://slate.com/human-interest/2016/07/when-white-parents-have-a-choice-they-choose-segregated-schools.html. Research cited in this article also suggests that some white parents desire what Nikole Hannah-Jones has dubbed "'carefully curated integration,' the kind that exposes white children to some poor peers of color but 'not too many.'"

150. For example, "school district succession," in which a community separates from their local district, is increasingly common. The new districts usually create new district boundaries that correspond to racial and/or economic borders. "It's white flight, without the actual flight." See Peter Greene, "White Flight, Without the Actual Flight," *Forbes,* Nov. 12, 2019. https://www.forbes.com/sites/petergreene/2019/11/12/white-flight-without-the-actual-flight/?sh=74f00c6253c6.

151. Dana Goldstein, "Where Civility Is a Motto, a School Integration Fight Turns Bitter," *New York Times,* Nov. 12, 2019. https://www.nytimes.com/2019/11/12/us/howard-county-school-redistricting.html.

152. Another account of the inventive ways whites work to secure the best public educational resources for themselves, especially within "school choice" systems, is detailed in the five-part podcast *Nice White Parents* (2020), produced by the *New York Times*.

153. Lawrie Balfour, *Democracy's Reconstruction: Thinking Politically with W. E. B. Du Bois* (Oxford: Oxford University Press, 2011) mobilizes Du Bois's reference to the "present-past" to explore how his thought "dwells in the space between the moment of emancipation and the withholding of freedom that followed" (11, 17).

154. Du Bois, "My Evolving Program," 55–56.

Chapter 3

1. W. E. B. Du Bois, *Black Reconstruction in America: An Essay Toward a History of the Part Which Black Folk Played in the Attempt to Reconstruct Democracy in America, 1860–1880* (Oxford: Oxford University Press, 2007 [1935]), 11.

2. See, for example, Du Bois, "Karl Marx and the Negro," *The Crisis* 40, no. 3 (March 1933): 55–56; Du Bois, "Marxism and the Negro Problem," *The Crisis* 40, no. 5 (May 1933): 103–4, 118.

3. The most well-known examples of these two perspectives are Bernie Sanders and Ta-Nehesi Coates. Even in 2019, when there was ample data to the contrary, Sanders

maintained that racism and sexism were minor factors in Trump's appeal and that the real issue was economic anxiety. In a televised town hall, he explained, "Many of these people are people who have worked hard their entire lives and their standard of living is going down, in many cases, they're making less today than they did 30 or 40 years ago." http://transcripts.cnn.com/TRANSCRIPTS/1902/25/se.01.html. On the other hand, Ta-Nehesi Coates argued that Trump was a "product of white supremacy," elected by a cross-class "white coalition" affronted by the two-term "n****r presidency" that preceded it. Ta-Nehesi Coates, "The First White President," *The Atlantic*, October 2017. https://www.theatlantic.com/magazine/archive/2017/10/the-first-white-president-ta-nehisi-coates/537909/.

4. W. E. B. Du Bois, "Revolution," in *Dusk of Dawn: An Essay Toward an Autobiography of the Race Concept* (Oxford: Oxford University Press, 2007 [1940]), 151. By 1961, of course, Du Bois's assessment was decidedly bleak. A month before he moved to Ghana he wrote in a letter to Grace Goens, "Chin up, and fight on, but realize that American Negroes can't win." Du Bois, "Letter from W. E. B. Du Bois to Grace Goens," September 13, 1961. W. E. B. Du Bois Papers (MS 312). Special Collections and University Archives, University of Massachusetts Amherst Libraries. https://credo.library.umass.edu/view/full/mums312-b153-i208.

5. W. E. B. Du Bois, "The White World," in *Dusk of Dawn*, 87.

6. For an illuminating interpretation of Du Bois's middle-period work that focuses on the notion of "white people's unconscious," see Shannon Sullivan, "Appropriate Habits of White Privilege," in her book *Revealing Whiteness: The Unconscious Habits of White Privilege* (Bloomington: Indiana University Press, 2006).

7. Du Bois, "Revolution," 141.

8. W. E. B. Du Bois, "The Colored World Within," in *Dusk of Dawn,* 98.

9. W. E. B. Du Bois, "Science and Empire," in *Dusk of Dawn,* 26.

10. Du Bois, "Science and Empire," 28.

11. W. E. B. Du Bois, "Propaganda and World War," in *Dusk of Dawn,* 111. In another *Dusk of Dawn* essay, Du Bois notes that "science" now recognizes that "most of [the individual's] actions are not rational and many of them arise from subconscious urges" ("The White World," 86).

12. Du Bois, "Science and Empire," 26.

13. Du Bois, "Revolution," 151.

14. Du Bois, "The Colored World Within," 98.

15. Du Bois, "Revolution," 141.

16. Du Bois, "Revolution," 142.

17. W. E. B. Du Bois, "The Plot," in *Dusk of Dawn,* 2. This important shift in Du Bois's thinking is overlooked by Cornel West's essay on Du Bois, "Black Strivings in a Twilight Civilization," in *The Cornel West Reader* (New York: Basic Books, 1999), 87–118. West maintains that for Du Bois, "the ultimate evil was stupidity. The cure for it was knowledge based on scientific investigation," which was only "momentarily shaken" by Sam Hose's murder (discussed later in this chapter). Du Bois's middle-period work, in which he becomes increasingly disenchanted with "the Enlightenment ethos," defies West's account.

18. Du Bois, "Revolution," 148.

19. W. E. B. Du Bois, "Apologia" (1954). http://www.webdubois.org/dbSAST-Apolo gia.html.

20. Du Bois, "Science and Empire," 28. In another essay in *Dusk of Dawn,* Du Bois writes of lynching as a "continuing and recurring horror during my college days" and reports "each death was a scar upon my soul" ("Education in the Last Decades of the Nineteenth Century," 15).

21. Du Bois, "Science and Empire," 34.

22. Du Bois, "Science and Empire," 47. On Du Bois's complex understanding of "propaganda," see Chapter 5.

23. Du Bois, "Propaganda and World War," 112.

24. Du Bois, "Propaganda and World War," 120–21.

25. Du Bois, "Propaganda and World War," 121.

26. Du Bois, "Propaganda and World War," 126. Du Bois also references here the East St. Louis riots of 1917 in which "one hundred twenty-five Negroes were killed by their fellow white laborers; their homes looted and destroyed; and hundreds of others maimed."

27. Du Bois, "Propaganda and World War," 123.

28. Du Bois, "Propaganda and World War," 132.

29. In "Propaganda and World War," Du Bois describes the East St. Louis riot as "notable for its passion, cruelty, and obvious economic motive" (126).

30. Du Bois, "Propaganda and World War," 132.

31. Du Bois, "The Souls of White Folk," in *Darkwater: Voices from Within the Veil* (Oxford: Oxford University Press, 2007 [1920]), 17.

32. Du Bois, "The Souls of White Folk," 17.

33. Du Bois, *Black Reconstruction,* 551.

34. Du Bois, *Black Reconstruction,* 551, 555.

35. Du Bois, *Black Reconstruction,* 550–58. Du Bois refers to "armed guerilla warfare" on 552.

36. Du Bois, *Black Reconstruction,* 573.

37. Du Bois, *Black Reconstruction,* 574. In an arresting remark earlier in the book, Du Bois declares, "Human nature does not deliberately choose blood—at least not black human nature" (53).

38. W. E. B. Du Bois and Martha Gruening, "The Massacre of East St. Louis," *The Crisis* 14, no. 5 (September 1917): 221, quoting the July 3, 1917, *St. Louis Post-Dispatch* article.

39. William Pickens, "A Roman Holiday," originally published in *The Crisis,* March 1929; reprinted in Nancy Cunard, ed., *Negro Anthology* (London: Wishart & Co., 1934), 32–35.

40. Du Bois and Gruening, "The Massacre," 219–38. The outbreak of bloody anti-Black violence was precipitated by rapidly growing numbers of Black workers in local factories (the Black population in the city had doubled in seven years) and, more specifically, according to some accounts, by the hiring of Black workers (along with white) to replace striking white workers in an aluminum plant in May. Tim O'Neil, "Look Back: Race Hatred, Workforce Tensions Explode in East St. Louis in 1917," *St. Louis*

Post Dispatch, Sept. 21, 2014. https://www.stltoday.com/news/local/history/race-hat
red-workforce-tensions-explode-in-east-st-louis-in-1917/article_9bfa1b5d-c627-
5dc7-b1da-6d58993f3ecb.html; Alex Park, "The St. Louis Area Has a Long History
of Shameful Racial Violence," *Mother Jones*, Aug. 18, 2014. https://www.motherjones.
com/politics/2014/08/riot-east-st-louis-ferguson-history-race/.

41. Du Bois and Gruening, "The Massacre," 228.
42. Du Bois and Gruening, "The Massacre," 221. Although I do not pursue this line of
    thought here, some of Du Bois's reflections on violence bring to mind Nietzsche's
    reflections on cruelty and pleasure in the second essay of the *Genealogy of Morals*.
    Claiming that "for most of human history" punishment took the form of the injured
    party acting out of anger at the source of the harm, Nietzsche traces this model to early
    creditor/debtor contracts that permitted the creditor to inflict "every kind of indignity
    and torture upon the body of the debtor" if he failed to pay. Crucially, on Nietzsche's
    telling, recompense here comes in the form of "pleasure"—namely, the pleasure of
    "*making* suffer," the "enjoyment of violation" (*Genealogy of Morals* II: 4–6). Beyond
    identifying this particular kind of pleasure, Nietzsche makes two further claims that
    might be worth exploring in relation to Du Bois's account of whites' persistent attacks
    on Blacks: Nietzsche indicates that, although it falls short of the enjoyment found in
    making others suffer, even *seeing* others suffer "does one good" (*Genealogy of Morals*
    II: 6); Second, he contends that the "voluptuous pleasure" that comes from hurting
    another "will be the greater the lower the creditor stands in the social order, and can
    easily appear to him as a most delicious morsel, indeed as a foretaste of higher rank."
    Nietzsche says that by inflicting pain on another person, the "creditor participates in
    a *right of the masters*: at last, he, too, may experience for once the exalted sensation
    of being allowed to despise and mistreat someone as 'beneath him'" (*Genealogy of
    Morals* II: 5). Friedrich Nietzsche, *On the Genealogy of Morals* and *Ecce Homo*, trans.
    and ed. Walter Kaufmann (New York: Vintage Books, 1989).
43. Du Bois and Gruening, "The Massacre," 220, 224.
44. Du Bois and Gruening, "The Massacre," 220–21. Italics are mine.
45. Sigmund Freud, "Instincts and Their Vicissitudes," trans. James Strachey, in *The
    Standard Edition of the Complete Psychological Works of Sigmund Freud,* Vol. 14
    (London: Hogarth Press, 1957), 127, 129. "Instinct" is the translation of the German
    Trieb, elsewhere translated as "drive." Freud's account of sadism changed significantly
    over time. In this text and the earlier *Three Essays on Sexuality* (1905), sadism is un-
    derstood as a sexual drive, but this shifts around 1920, when Freud posits a distinct
    death instinct, into which sadism is subsumed.
46. Du Bois makes both claims, for example, in *Black Reconstruction,* 554, and "Of Work
    and Wealth," in *Darkwater*, 43. Ida B. Wells advanced these arguments earlier in "A
    Red Record" (1895), exposing the supposed rape of white women as a hollow "ex-
    cuse" for the lynching of Black men. She writes, "To justify their own barbarism they
    assume a chivalry which they do not possess" and points out that that is "chivalry for
    white women only," since the widespread sexual assault of Black women is ignored.
    Ida B. Wells, "A Red Record," in *The Light of Truth: Writings of an Anti-Lynching
    Crusader,* ed. Mia Bay (New York: Penguin Books, 2014), 226, 277. Megan Ming

Francis, "The Battle for the Hearts and Minds of America," *Souls: A Critical Journal of Black Politics, Culture, and Society* 13, no. 1 (2011): 46–71 shows that Wells's "fight to end lynching shaped the focus and strategy of the NAACP from the outset," even though her impact is often left out of mainstream accounts of the organization (48, 49). This neglect mirrors Du Bois's own well-documented marginalization of Wells. See Paula Giddings, "Missing in Action: Ida B. Wells, the NAACP and the Historical Record," *Meridians* 1, no. 2 (Spring 2001): 1–17.

47. Du Bois refers to a specific case of castration (often part of the torture exacted upon lynching victims) in *Black Reconstruction,* 550.

48. Du Bois, "The Souls of White Folk," 17.

49. Du Bois and Gruening, "The Massacre," 222.

50. W. E. B. Du Bois, "The Damnation of Women," in *Darkwater,* 82. This essay is Du Bois's clearest indictment of the specific oppressions faced by Black women and a celebration of their "strength," "determination," and "sacrifice." In this text, Du Bois takes a strong stand in favor of women's rights (and, as Lawrie Balfour notes, subversively uses the unmodified "woman" to analyze the situation of Black women). He argues, "The future woman must have life work and economic independence. She must have knowledge. She must have the right of motherhood at her own discretion" (78). The gendered dimensions of Du Bois's thought are, of course, an important topic of debate, especially among Black feminists. Joy James's persuasive interpretation locates an abiding tension at the center of Du Bois's work. He is both "profeminist"—in the sense that he argues against sexism, works to dispel myths of female inferiority, and champions women's rights—*and* "masculinist," insofar as he "presents the male as normative" and "minimizes black female agency." Joy James, *Transcending the Talented Tenth: Black Leaders and American Intellectuals* (New York: Routledge, 1997), 35–36. James and Hazel V. Carby both point out that Du Bois did not seriously engage with, and even concealed the contributions of, contemporary Black women intellectuals, most notably Anna Julia Cooper and Ida B. Wells. Carby argues that Du Bois upholds a model of leadership with Black manhood at its center. Hazel V. Carby, *Race Men* (Cambridge, MA: Harvard University Press, 1998). See also Lawrie Balfour, *Democracy's Reconstruction: Thinking Politically with W. E. B. Du Bois* (Oxford: Oxford University Press, 2011), Ch. 5; Susan Gillman and Alys Eve Weinbaum, eds., *Next to the Color Line: Gender, Sexuality and Du Bois* (Minneapolis: University of Minnesota Press, 2007); Farah Jasmine Griffin, "Black Feminists and Du Bois: Respectability, Protection, and Beyond," *Annals of the American Academy of Political and Social Science* 586 (March 2000): 28–40.

51. Du Bois, *Black Reconstruction,* 574; W. E. B. Du Bois, " 'The Servant in the House,' " in *Darkwater,* 54.

52. Du Bois, *Black Reconstruction,* 569.

53. Du Bois, "The Souls of White Folk," 16.

54. Anthony Paul Farley, Saidiya Hartman, Frank Wilderson III, and Jared Sexton all refer to the "libidinal economy" of anti-Blackness. Wilderson elaborates his view in terms partially reminiscent of Du Bois, charging that white supremacy has always been (at least partly) "irrational": "the gratuitous terror of white supremacy is as much

contingent upon the irrationality of white fantasies and shared pleasures as it is upon a logic—the logic of capital." Moreover, as Du Bois intimated with the idea of white "joy," Wilderson argues that the affective valence of white supremacy combines an antipathy to Blackness with feelings of "pleasure" generated by racialized objectification and violence. Frank Wilderson III, "Gramsci's Black Marx: Whither the Slave in Civil Society?," *Social Identities* 9, no. 2 (2003): 225, 230.

55. For an overview of the effect that the Sam Hose case had on Du Bois, see David Levering Lewis, *W. E. B. Du Bois: Biography of a Race, 1868–1919* (New York: Henry Holt and Co., 1993), 226, 228, 230, 281–82, 408, 441.

56. Mary Louise Ellis, *"Rain Down Fire": The Lynching of Sam Hose* (PhD diss., Florida State University, 1992). See also Philip Dray, *At the Hands of Persons Unknown: The Lynching of Black America* (New York: Random House, 2002), Ch. 1 on the case of Sam Hose.

57. On the "souvenirs" collected and sold in the Sam Hose case, see Ellis, *"Rain Down Fire,"* 120, 131, 134; Dray, *At the Hands of Persons Unknown,* 14; Grace Elizabeth Hale, *Making Whiteness: The Culture of Segregation in the South, 1890–1940* (New York: Vintage Books, 1999), 213–15.

58. The pamphlet, originally published by Chicago Colored Citizens in 1899 is reprinted in Ida B. Wells, *The Light of Truth,* 313–34.

59. Ellis, *"Rain Down Fire,"* 200, quoting the *Chicago Tribune,* May 1, 1899.

60. Hale, *Making Whiteness,* 209.

61. This number is my own and the result of some sustained investigation. I have found many mentions of the Sam Hose story in the Du Bois secondary literature, but none of the sources I have consulted catalog the number of references Du Bois makes to Hose nor have they reflected upon the multiple citations as a group.

62. For a smart psychoanalytic reading of Du Bois's recollections concerning Sam Hose, see Jonathan Flatley, "'What a Mourning': Propaganda and Loss in Du Bois's *Souls of Black Folk,*" in *Affective Mapping: Melancholia and the Politics of Modernism* (Cambridge: Harvard University Press, 2008). Flatley interprets the story of Hose in Lacanian terms, as an "irruption of the real," and suggests that some of the inconsistencies in his retelling (particularly his misremembering the alleged victim of Hose to be a white woman) are part of Du Bois's effort to "cover the hole in the symbolic network" (110).

63. This text was not well known until it was republished as "A Pageant in Seven Decades," in *W. E. B. Du Bois Speaks,* ed. Philip S. Foner (New York: Pathfinder Press, 1970), 21–72.

64. Du Bois, "Science and Empire," 34.

65. It is difficult to corroborate whether Hose's knuckles were indeed on view in an Atlanta market, as Du Bois recalls, but Mary Louise Ellis's thorough account of the case notes that multiple newspapers in April 1899 (including the *Atlanta Constitution, Macon Telegraph, Newnan Herald and Advertiser, Griffin Daily News and Sun, Washington Post,* and *New York Herald*) reported that Hose's body was "cut to pieces" and that assorted "relics" including "pieces of bone" were taken and sold. Ellis explains, "All give essentially the same account, with only slight variation in detail" (120).

66. The *Macon Telegraph* in May 1899 reported that Sam Hose's ear, preserved in alcohol, was on display in Gainesville, Georgia, in the weeks after his death (Ellis, *"Rain Down Fire,"* 121). In his book on the case, Edwin Arnold notes that butcher shops in the Atlanta area would frequently display pig knuckles labeled "Sam Hose's knuckles" as a "joke and advertising gimmick." *What Virtue There Is in Fire: Cultural Memory and the Lynching of Sam Hose* (Athens: University of Georgia Press, 2009), 172.

67. This formulation is mine. Du Bois does not directly apply his language of "irrationality" to the Hose incident. Yet the repeated references to Hose begin at the same time that Du Bois also begins to speak of racism's "irrationality," and as I have suggested, the latter term seems to flag gratuitous anti-Black brutality in particular.

68. Hale, *Making Whiteness*, 214.

69. The first statement appears in Du Bois, "A Pageant in Seven Decades," 39, and in Du Bois, "Science and Empire," 34. The latter is from Du Bois, "My Evolving Program for Negro Freedom," in *What the Negro Wants* (Chapel Hill: University of North Carolina Press, 1944), 44.

70. William T. Ingersoll, Oral History Interview of W. E. B. Du Bois, ca. June 1960, W. E. B. Du Bois Papers (MS 312), Special Collections and University Archives, University of Massachusetts Amherst Libraries, 148.

71. This conversation is reported in Ralph McGill, "W. E. B. Du Bois," *Atlantic Monthly*, Nov. 1965. https://www.theatlantic.com/past/docs/unbound/flashbks/black/mcgil lbh.htm.

72. Joseph R. Winters, *Hope Draped in Black: Race, Melancholy, and the Agony of Progress* (Durham, NC: Duke University Press, 2016), Ch. 1. Winters's analysis is focused on *The Souls of Black Folk*, however, and makes no mention of the figure of Sam Hose.

73. Du Bois, "My Evolving Program," 44.

74. W. E. B. Du Bois, "The Class Struggle," in *The Emerging Thought of W. E. B. Du Bois*, ed. Henry Lee Moon (New York: Simon & Schuster, 1972), 269.

75. W. E. B. Du Bois, "The Plot," in *Dusk of Dawn*, 3, 2.

76. W. E. B. Du Bois, NAACP Board Minutes, Dec. 10, 1916, quoted in Francis, "Battle for the Hearts and Minds of America," 55.

77. Timothy Pachirat, *Every Twelve Seconds: Industrialized Slaughter and the Politics of Sight* (New Haven, CT: Yale University Press, 2011), 15.

78. W. E. B. Du Bois, "Hands of Ethiopia," in *Darkwater*, 35; Du Bois, "The Souls of White Folk," 17.

79. W. E. B. Du Bois, "Triumph," *The Crisis* 2, no. 5 (Sept. 19, 1911): 195; Gruening and Du Bois, "The Massacre," 224.

80. See Courtney R. Baker, *Humane Insight: Looking at Images of African American Suffering and Death* (Urbana: University of Illinois Press, 2015), which explores the tension between voyeurism and witnessing in relation to images of the Black body in pain. The book begins with the claim that looking is a "variegated" practice, but the project focuses on deliberate efforts by Black activists, beginning in 19th-century antebellum America, to "appeal to sentiment through the presentation of pain" (4). Baker is interested in how such actors try to elicit "humane insight"—an

"ethical look" that imagines the body in pain as human and worthy of protection. See especially Chapter 2 on "looking at the lynched body."

81. Du Bois, "The White World," 86. Hazel V. Carby has suggested that the bystander video recorded of police officer Derek Chauvin killing George Floyd on the street in Minneapolis serves as an enjoyable "snuff film" for some viewers. Hazel V. Carby and Adam Shatz, "The Colour Line in the Americas," *LRB Conversations* podcast, Jan. 12, 2021. https://www.lrb.co.uk/podcasts-and-videos/podcasts/lrb-conversations/the-colour-line-in-the-americas.

82. Robert Gooding-Williams, "Look! A Negro!," in *Reading Rodney King/Reading Urban Uprising,* ed. Robert Gooding-Williams (New York: Routledge, 1993), 165, 167.

83. Franz Fanon, *Black Skin, White Masks,* trans. Richard Philox (New York: Grove Press, 2008 [1952]), 111; Judith Butler, "Endangered/Endangering: Schematic Racism and White Paranoia," in *Reading Rodney King/Reading Racial Uprising.*

84. Dominic J. Capeci Jr. and Jack C. Knight, "Reckoning with Violence: W. E. B. Du Bois and the 1906 Atlanta Race Riot," *Journal of Southern History* 62, no. 4 (Nov. 1996): 727–66 stands out among the secondary literature for its claim that Du Bois's exposure to particular acts of white supremacist violence had an "enormous effect" on his thought and "militant strategies." Although their analysis centers on the 1906 riots, their larger point—that the "evolution of Du Bois's radicalism" was directly tied to acts of white violence—supports my claims in this chapter.

85. This is Walter Johnson's description of Barbara J. Fields' approach. Walter Johnson, "Brute Ideology," *Dissent* 61, no. 4 (Fall 2014): 129.

86. Barbara J. Fields, "Slavery, Race and Ideology in the United States of America," *New Left Review* 181 (May–June 1990): 101.

87. Fields, "Slavery, Race and Ideology," 102.

88. Fields, "Slavery, Race and Ideology," 104.

89. Fields, "Slavery, Race and Ideology," 106.

90. Karen E. Fields and Barbara J. Fields, *Racecraft: The Soul of Inequality in American Life* (London: Verso Books, 2012), 266–67.

91. Barbara J. Fields, "Whiteness, Racism, and Identity," *International Labor and Working-Class History* 60 (Fall 2001): 51.

92. Karen E. Fields and Barbara J. Fields, "How Race Is Conjured: An Interview with Barbara J. Fields and Karen E. Fields," *Jacobin,* June 29, 2015 https://www.jacobinmag.com/2015/06/karen-barbara-fields-racecraft-dolezal-racism/.

93. Fields and Fields, *Racecraft,* 277–78.

94. See, for example, Fields and Fields, *Racecraft,* 27, on the killing of a Black police officer, Omar Edwards, by a white police officer; Barbara J. Fields and Karen E. Fields, "Did the Color of His Skin Kill Philando Castille?," *Jacobin,* July 3, 2016 https://www.jacobinmag.com/2016/07/racecraft-barbara-karen-fields-philando-castile.

95. Fields and Fields, *Racecraft,* 283.

96. Fields and Fields, *Racecraft,* 268; Fields and Fields, "How Race Is Conjured."

97. Fields and Fields, *Racecraft,* 269, 272. This formulation resonates with Barbara J. Fields's earlier argument that "class and race are concepts of a different order,"

and therefore cannot be treated as "variables" in an explanation of American society. Class, Fields argues, has an "objective core" that race—a "purely ideological notion"—does not. Barbara J. Fields, "Ideology and Race in American History," in *Region, Race, and Reconstruction: Essays in Honor of C. Vann Woodward*, ed. J. Morgan Kausser and James M. McPherson (New York: Oxford University Press, 1982), 150–51.

98. Fields and Fields, *Racecraft*, 270. They allege that racecraft works "to the disadvantage of all working Americans, not just black or white ones" (289).

99. Fields and Fields, *Racecraft*, 269. See also 12, 286 on the lack of a meaningful language in the United States for talking about class inequality.

100. Frank Wilderson III, "The Black Liberation Army and the Paradox of Political Engagement," April 2014. https://illwill.com/the-black-liberation-army-the-paradox-of-political-engagement; Wilderson, "Gramsci's Black Marx," 231. Here Wilderson criticizes the tendency to treat white supremacy as a "derivative phenomenon of the capitalist matrix" and suggests that we should "think white supremacy as the base" (231, 225).

101. Frank Wilderson III, *Afropessimism* (New York: W. W. Norton & Co. 2020) asks, "Why must the world find its nourishment in Black flesh?" (15).

102. Frank Wilderson III, "Afro-Pessimism and the End of Redemption," Franklin Humanities Institute, 2016. https://humanitiesfutures.org/papers/afro-pessimism-end-redemption/. Frank Wilderson III, *Red, White, & Black: Cinema and the Structure of U.S. Antagonisms* (Durham, NC: Duke University Press, 2010).

103. Wilderson, *Red, White, & Black*, 9.

104. Wilderson, *Afropessimism*, 174. In an interview, Wilderson makes this point in slightly different terms, stating, "We, Afropessimists, believe that the essential antagonism is not between workers and bosses but between the Humans and the Blacks." Zamansele Nsele, Interview with Frank Wilderson III, "Part I: 'Afropessimism' and the Rituals of Anti-Black Violence," *Mail & Guardian*, June 24, 2020. https://mg.co.za/article/2020-06-24-frank-b-wilderson-afropessimism-memoir-structural-violence/.

105. The list of "degraded human entities" is from Wilderson, "Afro-Pessimism and the End of Redemption." Other quotes are from Wilderson, *Red, White, & Black*, 9. In that book, he writes of an "unbridgeable gap between Black being and Human life" (57).

106. Wilderson, "The Black Liberation Army." See also Wilderson, *Afropessimism*, 216.

107. Wilderson, "Gramsci's Black Marx," 229.

108. This is a prominent, recurring claim within Wilderson's oeuvre. He writes in his 2020 book *Afropessimism* that "Human life is dependent on Black death for its existence and for its coherence" (42).

109. Nsele, Interview with Frank Wilderson III, "Part I." Wilderson contends that the "pleasure of maiming Black bodies" generates a division between "two species: Blacks and Humans" (*Afropessimism*, 209).

110. Wilderson, *Afropessimism*, 224.

111. In prior writings, Wilderson addressed anti-Black oppression as part of "white supremacy" but later began to differentiate the two. For the earlier conceptualization, see Wilderson, "Gramsci's Black Marx," and Wilderson, "The Black Liberation Army." For the more recent schema, see Wilderson, "Afro-Pessimism and the End of Redemption," and Zamansele Nsele, Interview with Frank Wilderson III, "Part II: 'Afropessimism' and the Rituals of Anti-Black Violence," *Mail & Guardian,* June 27, 2020. https://mg.co.za/friday/2020-06-27-part-ii-afropessimism-and-the-rituals-of-anti-black-violence/.

112. Zamansele Nsele, Interview with Frank Wilderson III, "Part II." See also Wilderson, "Afro-Pessimism and the End of Redemption," and Wilderson, *Afropessimism,* 216–22.

113. Wilderson, *Afropessimism,* 219.

114. Wilderson, *Afropessimism,* 92. In earlier work, Wilderson conceptualized *white* life as dependent on anti-Blackness, but in more recent work, it is *human* life as such that is "dependent on Black death for its existence and coherence." In this latter rendering "human" includes both "white" and "non-Black" persons.

115. Wilderson, *Afropessimism,* 15, 92, 219–20. Wilderson writes, "Unlike violence against the working class, which secures an economic order, or violence against non-Black women, which secures a patriarchal order, or violence against Native Americans, which secures a colonial order, the jouissance that constitutes the violence of anti-Blackness secures the order of life itself; sadism in the service of the prolongation of life" (92).

116. Angela Davis, "Masked Racism: Reflections on the Prison Industrial Complex," *Colorlines,* Sept. 10, 1998. https://www.colorlines.com/articles/masked-racism-reflections-prison-industrial-complex.

See also Ruth Gilmore, "From the Military Industrial Complex to the Prison Industrial Complex," *Recording Carceral Landscapes,* Creative Commons, May 2005. https://pointsforponder.files.wordpress.com/2012/10/gilmore-nd2.pdf. Davis says of the "military industrial complex" and the "prison industrial complex": both "earn profit while producing the means to maim and kill human beings and devour social resources." Angela Davis, *Abolition Democracy: Beyond Empire, Prisons, and Torture* (New York: Seven Stories Press, 2005), 39. Although Gilmore, along with Davis, helped popularize the term "prison industrial complex," she also warns that although it was meant to be "conceptually expansive," over time its effect has been to limit "imaginative understanding of the system's apparent boundless boundary-making." Gilmore suggests that "carceral geographies" is preferable for directing attention to what "abolition is all about." Ruth Wilson Gilmore, "Abolition Geography and the Problem of Innocence," in *Futures of Black Radicalism* (London: Verso, 2017), 231.

117. Davis, "Masked Racism."

118. Angela Davis, *Are Prisons Obsolete?* (New York: Seven Stories Press, 2003), 91. Davis also describes "colored bodies" as the "main human raw material" by which prisons generate profits ("Masked Racism").

119. Davis, *Are Prisons Obsolete?*, 84, 95.

120. Gilmore, "Abolition Geography," 228. Gilmore develops this account in detail in the context of California in Ruth Gilmore, *Golden Gulag: Prisons, Surplus, Crisis, and Opposition in Globalizing California* (Berkeley: University of California Press, 2007).

121. Gilmore, "Abolition Geography," 228.

122. Angela Davis, *The Meaning of Freedom: And Other Difficult Dialogues* (San Francisco: City Lights Publishers, 2012), 50.

123. Davis, *Are Prisons Obsolete?*, 84.

124. Gilmore, *Golden Gulag*, 243. Gilmore is critical of the tendency to misrepresent mass incarceration as "something that only Black people experience" because this inaccurate rendering means "the necessary connection to be drawn from mass incarceration to the entire organization of capitalist space today falls out of the picture." Clément Petitjean, "Prisons and Class Warfare: An Interview with Ruth Wilson Gilmore," Aug. 2, 2018. https://www.versobooks.com/blogs/3954-prisons-and-class-warfare-an-interview-with-ruth-wilson-gilmore. See also Gilmore, "Abolition Geography," 234.

125. Jared Sexton, *Amalgamation Schemes: Antiblackness and the Critique of Multiracialism* (Minneapolis: University of Minnesota Press, 2005), 22.

126. Steve Martinot and Jared Sexton, "The Avant-Garde of White Supremacy," *Social Identities* 9, no. 2 (2003): 179.

127. Martinot and Sexton, "The Avant-Garde," 179.

128. Jared Sexton, "Racial Profiling and the Societies of Control," in *Warfare in the American Homeland: Policing and Prison in a Penal Democracy*, ed. Joy James (Durham, NC: Duke University Press, 2007), 210.

129. Michael Rogin, "American Political Demonology: A Retrospective," in *Ronald Reagan, The Movie, and Other Episodes in Political Demonology* (Berkeley: University of California Press, 1987), 277.

130. Du Bois, "The White World," 65.

131. Du Bois, "Apologia" (1954). http://www.webdubois.org/dbSAST-Apologia.html.

Chapter 4

1. An exception is Shannon Sullivan, *Revealing Whiteness: The Unconscious Habits of White Privilege* (Bloomington: Indiana University Press, 2006), Ch. 5.

2. W. E. B. Du Bois, "The Souls of White Folk," in *Darkwater: Voices from Within the Veil* (Oxford: Oxford University Press, 2007 [1920]), 15–25. This essay draws on two prior essays: "The Souls of White Folk," *The Independent* (Aug. 18, 1910): 339–42 and "Of the Culture of White Folk," *Journal of Race Development* 7, no. 4 (April 1917): 434–47.

3. Du Bois, "Souls of White Folk," 15.

4. Du Bois, "Souls of White Folk," 15–16.

5. Du Bois, "Souls of White Folk," 16.

6. Du Bois, "Souls of White Folk," 16, 18, 17.

7. Du Bois, "Souls of White Folk," 22.
8. On the centrality of slavery to the development of modern capitalism, see W. E. B. Du Bois, *Black Reconstruction in America: An Essay Toward a History of the Part Which Black Folk Played in the Attempt to Reconstruct Democracy in America, 1860–1880* (Oxford: Oxford University Press, 2007 [1935]), Ch. 1.
9. Du Bois, *Black Reconstruction*, 8. On Du Bois's understanding of the "present-past" as the condition of politics, see Lawrie Balfour, *Democracy's Reconstruction: Thinking Politically with W. E. B. Du Bois* (Oxford: Oxford University Press, 2011), Ch. 1.
10. Du Bois, *Black Reconstruction*, 7.
11. Du Bois, *Black Reconstruction*, 6.
12. Du Bois, *Black Reconstruction*, 8. He continues, "Negroes could be sold—actually sold as we sell cattle with no reference to calves or bulls, or recognition of family."
13. Walter Johnson, *Soul by Soul: Life Inside the Antebellum Slave Market* (Cambridge, MA: Harvard University Press, 1999).
14. The fugitive slave was paradoxically positioned in law as both property and person. As Saidiya Hartman explains, this duality defined enslavement broadly. Slaves were legally recognized as "absolutely subject to the will of another" *and* as "actional subjects" in the restricted sense of bearing criminal culpability. Saidiya Hartman, *Scenes of Subjection: Terror, Slavery, and Self-Making in 19th Century America* (Oxford: Oxford University Press, 1997), 80. See also Hortense Spillers, "Mama's Baby, Papa's Maybe: An American Grammar Book," *Diacritics* 17, no. 2 (1987): 64–81 on the "uneasy oxymoronic character" of slave codes that attempted to transform "*personality* into *property*" (78–79). I would add that this oxymoronic duality is evident in the US Constitution's fugitive slave clause (Article IV, Section II), which cast persons "held in service or labor" as simultaneously criminal agents (lawbreakers) and objects (property to be returned to their rightful owners). Stephen Best makes a similar point regarding the Fugitive Slave Law of 1850, noting that the law figured the fugitive as "pilfered property and indebted person, object of property and subject of contract." Stephen Best, *The Fugitive's Properties: Law and the Poetics of Possession* (Chicago: University of Chicago Press, 2004), 9.
15. Frederick Douglas, Address to the Massachusetts Anti-Slavery Society, quoted in *The Liberator* XII, no. 7 (February 18, 1842): 26. http://fair-use.org/the-liberator/1842/02/18/the-liberator-12-07.pdf
16. Du Bois, *Black Reconstruction*, 8–9.
17. Du Bois, *Black Reconstruction*, 136.
18. Du Bois, *Black Reconstruction*, 111.
19. Cheryl Harris, "Whiteness as Property," *Harvard Law Review* 106, no. 8 (June 1993): 1720.
20. Saidiya Hartman notes, "Slaves were subjected to the absolute control and authority of any and every member of the dominant race . . . Chattel slavery enhanced whiteness by granting all whites, not just slaveowners, dominion over blacks" (*Scenes of Subjection*, 119).
21. Du Bois, "Souls of White Folk," 15.
22. Du Bois, "Souls of White Folk," 15.

23. C. Vann Woodward, "The Price of Freedom," in *What Was Freedom's Price?*, ed. David Sansing (Columbia: University Press of Missouri, 1978), 93–113.

24. Du Bois, "Souls of White Folk," 16.

25. W. E. B. Du Bois, "The Hands of Ethiopia," in *Darkwater*, 35; Du Bois, "Souls of White Folk," 25.

26. Harris, "Whiteness as Property," 1713, 1745. George Lipsitz also theorizes whiteness as a form of property or a collection of assets. George Lipsitz, *The Possessive Investment in Whiteness* (Philadelphia: Temple University Press, 1998).

27. Harris, "Whiteness as Property," 1731, 1734.

28. Harris, "Whiteness as Property," 1736.

29. Harris, "Whiteness as Property," 1724.

30. Derrick Bell, "White Superiority in America: Its Legal Legacy, Its Economic Costs," *Villanova Law Review* 33 (1988): 773.

31. Harris, "Whiteness as Property," 1741.

32. Joel Olson, "W. E. B. Du Bois and the Race Concept," *Souls* 7, no. 3–4 (2005): 118–28.

33. W. E. B. Du Bois, "The White World," in *Dusk of Dawn: An Essay Toward an Autobiography of the Race Concept* (Oxford: Oxford University Press, 2007 [1940]), 69.

34. Harris, "Whiteness as Property," 1720.

35. Du Bois, "The Concept of Race," in *Dusk of Dawn*, 59.

36. Du Bois, *Black Reconstruction,* 574. Du Bois's invocation of the "badges" of race and the "sign of slavery" references and challenges the 1883 Civil Rights Cases and *Plessy v. Ferguson* (1896), which denied that segregation functioned as a "badge of slavery" and "badge of inferiority," respectively.

37. Although my reading here emphasizes Du Bois's account of how the sign "black" is deployed to enforce white supremacy, any reader of Du Bois knows that his work also offers a powerful celebration of Black existence. His characterization of Blackness, then, is not simply negative. Although he rejects the reigning "system of marks" that degrades those bearing the sign "black," his vast body of work consistently affirms and even reveres Black people and their distinctive "gifts." See especially *The Souls of Black Folk* (Oxford: Oxford University Press, 2007 [1903]); *The Gift of Black Folk: The Negroes in the Making of America* (Oxford: Oxford University Press, 2014 [1924]); *Black Reconstruction*. On this feature of Du Bois's work, see Balfour, *Democracy's Reconstruction,* Ch. 2; John Shuford, "Four Du Boisean Contributions to Critical Race Theory," *Transactions of the Charles S. Peirce Society* 37, no. 3 (2001): 301–37; Sullivan, *Revealing Whiteness,* Ch. 5.

38. Du Bois, "The Concept of Race," 59.

39. Du Bois, "The White World," 69. Italics mine.

40. Du Bois, "The White World," 77.

41. Du Bois, "Souls of White Folk," 25. Addressing how the "national 'we'" has been reshaped over time, Nikhil Pal Singh writes, "The question remains, how does this process work—or does it—for groups who have remained more durably caught within the world-system of racial marks, particularly people of African descent?" Singh, *Black Is a Country: Race and the Unfinished Struggle for Democracy* (Cambridge, MA: Harvard University Press, 2004), 21.

42. Du Bois, "'The Servant in the House,'" in *Darkwater*, 56. Du Bois also writes that Negro servants wear "this hateful badge of slavery" (54).

43. Hartman, *Scenes of Subjection*, 119. Du Bois's attention to "signs" and "badges" resonates with Anthony Paul Farley's theorization of race as an enduring "system of marks" established under slavery to divide the "otherwise common flesh of the human" into "owners and owned." Anthony Paul Farley, "The Apogee of the Commodity," *DePaul Law Review* 53 (2003–04): 1231.

44. Balfour, *Democracy's Reconstruction*, 115; Du Bois, *The Souls of Black Folk*, 8. "The Color Line Belts the World" is the title of an essay by Du Bois published in *Collier's* (Oct. 20, 1906).

45. "Global orientation" is from Balfour, *Democracy's Reconstruction*, 117. See Singh, *Black Is a Country*, Ch. 3, on Du Bois's role in the growth of Black internationalism during and after World War II. Du Bois's famous 1946 *An Appeal to the World* explicitly casts African Americans' struggle for civil rights as part of a worldwide quest for the protection of minorities' human rights.

46. W. E. B. Du Bois, "The African Roots of War," *The Atlantic*, May 1915. https://www.theatlantic.com/magazine/archive/1915/05/the-african-roots-of-war/528897/. Du Bois's 1915 essay anticipates the *Darkwater* essays addressed here, especially "The Souls of White Folk" and "The Hands of Ethiopia" and their shared analysis of white dominion. In "The African Roots of War," Du Bois depicts the "undisguised robbery of the land of 7 million natives" as part of a sweeping racial-colonial capitalist project. He interprets the "current war" in these terms as well: "the ownership of materials and men in the darker world is the real prize that is setting the nations of Europe at each other's throats to-day."

47. Charles Mills, "The Racial Polity," in *Blackness Visible: Essays on Philosophy and Race* (Ithaca: Cornell University Press, 1998), 126. Mills says that the commitment to analyzing race "at the global level" is a hallmark of the "oppositional black tradition," running from Martin Delaney to Du Bois and C. L. R. James to Frantz Fanon.

48. Du Bois, "Souls of White Folk," 22. In a 1944 paper, Du Bois wrote that "Negroes in the United States" were living in a "semicolonial" situation. "Colonialism, Democracy, and Peace After the War," in W. E. B. Du Bois, *Against Racism: Unpublished Essays, Papers, Addresses* (Amherst: University of Massachusetts Press, 1985), 229.

49. Balfour, *Democracy's Reconstruction*, Ch. 6; Juliet Hooker, *Theorizing Race in the Americas: Douglass, Sarmiento, Du Bois and Vasconcelos* (Oxford: Oxford University Press, 2017), Ch. 3; Reiland Rabaka, "The Souls of White Folk: W. E. B. Du Bois's Critique of White Supremacy and Contributions to Critical White Studies," *Journal of African American Studies* 11 (2007): 1–15; Robinson, *Black Marxism*, Ch. 9; Singh, *Black Is a Country*; Inés Valdez, *Transnational Cosmopolitanism: Kant, Du Bois, and Justice as a Political Craft* (Cambridge: Cambridge University Press, 2019).

50. Du Bois, "Souls of White Folk," 20.

51. Du Bois, "Souls of White Folk," 21.

52. Du Bois's responses to the First World War were notoriously mixed. Despite his scathing account of the war in 1915's "The African Roots of War" and his longtime anti-war activism, in July 1918 Du Bois called on Black Americans "to close ranks"

in support of the US military effort in an infamous essay published in *The Crisis*. His hope that Black Americans' participation in the conflict would secure them an undeniable claim to full inclusion in the US society and polity was dashed, however, by continued segregation of the US Armed Forces and white racist violence in US cities. (Du Bois participated in the 1917 Silent Parade in New York, which protested the anti-Black riots in East St. Louis. Protesters highlighted the hypocrisy of the United States, carrying signs that called on President Wilson to "Make America Safe for Democracy.") By the time of *Darkwater*'s publication in 1920, Du Bois's condemnation of the war as a racist-colonialist "nightmare" was unwavering.

53. Du Bois, "Souls of White Folk," 19.

54. Du Bois, "Souls of White Folk," 19. Alberto Toscano notes that Du Bois's claim, also made earlier in "The African Roots of War," articulates what would be a "founding tenet of much anti-colonial critique (most eloquently in Césaire's *Discourse on Colonialism*) . . . [T]he war represented the return onto (white) European soil of the systematic violence and repression that had thereto taken place on the other side of the geographical colour line—in the colonies, among 'the savages.' This was the boomerang effect of imperialism." Alberto Toscano, "'America's Belgium': W. E. B. Du Bois on Race, Class, and the Origins of World War I," in *Cataclysm 1914: The First World War and the Making of Modern World Politics,* ed. Alexander Anievas (Leiden: Brill, 2015), 237.

55. Du Bois, "Souls of White Folk," 19.

56. Du Bois, "Souls of White Folk," 23.

57. Du Bois, "Souls of White Folk," 21. This statement is echoed in the penultimate paragraph of *Black Reconstruction* (596).

58. John Carlos Rowe makes this point in *Literary Culture and US Imperialism: From the Revolution to WWII* (Oxford: Oxford University Press, 2000), 203–4.

59. David Luis-Brown, *Waves of Decolonization: Discourses of Race and Hemispheric Citizenship in Cuba, Mexico, and the United States* (Durham, NC: Duke University Press, 2008), 70.

60. Adom Getachew, *Worldmaking After Empire: The Rise and Fall of Self-Determination* (Princeton, NJ: Princeton University Press, 2019), Ch. 3. Getachew shows that the empire-as-enslavement framing was advanced by key anti-colonial figures in the 20th century—including Du Bois as well as George Padmore and Kwame Nkrumah (79–87).

61. Du Bois, "Hands of Ethiopia," 29.

62. Du Bois, "Hands of Ethiopia," 31.

63. Du Bois, *Black Reconstruction*, 6.

64. Robinson writes in *Black Marxism*, "For Du Bois, America in the first half of the 19th century, a society in which manufacturing and industrial capitalism had been married to slave production, had been a microcosm of the world system." It was a "forewarning" (239).

65. Getachew, *Worldmaking After Empire*, 80.

66. Du Bois, "Souls of White Folk," 21.

67. Du Bois, "Souls of White Folk," 21. See also his earlier "The African Roots of War" on this point.

68. Du Bois, "Souls of White Folk," 23.

69. This feature of Du Bois's analysis complicates Getachew's claim that "the anticolonial emphasis on slavery"—to which Du Bois contributed—"ignored the problem of dispossession so central to settler colonial formations" (*Worldmaking After Empire*, 86). In the case of Du Bois, his empire-as-enslavement framing emphasized labor exploitation but did not "ignore" dispossession as a distinctive form of injustice. Or at least, this is the case in his treatment of Africa. (As I discuss in this chapter, Du Bois overlooks the settler colonial character of the United States entirely and even contributes to Indigenous erasure in his representations of "land" in *Black Reconstruction*.)

70. Du Bois, "Hands of Ethiopia," 22, 23.

71. Du Bois, "Hands of Ethiopia," 29. Du Bois's treatment of African colonization resonates with Robin D. G. Kelley's description of the same phenomenon: "They wanted the land *and* the labor, but not the *people*—that is to say, they sought to eliminate stable communities and their structures of resistance." Robin D. G. Kelley, "The Rest of Us: Rethinking Settler and Native," *American Quarterly* 69, no. 2 (June 2017): 269.

72. Glen Coulthard argues that Marx's account of primitive accumulation—with its emphasis on the violent appropriation of land—is important because it "links the totalizing power of *capital* to that of *colonialism*." Glen Coulthard, *Red Skin, White Masks: Rejecting the Colonial Politics of Recognition* (Minneapolis: University of Minnesota Press, 2014), 7.

73. Robert Nichols, "Disaggregating Primitive Accumulation," *Radical Philosophy* 194 (November/December 2015): 21; Onur Ulas Ince, "Primitive Accumulation and Global Land Grabs," *Rural Sociology* 79, no. 1 (2014): 104–31.

74. Rosa Luxemburg, *The Accumulation of Capital*, trans. Agnes Schwarzschild (London: Routledge and Kegan Paul, 1951 [1913]), 185, 294, 452.

75. Du Bois, "Hands of Ethiopia," 29; Du Bois, "Souls of White Folk," 22.

76. Toscano, "'America's Belgium,'" 237.

77. Siddhant Issar, "Theorising 'Racial/Colonial Primitive Accumulation': Settler Colonialism, Slavery and Racial Capitalism," *Race & Class* 63, no. 1 (2021): 23–50.

78. Du Bois, "Souls of White Folk," 23, 24.

79. Du Bois, "Souls of White Folk," 22.

80. Aileen Moreton-Robinson, *The White Possessive: Property, Power, and Indigenous Sovereignty* (Minneapolis: University of Minnesota Press, 2015), 50–53. Harris, "Whiteness as Property."

81. Du Bois, "Hands of Ethiopia," 29; Patrick Wolfe, "Settler Colonialism and the Elimination of the Native," *Journal of Genocide Research* 8, no. 4 (2006): 387–409.

82. Du Bois thus captures the reality of settler colonialism in Africa, a phenomenon that is overlooked in Patrick Wolfe's influential account, according to Kelley, "The Rest of Us," 268–69.

83. Du Bois, *Black Reconstruction*, 54.

84. Du Bois, *Black Reconstruction,* 494. See also 323, 493.

85. Du Bois, *Black Reconstruction*, 493.

86. Moreton-Robinson, *The White Possessive*, 51.

87. Du Bois, *Black Reconstruction,* refers often to the abundance of "free" and "unoccupied" land in America (2, 3, 14, 15, 224). The reference to "endless land" quoted here appears on p. 23. Tacuma Peters, "Revisiting *Black Reconstruction*: Chattel Slavery, Native Lands, and the Color Line" (paper, Western Political Science Association meeting, Vancouver, BC, 2017) explores the erasure of Indigenous people and lands in Du Bois's *Black Reconstruction.*

88. Du Bois, *Black Reconstruction,* 15.

89. Du Bois, "Souls of White Folk," 23, 20, 21.

90. Du Bois, "Souls of White Folk," 21, 23.

91. Du Bois, "Souls of White Folk," 16, 22.

92. Du Bois, "Souls of White Folk," 23, 25.

93. Du Bois, "Souls of White Folk," 24.

94. In an early essay, Du Bois writes of an "eleventh" commandment that declares, "Though shalt not Cross the [Color] Line" and notes that while people break other commandments with little consequence, "when the eleventh is broken, *the world heaves.*" W. E. B. Du Bois, "The Development of a People [1904]," *Ethics* 123, no. 3 (April 2013): 530. For the purposes of this discussion, I bracket the question of Du Bois's personal religious beliefs, the answer to which is much disputed, with major scholars including David Levering Lewis and Manning Marable taking opposing views (depicting Du Bois as plainly irreligious and as devoted to traditional Black Christianity, respectively). Regardless, I agree with Anthony B. Pinn's assessment that the significance of "Du Bois's thinking on and use of religion" does not depend upon his personal religious beliefs. Anthony B. Pinn, "Reading Du Bois Through Religion and Religious Commitment," *Journal of Religion* 94, no. 3 (July 2014): 382.

95. J. R. Kerr-Ritchie notes that many scholars have recognized "Du Bois's dichotomous treatment of white and black religion." J. R. Kerr-Ritchie, "Review of Edward J. Blum, *W. E. B. Du Bois: American Prophet,*" *Journal of African American History* 94, no. 1 (Winter 2009): 124. For important analyses of both strains of Du Bois's thought, see Edward J. Blum, *W. E. B. Du Bois: American Prophet* (Philadelphia: University of Pennsylvania Press, 2007); Pinn, "Reading Du Bois"; Phillip Luke Sinitiere, "W. E. B. Du Bois's Prophetic Propaganda: Religion and *The Crisis* 1910–1934," in *Protest and Propaganda: W. E. B. Du Bois, the Crisis and American History,* ed. Amy Helene Kirschke and Phillip Luke Sinitiere (University of Missouri Press, 2019), 190–207. These works explore how Du Bois consistently condemned the white Christian church for its role in maintaining racial caste, even as he also articulated a distinctive version of Black Christianity—replete with a Black Christ and Black God—that offered a redemptive vision of Black existence and was meant to serve as a "public vehicle for transformation" (Pinn, "Reading Du Bois," 372). An important element in this reimagining was Du Bois's "countercreation" of a Black Christ living in the contemporary United States. He wrote many narratives of this type, including *Darkwater*'s "Jesus Christ in Texas" and dozens of pieces published in *The Crisis.* On

the significance of this figure, particularly in relation to the practice of lynching, see Blum, *American Prophet*, Ch. 4, and Sinitiere, "Prophetic Propaganda." Blum argues that Du Bois's development of a "countertheology"—especially one that linked Christ's crucifixion to the lynching of Black men—"presaged the black liberation theological revolution of the late 60s" (139). The key work of Black liberation theology that explores biblical symbols in relation to racial violence is James H. Cone, *The Cross and the Lynching Tree* (Maryknoll, NY: Orbis Books, 2011).

96. This is a relatively unexplored dimension of Du Bois's thought, although Edward J. Blum's *American Prophet* addresses Du Bois's challenge to the "theology of white supremacy" (8; see also Ch. 3). Blum's central concept, however—what he calls a "spiritual wage of whiteness"—implies a more self-conscious, transactional relationship than is consistent with the workings of a comprehensive cosmology.

97. William Connolly, *Pluralism* (Durham, NC: Duke University Press, 2005), 25–27.

98. "Horizon of white perception" is from Judith Butler, "Endangered/ Endangering: Schematic Racism and Racial Paranoia," in *Reading Rodney King, Reading Urban Uprising*, ed. Robert Gooding-Williams (New York: Routledge, 1993), 16.

99. Toni Morrison, *Playing in the Dark: Whiteness and the Literary Imagination* (New York: Vintage Books, 1992); George Yancy, *Black Bodies, White Gazes: The Continuing Significance of Race* (Lanham, MD: Rowman & Littlefield, 2008); Claudia Rankine's Racial Imaginary Institute, https://theracialimagin ary.org; Joe Feagin, *The White Racial Frame: Centuries of Racial Framing and Counter-Framing* (New York: Taylor & Francis, 2009); Charles W. Mills, "White Ignorance," in *Race and Epistemologies of Ignorance*, ed. Shannon Sullivan and Nancy Tuana (Ithaca: State University of New York Press, 2007), 13–38 and "Global White Ignorance," in *Routledge International Handbook of Ignorance Studies* (New York: Taylor and Francis, 2015), 217–27. Mills's important and influential writings depict this racialized "optic" or worldview as a matter of "white ignorance" (see Ch. 1). I cannot adequately address that argument here but would point out that Mills adopts a more epistemological approach than does Du Bois. Although Du Bois and Mills both characterize a particular white interpretive schema as delusional and fantastical, Du Bois presents whiteness less as a form of "non-knowing" or a "particular cognitive orientation" (Mills) and more as a lived faith or ethos.

100. Frantz Fanon, *Black Skin, White Masks*, trans. Richard Philcox (New York: Grove Press, 2008 [1952]).

101. Fanon's analysis of a "historico-racial schema" that casts Black persons as "being for others" includes a passage that presents the "white gaze" as specifically proprietary: "The white man wants the world; he wants it for himself. He discovers he is the predestined master of the world. He enslaves it. His relationship with the world is one of appropriation" (*Black Skin, White Masks*, 107).

102. Du Bois, "Souls of White Folk," 23.

103. Benjamin Wallace-Wells, "Why the Bundys and Their Heavily Armed Supporters Keep Getting Away with It," *New Yorker*, Aug. 25, 2017. https://www.newyorker.

com/news/news-desk/why-the-bundys-and-their-heavily-armed-supporters-keep-getting-away-with-it.

104. Wallace-Wells, "Why the Bundys."

105. Wallace-Wells, "Why the Bundys." Even the defense attorneys could not believe what had happened. "I'm speechless," Robert Salisbury, a defense attorney for one of the accused Bundy conspirators, said at the time. "It's a stunning victory."

106. Kirk Siegler, "Roots of US Capitol Insurrectionists Run Through American West," NPR, Jan. 12, 2021. https://www.npr.org/2021/01/12/955665162/roots-of-u-s-capitol-insurrectionists-run-through-american-west. In 2020, a federal appeals court upheld the dismissal of the case.

107. This is a worldview seemingly shared not just by the Bundys and their direct and indirect supporters but also by the judge and juries who repeatedly sanctioned their actions.

108. Joshua F. J. Inwood and Anne Bonds, "Property and Whiteness: The Oregon Standoff and the Contradictions of the US Settler State," *Space and Polity* 21, no. 3 (2017): 254.

109. Wolfe, "Settler Colonialism"; Moreton-Robinson, *The White Possessive*.

110. Dan Hernandez and Joseph Langdon. "Federal Rangers Face Off Against Armed Protesters in Nevada 'Range War,'" *The Guardian*, April 13, 2014. Bundy's family began grazing cattle there years after the Bureau of Land Management was established. Jacqueline Keeler, "On Calvin Bundy's 'Ancestral Rights,'" *The Nation*, April 29, 2014.

111. Inwood and Bonds, "Property and Whiteness," 262. The description of Manifest Destiny ideology comes from Matthew Baigell, "Territory, Race, Religion: Images of Manifest Destiny," *Smithsonian Studies in American Art* 4, no. 3/4 (1990): 7.

112. Anne Bonds and Joshua Inwood, "Beyond White Privilege: Geographies of White Supremacy and Settler Colonialism," *Progress in Human Geography* 40, no. 6 (2016): 725.

113. Keeler, "On Calvin Bundy's 'Ancestral Rights.'"

114. Bonds and Inwood, "Beyond White Privilege," 726.

115. Jedediah Purdy, "The Bundys and the Irony of American Vigilantism," *New Yorker*, Jan. 5, 2016, describes anti-Blackness and anti-Indigeneity as "the twin American ideologies" animating the Bundy case.

116. Bundy said, "And because they were basically on government subsidy, so now what do they do? They abort their young children, they put their young men in jail, because they never learned how to pick cotton." Adam Nagourney, "A Defiant Rancher Savors the Audience That Rallied to His Side," *New York Times*, April 24, 2014. https://www.nytimes.com/2014/04/24/us/politics/rancher-proudly-breaks-the-law-becoming-a-hero-in-the-west.html.

Several commentators noted that whiteness was central to the occupiers' self-understanding and the reception they received. Jamelle Bouie, "What If Bundy Ranch Were Owned by a Bunch of Black People?," *Slate*, April 15, 2014. https://www.nytimes.com/2014/04/24/us/politics/rancher-proudly-breaks-the-law-becoming-a-hero-in-the-west.html; Ta-Nehisi Coates, "Cliven Bundy and the Tyranny All

.Around Us," *The Atlantic,* April 22, 2014. https://www.theatlantic.com/politics/arch ive/2014/04/clive-bundy-and-the-tyranny-all-around-us/361039/.

117. Inwood and Bonds, "Property and Whiteness," 256.

118. Inwood and Bonds, "Property and Whiteness," 254, 263, 258.

119. Inwood and Bonds, "Property and Whiteness" offers further historical context.

120. Inwood and Bonds, "Property and Whiteness," 259.

121. Bonds and Inwood, "Beyond White Privilege," 725.

122. Taja-Nia Y. Henderson and Jamila Jefferson-Jones, "#LivingWhileBlack: Blackness as Nuisance," *American University Law Review* 69, no. 3 (2020): 863. Chan Tov McNamarah, "White Caller Crime: Racialized Police Communication and Existing While Black," *Michigan Journal of Race and Law* 24 (2019): 335–415 distinguishes between two kinds of "racialized police communication": "racially motivated" calls are made when behavior that wouldn't be considered suspicious for a white person is reported due to the person's race; "racially weaponized" calls are when the caller exaggerates behavior because they know an outsized police response can cause a Black person harm. McNamarah points out that white calls to police to report on the normal activities of Black people have played a prominent role in landmark Supreme Court cases. *Loving v. Virginia* (1967), the case that struck down anti-miscegenation laws, "was instigated when a White neighbor called the police to anonymously report their neighbors' interracial relationship." *Lawrence v. Texas* (2003), which struck down anti-homosexuality laws, began when a white man, angered that his partner was sleeping with another man, who was Black, called police and "falsely reported that 'a Black man was going crazy with a gun' at their apartment" (345–46).

123. These are examples compiled from news coverage. McNamarah, "White Caller Crime," notes, "At the time of this writing LexisNexis and WestLaw searches have no results for persons criminally prosecuted for false or exaggerated reports to the police against Black Americans" (342n36). The appendix to McNamarah's article catalogs 92 reported cases of "racialized police communication" regarding ordinary activities by Black people in the year 2018 (399–415). Henderson and Jefferson-Jones, "#LivingWhileBlack" also cites multiple cases and discusses several in detail.

124. Henderson and Jefferson-Jones, "#LivingWhileBlack," 863. #LivingWhileBlack is to be continually vulnerable—not only to the harassment or humiliation evident in these examples of "white caller crime," but also to fatal police and vigilante violence as well. Claudia Rankine captures the precarity that infuses the ordinary activities of Black Americans: "Though the white liberal imagination likes to feel temporarily bad about Black suffering, there really is no mode of empathy that can replicate the daily strain of knowing that as a Black person you can be killed for simply being Black: no hands in your pockets, no playing music, no sudden movements, no driving your car, no walking at night, no walking in the day, no turning onto this street, no entering this building, no standing your ground, no standing here, no standing there, no talking back, no playing with toy guns, no living while black." Claudia Rankine, "The Condition of Black Life Is One of Mourning," *New York Times,* June 22, 2015. https://www.nytimes.com/2015/06/22/magazine/the-condit ion-of-black-life-is-one-of-mourning.html.

125. Michael Harriot, "White Caller Crime: The Worst Wypipo Police Calls of All Time," *The Root*, May 15, 2018. https://www.theroot.com/white-caller-crime-the-worst-wypipo-police-calls-of-1826023382.

126. Junia Howell, Marie Skoczylas, and Shatae DeVaughn. "Living While Black," *American Sociological Association Contexts* 18, no. 2 (2019): 68–69.

127. Michael Andor Brodeur, "Our Memes, Ourselves: The Year in Things," *Boston Globe*, Dec. 23, 2018. https://www.bostonglobe.com/arts/2018/12/20/our-memes-our-sel ves-year-things/MtTpjtyap9fejL6eg2YikN/story.html. This list references actual cases, some of which happened more than once. Benjamin Fearnow, "Video: White Woman Calls Police on Black Family's BBQ for 'Trespassing' in Oakland Park," *Newsweek*, May 10, 2018. https://www.newsweek.com/lake-merritt-bbq-barbecue-video-oakland-racist-charcoal-east-bay-black-family-919355 (grilling in park); Sebastian Murdock, "White Woman Threatened to Call Cops on 8-Year-Old Girl Selling Water," *HuffPost*, June 23, 2018. https://www.huffpost.com/entry/white-woman-sees-black-girl-selling-water-allegedly-calls-police_n_5b2e94a5e4b00295f 15cf35f (selling bottled water); Hayley Fowler, "Hampton Inn Worker Calls Police on Black Guests at Hotel Pool in NC, Video Shows," *News & Observer*, June 30, 2020. https://www.newsobserver.com/news/state/north-carolina/article243897702.html (swimming at hotel pool); Eli Rosenberg, "A Black Former White House Staffer Was Moving into a New Apartment. Someone Reported a Burglary," *Washington Post*, May 1, 2018. https://www.washingtonpost.com/news/post-nation/wp/2018/05/ 01/a-black-former-white-house-staffer-was-moving-into-a-new-apartment-some one-reported-a-burglary/?utm_term=.2823dc07c572.11 (moving into apartment); Christina Caron, "A Black Yale Student Was Napping, and a White Student Called the Police," *New York Times*, May 9, 2018. https://www.nytimes.com/2018/05/09/ nyregion/yale-black-student-nap.html (student sleeping in common room).

128. Henderson and Jefferson-Jones, "#LivingWhileBlack." "Third space," a term coined by Ray Oldenburg, describes "a distinctive, informal public gathering place." See Henderson and Jefferson-Jones, "#LivingWhileBlack," 895–97, for discussion of this concept in relation to Starbucks, the site of a well-known incident in which a white Starbucks employee at a Philadelphia shop called the cops on two Black men sitting at a table.

129. Elijah Anderson, "The White Space," *Sociology of Race and Ethnicity* 1, no. 1 (2015): 10–21. Anderson defines white space as a "perceptual category" for Black people. He argues, "White people typically avoid black space, but black people are required to navigate the white space as a condition of their existence" (10). Angela Onwuachi-Willig, "Policing the Boundaries of Whiteness: The Tragedy of Being 'Out of Place' from Emmet Till to Trayvon Martin," *Iowa Law Review* 102, no. 1113 (2017) argues that protecting "white space" has become a key tactic for securing racialized benefits in the post–civil rights era (1156).

130. Elise C. Boddie, "Racial Territoriality," *UCLA Law Review* 58, no. 401 (2010): 433. Boddie is referring to the "spatial system" linking slavery to Jim Crow, which in-volved the physical separation of Blacks and whites across "a seemingly limitless range of institutions." The white perception of a Black person being "out of place"

and the disciplinary responses that attempt to "put them in their place" are also explored in McNamarah, "White Caller Crime," which addresses white callers' reliance on police to "keep black people in their place" (358), and Onwuachi-Willig, "Policing the Boundaries of Whiteness," which connects the murders of Emmett Till and Trayvon Martin through the notion of "being out of place." Anderson, "White Space" talks about a kind of "cognitive dissonance" felt by some whites encountering Blacks in "white space," the response to which is to "try to put the black person 'back in his place'" in the interest of "consonance" (14).

131. Boddie, "Racial Territoriality," 401.

132. Boddie, "Racial Territoriality," 410. Boddie's central example for thinking about this form of discrimination is the barring of a group of Black people (seeking refuge from Hurricane Katrina) from crossing a bridge connecting New Orleans and a predominantly white town, Gretna, in 2005. Boddie persuasively argues that this amounts to an act of discrimination and proposes that anti-discrimination law should "incorporat[e] claims for racial territoriality" (407).

133. Boddie, "Racial Territoriality," 426. Limitations on mobility were not necessarily confined to the South. During the period of slavery in the North, some states imposed physical restrictions on slaves and free Blacks in order to limit the threat of rebellion. On this point, Boddie cites Michael J. Klarman, *Unfinished Business: Racial Equality in American History* (Oxford: Oxford University Press, 2007).

134. Boddie, "Racial Territoriality," 427.

135. Boddie, "Racial Territoriality," 429–30.

136. Henderson and Jefferson-Jones, "#LivingWhileBlack" presents illuminating interpretations of several recent incidents—at Yale University and at two community swimming pools—that connect these encounters, respectively, to the history of racially exclusionary policies at US universities and to the history of swimming pools as sites of "violent efforts to uphold and reinforce racist cultural norms" (881–88).

137. "Spacism" comes from Onwuachi-Willig, "Policing the Boundaries of Whiteness."

138. Henderson and Jefferson-Jones, "#LivingWhileBlack," 870.

139. Henderson and Jefferson-Jones, "#LivingWhileBlack," 872.

140. See Apryl Williams, "Black Memes Matter: #LivingWhileBlack with Becky and Karen," *Social Media and Society,* December 2020 for a smart critical discourse analysis of over 15,000 BBQ Becky–related memes on Twitter. Williams argues that these memes—like other #LivingWhileBlack memes in her database of 89,000—serve as a "cultural critique of White surveillance and White racial dominance" (1).

141. These two cases are discussed in Henderson and Jefferson-Jones, "#LivingWhileBlack," 873–78.

142. Henderson and Jefferson-Jones, "#LivingWhileBlack," 870; see also 863.

Chapter 5

1. W. E. B. Du Bois, "The Souls of White Folk," in *Darkwater: Voices from Within the Veil* (Oxford: Oxford University Press, 2007 [1920]), 22.

2. W. E. B. Du Bois, "The Hands of Ethiopia," in *Darkwater,* 35. Du Bois continues: "One cannot ignore the extraordinary fact that a world campaign beginning with the slave-trade and ending with the refusal to capitalize the word 'Negro,' leading through a passionate defense of slavery by attributing every bestiality to blacks and finally culminating in the evident modern profit which lies in degrading blacks,—all this has unconsciously trained millions of honest, modern men into the belief that black folk are sub-human" (35).

3. W. E. B. Du Bois, *Black Reconstruction in America: An Essay Toward a History of the Part Which Black Folk Played in the Attempt to Reconstruct Democracy in America, 1860–1880* (Oxford: Oxford University Press, 2007 [1935]), 584, 587.

4. Du Bois, *Black Reconstruction,* 582–83.

5. Du Bois, *Black Reconstruction,* 595.

6. Du Bois, "Hands of Ethiopia," 35.

7. W. E. B. Du Bois, "The Colored World Within," in *Dusk of Dawn: An Essay Toward an Autobiography of the Race Concept* (Oxford: Oxford University Press, 2007 [1940]), 97.

8. W. E. B. Du Bois, "Science and Empire," in *Dusk of Dawn,* 47.

9. W. E. B. Du Bois, "Propaganda and World War," in *Dusk of Dawn,* 114. On the "vanguard role" played by Black periodical culture in combatting white supremacist thought in the 20th century, see Bill V. Mullen, "A World to Win: Propaganda and African American Expressive Culture," in *The Oxford Handbook of Propaganda Studies,* ed. Jonathan Auerbach and Russ Castronovo (Oxford: Oxford University Press, 2013), 49–66.

10. Mark Crispin Miller, Introduction to Edward Bernays, *Propaganda* (New York: Ig Publishing, 2004), 9–33; Jonathan Auerbach and Russ Castronovo, "Introduction: Thirteen Propositions about Propaganda," in *The Oxford Handbook of Propaganda Studies,* 1–16.

11. Auerbach and Castronovo, "Introduction," 5.

12. Striking recent examples are *The 1619 Project,* first published in the *New York Times* and "The 1776 Report" issued by the Trump administration in 2021. Nikole Hannah-Jones, Mary Elliott, Jazmine Hughes, and Jake Silverstein, eds., "The 1619 Project," *New York Times Magazine,* Aug. 18, 2019. https://www.nytimes.com/interactive/2019/08/14/magazine/1619-america-slavery.html. "The 1776 Report" advances an account of American history not unlike the one Du Bois criticized in *Black Reconstruction*'s final chapter, "The Propaganda of History."

13. W. E. B. Du Bois, "Criteria of Negro Art" (1926), para 1–2, http://www.webdubois.org/dbCriteriaNArt.html.

14. Du Bois, "Criteria," para 6.

15. For sustained reflection on this theme in Du Bois's work, see Andrew J. Douglas, *W. E. B. Du Bois and the Critique of Competitive Society* (Athens: University of Georgia Press, 2019).

16. Du Bois, "Criteria," para 7.

17. Du Bois, "Criteria," para 11.

18. Du Bois, "Criteria," para 27.

19. Ross Posnock, "The Distinction of Du Bois: Aesthetics, Pragmatism, Politics," in Ross Posnock, *Color and Culture: Black Writers and the Making of the Modern Intellectual* (Cambridge, MA: Harvard University Press, 2000), 144.

20. Du Bois, "Criteria," para 29.

21. On Du Bois's use of interracial romance, including the novel *Dark Princess*, as "propaganda" for Black internationalism, see Alys Eve Weinbaum, "Interracial Romance and Black Internationalism," in *Next to the Color Line: Gender, Sexuality and Du Bois*, ed. Susan Gillman and Alys Eve Weinbaum (Minneapolis: University of Minnesota Press, 2007), 96–123.

22. Du Bois, "Criteria," para 32.

23. Melvin Rogers, "Propaganda and Rhetoric: On W. E. B. Du Bois' 'Criteria of Negro Art,'" in *The Darkened Light of Faith: Race, Democracy, and Freedom in African American Political Thought*, book manuscript, forthcoming from Princeton University Press.

24. See Posnock, "Distinction of Du Bois"; Rogers, "Propaganda and Rhetoric."

25. On Du Bois's aestheticized politics, see Jonathan Flatley, "'What a Mourning': Propaganda and Loss in W. E. B. Du Bois's *Souls of Black Folk*," in *Affective Mapping: Melancholia and the Politics of Modernism* (Cambridge, MA: Harvard University Press, 2008), 105–57; Posnock, "Distinction of Du Bois"; Rogers, "Propaganda and Rhetoric"; Shawn Michelle Smith, *Photography on the Color Line: W. E. B. Du Bois, Race, and Visual Culture* (Durham, NC: Duke University Press, 2004); Joseph R. Winters, *Hope Draped in Black: Race, Melancholy, and the Agony of Progress* (Durham, NC: Duke University, 2016).

26. Posnock, "Distinction of Du Bois," 113.

27. Rogers, "Propaganda and Rhetoric."

28. Winters, *Hope Draped in Black*, 81. See also Eric King Watts, "Cultivating a Public Voice: W. E. B. Du Bois and the 'Criteria of Negro Art,'" *Rhetoric & Public Affairs* 4, no. 2 (Summer 2001) on Du Bois's belief that "cultural expression" is a key method "to get white folk to recognize and hear a black public voice" (193).

29. Paul Gilroy, *The Black Atlantic: Modernity and Double Consciousness* (Cambridge, MA: Harvard University Press, 1993), 115.

30. Susan Gillman and Alys Eve Weinbaum, "Introduction: W. E. B. Du Bois and the Politics of Juxtaposition," in *Next to the Color Line*, 6.

31. Posnock, "Distinction of Du Bois," 144. Posnock cites Harold Cruse, who claimed that "Criteria" was the first time a Black intellectual described Negro art in "functional" relation to the US civil rights movement (144).

32. Rogers, "Propaganda and Rhetoric."

33. Du Bois, "The Plot," in *Dusk of Dawn*, 2.

34. Du Bois, "The White World," in *Dusk of Dawn*, 86.

35. Du Bois, "The Colored World Within," in *Dusk of Dawn*, 98.

36. Du Bois, *The Crisis* (November 1910). https://teachingamericanhistory.org/library/document/the-crisis/.

37. Jenny Woodley, *Art for Equality: The NAACP's Cultural Campaign for Civil Rights* (Lexington: University Press of Kentucky, 2014), 2.

38. Woodley, *Art for Equality*, 10.

39. Amy Helene Kirschke, "Art in *Crisis* During the Du Bois Years," in *Protest and Propaganda: W. E. B. Du Bois, The Crisis, and American History*, ed. Helene Kirschke and Phillip Luke Sinitiere (Columbia: University of Missouri Press, 2019), 49–117 . This essay contains a detailed account of lynching imagery published in *The Crisis* in the 1910s–1930s, with many examples, including photos and political cartoons. Both types of images, Kirschke shows, drew on recurring themes—Christianity, American patriotism, and ideals of "civilization"—in an effort to expose the "Shame of America" (the title of a special section of *The Crisis* published in 1922). See also Woodley, *Art for Equality*, Ch. 3.

40. Du Bois, "Revolution," in *Dusk of Dawn*, 141.

41. Du Bois, "The White World," 87.

42. Du Bois, "The Colored World Within," in *Dusk of Dawn*, 98. See Robert Gooding-Williams, "Autobiography, Political Hope, Racial Justice," *Du Bois Review* 11, no. 1 (2014): 159–75, which emphasizes Du Bois's conviction in 1940's *Dusk of Dawn* that "undoing racial domination"—if possible—will require "a long siege . . . careful planning and subtle campaign with the education of growing generations and propaganda" (169, quoting Du Bois, *Dusk of Dawn*, 3). Gooding-Williams reads *Dusk of Dawn* alongside Barack Obama's autobiography, observing the extent to which Du Bois's thinking calls into question Obama's belief in a normative common ground that can bring about racial reconciliation.

43. Oral history interview of W. E. B. Du Bois by William T. Ingersoll (June 1960) in W. E. B. Du Bois Papers (MS 312), Special Collections and University Archives, University of Massachusetts Amherst Libraries, 146–47.

44. Kirschke, "Art in *Crisis* During the Du Bois Years," 59–60.

45. Larry Buchanan, Quoctrung Bui, and Jugal K. Patel, "Black Lives Matter May Be the Largest Movement in US History," *New York Times*, July 3, 2020. https://www.nytimes.com/interactive/2020/07/03/us/george-floyd-protests-crowd-size.html.

46. Alicia Garza, "A Herstory of the #BlackLivesMatter Movement by Alicia Garza," *Feminist Wire*, Oct. 7, 2014. https://www.thefeministwire.com/2014/10/blacklivesmatter-2/.

47. Buchanan et al., "Black Lives Matter May Be the Largest Movement in US History."

48. Audra D. S. Burch, Weiyi Cai, Gabriel Gianordoli, Morrigan McCarthy, and Jugal K. Patel, "How Black Lives Matter Reached Every Corner of the United States," *New York Times*, June 16, 2020. https://www.nytimes.com/interactive/2020/06/13/us/george-floyd-protests-cities-photos.html.

49. Burch et al., "How Black Lives Matter Reached Every Corner of the United States."

50. On white participation, see Jennifer Chudy, "Many Whites Are Protesting with Black Lives Matter. How Far Will Their Support Go?" *Washington Post*, June 15, 2020. https://www.washingtonpost.com/politics/2020/06/15/many-whites-are-protesting-with-black-lives-matter-how-far-will-their-support-go/. See also the Epilogue.

51. Burch et al., "How Black Lives Matter Reached Every Corner of the United States." In June 2020, Pew Research found that in the midst of the protests, "majorities across racial and ethnic groups express support" for BLM. See Kim Parker, Juliana Menasce Horowitz, and Monica Anderson, "Amid Protests, Majorities Across Racial and Ethnic Groups Express Support for the Black Lives Matter Movement," Pew Research Center, June 12, 2020. https://www.pewsocialtrends.org/2020/06/12/amid-protests-majorities-across-racial-and-ethnic-groups-express-support-for-the-black-lives-matter-movement/. That support appeared to weaken over the next few months and over the next year, however. See Deja Thomas and Juliana Menasce Horowitz, "Support for Black Lives Matter Has Decreased Since June but Remains Strong Among Black Americans," Pew Research Center, Sept. 16, 2020. Jennifer Chudy and Hakeem Jefferson, "Support for Black Lives Matter Surged Last Year. Did It Last?," *New York Times*, May 22, 2021. https://www.nytimes.com/2021/05/22/opinion/blm-movement-protests-support.html.

52. Barbara Ransby, *Making All Black Lives Matter: Reimagining Freedom in the 21st Century* (Oakland: University of California Press, 2018), 7. Ransby describes the important role that certain organizations play in "political quilting"—the practice of building "bridges and responsiveness among different sectors of the national progressive community of scholars, activists, and artists" (148).

53. Alicia Garza characterizes Black Lives Matter as "an organization, and a movement bigger than our organization" (259) in her book, *The Purpose of Power: How We Come Together When We Fall Apart* (New York: One World, 2020).

54. Garza, *Purpose of Power*, 161–62, 163. This "leaderless" model defies what some readers of Du Bois take to be his lifelong elitist vision of Black politics (even across other ideological shifts in his thinking). This interpretation is advanced by Adolph Reed, *W. E. B. Du Bois and American Political Thought: Fabianism and the Color Line* (New York: Oxford University Press, 1997).

55. Garza, *Purpose of Power*, 164.

56. BLM protests have also targeted vigilantism directed at Black persons—such as the killing of Trayvon Martin in 2012 and of Ahmaud Arbery in 2020.

57. Garza, "A Herstory of the Black Lives Matter Movement."

58. Ransby, *Making All Black Lives Matter*, 8.

59. Movement for Black Lives (M4BL) Platform, 2020. https://m4bl.org/policy-platforms/.

60. M4BL Platform; Garza, *Purpose of Power*, 46. On BLM's roots in Black and intersectional feminism, see Garza, *The Purpose of Power* and Christopher J. Lebron, *The Making of Black Lives Matter: A Brief History of an Idea* (Oxford: Oxford University Press, 2017).

61. The M4BL Platform states: "We are intentional about amplifying the particular experiences of racial, economic, and gender-based state and interpersonal violence

that Black women, queer, trans, gender nonconforming, intersex, and disabled people face. Cisheteropatriarchy and ableism are central and instrumental to anti-Blackness and racial capitalism, and have been internalized within our communities and movements."

62. Garza, *Purpose of Power*, 148. Some prominent scholar-activists, including Barbara Ransby and Keeanga-Yamahtta Taylor, emphasize the role that BLM has to play in a "class struggle" against capitalism, while noting that this struggle is "bound up with the struggle against all other major forms of oppression" (Ransby, *Making All Black Lives Matter*, 158). Both Ransby and Taylor explicitly connect BLM, whose platform identifies "racial capitalism" as a target for transformation, with the thought and practice of the Combahee River Collective (CRC). As Ransby explains, the collective—a 1970s Boston-based activist group of Black feminists—were "unapologetically socialist" (160). Taylor points out that CRC's analysis linked "the oppression of Blacks and women to capitalism." Keeanga-Yamahtta Taylor, *From #BlackLivesMatter to Black Liberation* (Chicago: Haymarket Books, 2016), 198. Both Ransby and Taylor believe BLM is at its most powerful and promising when organizing against the political-economic system of capitalism and in favor of socialism. Both underscore CRC's claim about the impossibility and undesirability of a "class only" agenda, however. As CRC wrote in 1977, "We are socialists because we believe that work must be organized for the collective benefit of those who do the work and create the products, and not for the profit of bosses.... We are not convinced, however, that a socialist revolution that is not also a feminist and anti-racist revolution will guarantee our liberation" (Combahee River Collective, "The Combahee River Collective Statement" [1977], in *Home Girls: A Black Feminist Anthology*, ed. Barbara Smith [New York: Kitchen Table – Women of Color Press, 1983], 276). This passage is quoted in Ransby, *Making All Black Lives Matter*, 161, and Taylor, *#BlackLivesMatter*, 198–99.

63. The title of this section, "mosaic of struggle," comes from Donna Murch's essay, "Ferguson's Inheritance," *Jacobin*, Aug. 5, 2015. https://www.jacobinmag.com/2015/08/ferguson-police-black-lives-matter/.

64. Nimalan Yoganathan, "Black Lives Matter Movement Uses Creative Tactics to Confront Systemic Racism," *The Conversation*, July 30, 2020. https://theconversation.com/black-lives-matter-movement-uses-creative-tactics-to-confront-systemic-racism-143273. Nicholas Mirzoeff, "Tactics of Appearance for Abolition Democracy #BlackLivesMatter," *Critical Inquiry*, 2018. https://criticalinquiry.uchicago.edu/tactics_of_appearance/.

65. Examples of such photos can be found in Yoganathan, "Black Lives Matter" and Mirzoeff, "Tactics."

66. bell hooks, *Black Looks: Race and Representation* (Boston: South End Press, 1992), 168.

67. Mirzoeff, "Tactics"; hooks, *Black Looks*, 168.

68. See "The Rise and Fall of Jim Crow," PBS Thirteen: Media with Impact, 2002. https://www.thirteen.org/wnet/jimcrow/tools_unwritten.html.

69. Mirzoeff, "Tactics." Mirzoeff mentions that "looking" was used to aggravate sexual assault charges as recently as the Matt Ingram case in 1952. See Mary-Francis Berry,

"'Reckless Eyeballing': The Matt Ingram Case and the Denial of African American Sexual Freedom," *Journal of African American History* 93, no. 2 (Spring 2008): 223–34.

70. Stacia L. Brown, "Looking While Black," *New Republic,* April 30, 2015. https://newr epublic.com/article/121682/freddie-grays-eye-contact-police-led-chase-death. Brown stresses that Gray "locked eyes" with at least one police officer patrolling the public housing complex where he lived but doubts that the police considered his gaze a challenge. She explains: "Though historically black male eye contact has been considered aggressive or defiant—averting eye contact when confronted with whites was one of the *unwritten rules* of Jim Crow—no black man is eager to initiate a staring contest with the cops, especially not a man with prior arrests."

71. Mirzoeff, "Tactics."

72. Brown, "Looking While Black." The next lines of the eulogy are notably masculinist: "And when he looked the police in the eye, they knew that there was a threat, because they're used to black men with their head bowed down low, with their spirit broken. He was a threat simply because he was man enough to look somebody in authority in the eye. I want to tell this grieving mother . . . you are not burying a boy, you are burying a grown man. He knew that one of the principles of being a man is looking somebody in the eye."

73. The term "repertoire of contention" originates in the work of sociologist Charles Tilly and refers to a set of cultural tools that are learned, shared, and enacted by collective action participants.

74. Randy Shaw, "How Black Lives Matter Is Building New Activist Strategies in a New Era," *UC Press Blog,* July 7, 2020. https://www.ucpress.edu/blog/51174/how-black-lives-matter-is-building-new-activist-strategies-in-a-new-era/.

75. Large BLM die-ins have taken place in many locations, including national and state capitols and major transportation hubs such as New York's Grand Central Station.

76. Dora Apel, "'Hands Up, Don't Shoot': Surrendering to Liberal Illusions," *Theory & Event* 17, no. 3 (July 2014).

77. Juliet Hooker, "Black Lives Matter and the Paradoxes of US Black Politics: From Democratic Sacrifice to Democratic Repair," *Political Theory* 44, no. 4 (2016): 462.

78. Hooker, "Black Lives Matter," 462.

79. Mirzoeff, "Tactics." Mirzoeff also suggests that the gesture in Ferguson was not solely directed at the police. The protestors were also addressing one another, exposing themselves as "political bodies that can be wounded, even die, but do not submit and are open to others" (n.p.).

80. W. E. B. Du Bois, "The Perfect Vacation," *The Crisis* 40, no. 8 (August 1931): 279.

81. Lisa M. Perhamus and Clarence W. Joldersma, "What Might Sustain the Activism of This Moment? Dismantling White Supremacy, One Monument at a Time," *Journal of Philosophy of Education* 54, no. 5 (2020): 1316; Verity Platt, "Why People Are Toppling Monuments to Racism," *Scientific American*, July 3, 2020. https://www.scientificameri can.com/article/why-people-are-toppling-monuments-to-racism/.

82. Ben Davis, "Monuments Across the United States Re-Emerged as Targets of Rage over a Weekend of Widespread Protest," *Artnet News,* June 1, 2020. https://news. artnet.com/art-world/monuments-across-the-united-states-re-emerged-as-targ

ets-of-fury-over-a-weekend-of-widespread-protest-1876542; Claire Selvin and Tessa Solomon, "Toppled and Removed Monuments: A Continually Updated Guide to Statues and the Black Lives Matter Protests," *ARTnews,* June 11, 2020. https://www. artnews.com/art-news/news/monuments-black-lives-matter-guide-1202690845/. "The movement initially set its sights on Confederate symbols and examples of racism against African-Americans, but has since exploded into a broader cultural moment, forcing a reckoning over such issues as European colonization and the oppression of Native Americans." Sarah Mervosh, Simon Romero, and Lucy Tompkins, "Reconsidering the Past, One Statue at a Time," *New York Times,* June 17, 2020. https://www.nytimes.com/2020/06/16/us/protests-statues-reckoning.html.

83. Quote from Julian Hayter, a historian at the University of Richmond, in Tariro Mzezewa, "The Woman Who Took Down a Confederate Flag on What Came Next," *New York Times*, June 14, 2020. https://www.nytimes.com/2020/06/14/us/politics/bree-newsome-bass-confederate-flag.html.

84. Perhamus and Joldersma, "What Might Sustain," 54.

85. In addition to destroying and remaking existing monuments, BLM supporters have created public works of art in a range of styles. See Julia Jacobs, "The 'Black Lives Matter' Street Art That Contains Multitudes," *New York Times,* July 16, 2020. https://www.nytimes.com/2020/07/16/arts/design/black-lives-matter-murals-new-york.html.

86. Mervosh et al., "Reconsidering the Past"; Danielle Kurtzleben and Miles Parks, "Trump Defends 'Beauty' of Confederate Memorials," *NPR,* Aug. 17, 2017. https://www.npr.org/2017/08/17/544137751/trump-defends-beauty-of-confederate-memorials.

87. Platt, "Why People Are Toppling Monuments to Racism."

88. Bruno Latour, "What Is Iconoclash?," in *Iconoclash: Beyond the Image Wars in Science, Religion, and Art*, ed. Bruno Latour and Peter Weibel (Cambridge, MA: MIT Press, 2002), 17.

89. The photo on this book's cover was taken during this period. The statue was completely removed in September 2021 and moved to Richmond's Black History Museum.

90. Ezra Marcus, "Will the Last Confederate Statue Standing Turn Off the Lights?," *New York Times,* June 23, 2020. https://www.nytimes.com/2020/06/23/style/statue-richmond-lee.html.

91. David A. Snow and Robert D. Benford, "Master Frames and Cycles of Protest," in *Frontiers in Social Movement Theory*, ed. Aldon D. Morris and Carol McClurg Mueller (New Haven, CT: Yale University Press, 1992), 137.

92. Doug McAdam, "The Framing Function of Movement Tactics: Strategic Dramaturgy in the American Civil Rights Movement," in *Comparative Perspectives on Social Movements: Political Opportunities, Mobilizing Structures, and Cultural Framings*, ed. Doug McAdam, John D. McCarthy, and Mayer N. Zald (Cambridge: Cambridge University Press, 1996), 338–55.

93. Snow and Benford, "Master Frames," 138.

94. Snow and Benford, "Master Frames," 145. That master frame "accented the principle of equal rights and opportunities regardless of ascribed characteristics and articulated it with the goal of integration through nonviolent means."

95. Snow and Benford, "Master Frames," 140. They interpret the nuclear freeze movement of the 1980s as advancing a "highly restrictive master frame" (147).

96. Snow and Benford, "Master Frames," 141.

97. By the summer of 2020, there were worries that BLM's master frame, or at least its governing vocabulary, had become so ubiquitous that its political message was becoming watered down. Many major corporations, small businesses, sports teams, and educational institutions aligned themselves with BLM—in official statements, advertisements, and social media accounts. Political candidates were consistently pressed on questions about the movement and the summer's protests, products with anti-Black iconography were pulled from shelves, and sports teams and musical acts changed their racist names—all purportedly to demonstrate that "Black Lives Matter." Some of these moves—especially efforts by abusive corporations like Amazon to claim a commitment to Black lives—warrant cynicism. Taken together, however, they testify to BLM's reach and the relatively quick ascendance of its master frame.

98. Snow and Benford, "Master Frames," 141.

99. "Strategic dramaturgy" comes from Doug McAdam, who uses it when describing the "signifying *actions*" used by the Southern Christian Leadership Conference during the US civil rights movement. McAdam, "The Framing Function of Movement Tactics."

100. Jacques Rancière, *Dis-agreement: Politics and Philosophy,* trans. Julie Rose (Minneapolis: University of Minnesota Press, 1999), 29.

101. Rancière, *Dis-agreement,* 29.

102. Rancière describes this as a process that "makes visible what had no business being seen, and makes heard a discourse where there was once only place for noise" (*Dis-agreement*, 30).

103. For the argument that BLM activists are engaged in disruption to the exclusion of persuasion, see Courtenay W. Daum, "Counterpublics and Intersectional Radical Resistance: Agitation as Transformation of the Dominant Discourse," *New Political Science* 39, no. 4 (2017): 523–37 and Yoganathan, "Black Lives Matter Movement".

104. Glenn Mackin, "Black Lives Matter and the Concept of the Counterworld," *Philosophy & Rhetoric* 49, no. 4 (2016): 462, quoting "The Thinking of Dissensus," 7.

105. Mackin, "Black Lives Matter," 477.

106. Mackin, "Black Lives Matter," 473.

107. Mackin, "Black Lives Matter," 473. He explains that BLM activists present facts about "the history of slavery, debt peonage, Jim Crow, and the ongoing forms of police violence, mass incarceration, poorly served neighborhoods, exposure to toxic environmental conditions, racist media depictions, and so on. Yet the facts alone do not necessarily challenge dominant perceptions . . . Aesthetic transformation comes not just from reciting the facts but in connecting them to the claim that black lives matter" (473–74).

Epilogue

1. For an insightful re-reading of Du Bois's late life and work (usually ignored by scholars), see Bill V. Mullen, *Un-American: W. E. B. Du Bois and the Century of World Revolution* (Philadelphia: Temple University Press, 2015). Du Bois's joining the Communist Party and moving to Ghana in 1961 express key ideas in his late writings, according to Mullen: "disidentification with the US nation-state" and an affirmation of the project of "world revolution" (6). Du Bois's disillusionment concerning the prospects for Black freedom in the United States is announced in a 1961 letter he wrote to his friend Grace Goens explaining his plan to move to Ghana in a month: "Chin up, and fight on, but realize that American Negroes can't win." W. E. B. Du Bois, "Letter from W. E. B. Du Bois to Grace Goens," September 13, 1961. W. E. B. Du Bois Papers (MS 312). Special Collections and University Archives, University of Massachusetts Amherst Libraries. https://credo.library.umass.edu/view/full/mums312-b153-i208. Saidiya Hartmann's reading of Du Bois emphasizes the themes of disappointment and failure found even in his first book and in 1903's *Souls of Black Folk*. Saidiya Hartman, "Introduction" to W. E. B. Du Bois, *The Suppression of the African Slave Trade to the United States of America, 1638–1870* (Oxford: Oxford University Press, 2007 [1896]), xxv–xxx.
2. W. E. B. Du Bois, "A Negro Nation Within a Nation" (1934). Du Bois gave this speech in New York City on June 26, 1934, as he resigned from the NAACP. https://www.blackpast.org/african-american-history/speeches-african-american-history/1934-w-e-b-du-bois-negro-nation-within-nation/.
3. Michael Tesler, "The Floyd Protests Will Likely Change Public Attitudes About Race and Policing," *Washington Post,* June 5, 2020. https://www.washingtonpost.com/polit ics/2020/06/05/floyd-protests-will-likely-change-public-attitudes-about-race-polic ing-heres-why/. The dramatic surge in white support for BLM in 2020 around the George Floyd protests does not seem to have lasted, especially among Republicans. Jennifer Chudy and Hakeem Jefferson, "Support for Black Lives Matter Surged Last Summer. Did It Last?," *New York Times,* May 22, 2021. https://www.nytimes.com/2021/05/22/opinion/blm-movement-protests-support.html.
4. For a sustained examination of the problems afflicting "the production and display of white middle-class moral goodness," see Shannon Sullivan, *Good White People: The Problem with Middle Class White Anti-Racism* (Albany: State University of New York Press, 2014). Sullivan's analysis focuses on how white middle-class people engage in performances of anti-racism that are primarily about "establishing the moral badness of poor and lower-class white people." This move "secures white liberals' status as good," Sullivan says, but does little to eliminate racial injustice. According to Sullivan, white middle-class liberalism is not driven by a serious commitment or will to end racial injustice but rather a desire "to be recognized as Not Racist, perhaps especially by people of color" (5).
5. Ailsa Chang, Rachel Martin, and Eric Marrapodi, "Summer of Racial Reckoning," *NPR,* Aug. 16, 2020. https://www.npr.org/2020/08/16/902179773/summer-of-rac

ial-reckoning-the-match-lit. John Eligon and Audra D. S. Burch, "After a Summer of Racial Reckoning, Race Is on the Ballot," *New York Times*, Oct. 30, 2020. https://www.nytimes.com/2020/10/30/us/racial-justice-elections.html.

6. Chudy and Jefferson, "Support for Black Lives Matter" states that the unusually large protests in response to George Floyd's murder may have been enhanced by "a global pandemic that provided an unusually attentive and emotional audience."

7. Some theorists of American whiteness, most notably Shannon Sullivan, have rejected the language of "anti-racism" on the grounds that it is little more than "virtue signaling"—that is, the term accompanies performances of supposed moral enlightenment for social approval that do little to actually combat racial domination. See Sullivan, *Good White People.* I am sympathetic to this concern but choose to use the terminology, both because it is used by committed racial justice activists who are engaged in important community organizing efforts and because I regard its popular circulation as a potential opportunity for politicization.

8. The debate over whether it is possible or desirable to "abolish whiteness" is not my focus here. My commentary presumes that to be marked as "white" today in the United States remains a salient social fact (mediated by many other variables) *and* that it is possible for white people to take action on behalf of a more racially just future, despite the "gratifications of whiteness" that pave the path of least resistance. I generally share Shannon Sullivan's and Linda Alcoff's skepticism toward the "abolish whiteness" position articulated by Noel Ignatiev and John Garvey. Like Sullivan, I think the eliminativist view "underestimates the significance of whiteness to many white people's identities and habits, and not just those who are avowed white supremacists" (Sullivan, *Good White People,* 41). Like Alcoff, I believe the "desire to eliminate whiteness in the future may in fact be motivated by a desire for escape from uncomfortable histories that bear on present-day material distributions." Linda Alcoff, "The Future of Whiteness," in *Living Alterities: Phenomenology, Embodiment, Race,* ed. Emily S. Lee (Albany: State University of New York Press, 2014), 157. See Mark B. Brown, "James Baldwin and the Politics of White Identity," *Contemporary Political Theory* 20, no. 1 (2020): 1–22 which argues for the importance of "politicizing" rather than "abolishing" white identity and draws on Baldwin's work to develop an account of "antiracist white identity politics."

9. W. E. B. Du Bois, "The Colored World Within," in *Dusk of Dawn: An Essay Toward an Autobiography of the Race Concept* (Oxford: Oxford University Press, 2007 [1940]), 101. See also 105, 110.

10. Kwame Ture and Charles V. Hamilton, *Black Power: The Politics of Liberation* (New York: Vintage Books, 1992 [1967]), 81.

11. Ture and Hamilton, *Black Power,* 82. A 1966 SNCC statement explaining Black Power reads: "It is meaningless to talk about coalition if there is no one to align ourselves with, because of the lack of organization in white communities" ("Excerpts from Paper on Which the 'Black Power' Philosophy Is Based," *New York Times,* Aug. 5, 1966). In a 1968 interview, Huey Newton explained that the Black Panther Party, unlike SNCC, had always been a Black group and further clarified, "Our alliance is one of organized black groups with organized white groups" (Students for a Democratic

Society, "Huey Newton Talks to the Movement," *The Movement*, August 1968. https://omeka.library.kent.edu/special-collections/items/show/3176).

12. Ture and Hamilton, *Black Power*, 83–84.

13. Jeb Aram Middlebrook, "The Ballot Box and Beyond: On the (Im)Possibilities of White Antiracist Organizing," *American Quarterly* 62, no. 2 (June 2010): 236. This characterization comes from white racial justice activist Anne Braden, who wrote in 1964 about the organizational relationship between the white-led Southern Student Organizing Committee and SNCC (prior to the formal expulsion of white members from SNCC in 1966).

14. See the SURJ website at https://surj.org/.

15. See the AWARE-LA website at https://www.awarela.org/. Jeb Aram Middlebrook, "The Ballot Box and Beyond"; and Sam Royall, " 'The Well-Meaning White People': A Comparative Case Study of the White Anti-Racist Organizing Models of the Southern Student Organizing Committee and Alliance of White Anti-Racists Everywhere, Los Angeles" (Senior thesis, Occidental College, 2018) https://www.oxy.edu/sites/defa ult/files/assets/UEP/Comps/Sam%20Royall_The%20Well-Meaning%20White%20 People.pdf.

16. Lauren Michele Jackson, "What's Missing from 'White Fragility,'" *Slate*, Sept. 4, 2019. https://slate.com/human-interest/2019/09/white-fragility-robin-diangelo-works hop.html.

17. Jackson, "What's Missing from 'White Fragility.'" For a critique of "antiracism as a speech act," see Sara Ahmed, "The Nonperformativity of Antiracism," *Meridians: Feminism, Race, Transnationalism* 7, no. 1 (2006): 104–26.

18. Middlebrook, "The Ballot Box and Beyond," 249–50.

19. In various interviews, Ruth Wilson Gilmore enunciates the claim, "Where life is precious, life is precious" to conjure a society, unlike our own at present, that embodies this principle.

20. Mariame Kaba explains, "Our work isn't just a movement *against* cages and cops. It's a movement *for* different ways of living together." Quoted in Dan White, "Hope, Mutual Aid, and Abolition," *UC Santa Cruz News*, Feb. 16, 2021. https://news.ucsc.edu/2021/02/kaba-mlk-coverage-2021.html. Fred Moten and Stefano Harvey write, "What is, so to speak, the object of abolition? Not so much the abolition of prisons but the abolition of a society that could have prisons, that could have slavery, that could have the wage, and therefore not abolition as the elimination of anything but abolition as the founding of a new society." Fred Moten and Stefano Harvey, "The University and the Undercommons: Seven Theses," *Social Text* 22, no. 2 (2004): 114.

21. Ruth Wilson Gilmore credits Du Bois's *Black Reconstruction* with showing that "abolition is a fleshly and material presence of social life lived differently." Clément Petitjean, "Prisons and Class Warfare: An Interview with Ruth Wilson Gilmore," Aug. 2, 2018. https://www.versobooks.com/blogs/3954-prisons-and-class-warfare-an-interview-with-ruth-wilson-gilmore.

22. Angela Davis, *Abolition Democracy: Beyond Empire, Prisons, and Torture* (New York: Seven Stories Press, 2005), 73 (on Du Bois's abolition-democracy and institution building, see also 95–96); Angela Davis, *Freedom Is a Constant*

Struggle: Ferguson, Palestine, and the Foundations of a Movement (Chicago: Haymarket Books, 2016), 25, 73; Angela Davis, *The Meaning of Freedom: And Other Difficult Dialogues* (San Francisco: City Lights Publishers, 2012), 115–16.

23. Davis, *Freedom Is a Constant Struggle*, 25. Davis elaborates the connection: "In thinking specifically about the abolition of prisons using the approach of abolition democracy, we would propose the creation of an array of social institutions that would begin to solve the social problems that set people on the track to prison, thereby helping to render the prison obsolete. There is a direct connection with slavery: when slavery was abolished, black people were set free, but they lacked access to the material resources that would enable them to fashion new, free lives" (Davis, *Abolition Democracy*, 96).

24. W. E. B. Du Bois, "Of Work and Wealth," in *Darkwater: Voices from Within the Veil* (Oxford: Oxford University Press, 2007 [1920]), 48.

25. As Tommie Shelby discusses, Du Bois believes it is the "world-historical mission of African-Americans" to "perfect the ideals of American democracy." Tommie Shelby, *We Who Are Dark* (Cambridge, MA: Harvard University Press, 2007), 67.

26. Joel Olson, *The Abolition of White Democracy* (Minneapolis: University of Minnesota Press, 2004), 129. Olson argues that the Black radical tradition, including Du Bois's middle-to-late work, can push contemporary democratic theory in a radical-utopian direction.

27. W. E. B. Du Bois, "Criteria of Negro Art" (1926). http://www.webdubois.org/dbCrite riaNArt.html.

28. Du Bois, "Criteria." In a similar vein, when Du Bois advocated the establishment of Black consumer cooperatives in the 1930s, he maintained that doing so would give Black Americans the chance to "teach industry and culture to a world that bitterly needs it" (W. E. B. Du Bois, "Colored World," in *Dusk of Dawn,* 110).

29. Ruth Wilson Gilmore and James Kilgore, "The Case for Abolition," June 19, 2019. https://www.themarshallproject.org/2019/06/19/the-case-for-abolition.

30. Rachel Kushner, "Is Prison Necessary? Ruth Wilson Gilmore Might Change Your Mind," *New York Times*, April 17, 2019. https://www.nytimes.com/2019/04/17/magaz ine/prison-abolition-ruth-wilson-gilmore.html.

31. Du Bois was an outspoken defender of women's rights who also ignored or marginalized the Black women intellectuals and activists of his time, most notably Anna Julia Cooper and Ida B. Wells, and adhered to a masculinist conception of leadership. See especially Joy James, *Transcending the Talented Tenth: Black Leaders and American Intellectuals* (New York: Routledge, 1997).

32. Mariame Kaba, *We Do This Til We Free Us: Abolitionist Organizing and Transforming Justice* (Chicago: Haymarket Books, 2021), 2.

33. Kushner, "Is Prison Necessary?" The tradition Davis references includes Anna Julia Cooper, the 19th-century Black feminist who famously declared, "Only the black woman can say, "When and where I enter, in the quiet undisputed dignity of my womanhood . . . then and there the *whole Negro race enters with me*," in *A Voice From the South* (1892), https://docsouth.unc.edu/church/cooper/cooper.html, and "The Combahee River Collective Statement" (1977), in *Home Girls: A Black Feminist*

Anthology, ed. Barbara Smith (New York: Kitchen Table – Women of Color Press, 1983), which states: "If Black women were free it would mean that everyone would else would have to be free since our freedom would necessitate the destruction of all the systems of oppression" (278).

34. See the "Invest-Divest" policy platform of the Movement 4 Black Lives at https://m4bl.org/policy-platforms/invest-divest/.

35. Keeanga-Yamahtta Taylor, *From #BlackLivesMatter to Black Liberation* (Chicago: Haymarket Books, 2016), 168. In a June 2020 interview, Ruth Wilson Gilmore commented that the popularization of demands to defund or abolish the police—"however thought through or not thought through they are"—are ways of declaring "this society absolutely does not work." "Transcript: In Conversation with Ruth Wilson Gilmore," University College London. https://www.ucl.ac.uk/racism-racialisation/transcript-conversation-ruth-wilson-gilmore.

36. On the significance of "worldly things" as the third terms of associative democratic politics, see Ella Myers, *Worldly Ethics: Democratic Politics and Care for the World* (Durham, NC: Duke University Press, 2013), Ch. 3.

37. Olson, *The Abolition of White Democracy* , Ch. 5. See also Dean Spade, "Solidarity, Not Charity: Mutual Aid for Mobilization and Survival," *Social Text* 38, no. 1 (March 2020):131–51 for an abolitionist critique of reformism.

38. Michael C. Dawson and Megan Ming Francis, "Black Politics and the Neoliberal Order," *Public Culture* 28, no. 1 (2015): 23–62. Black neoliberalism, according to Dawson and Francis, is defined by "an individualism where hedonistic, consumerist, capitalist actions/achievements" are regarded as "advances in the crusade for black progress" (47).

39. Andrew Douglas, *W. E. B. Du Bois and the Critique of the Competitive Society* (Athens: University of Georgia Press, 2019), 37.

40. Jodi Melamed, "Racial Capitalism," *Critical Ethnic Studies* 1, no. 1 (Spring 2015): 77.

41. Du Bois, "Of Work and Wealth," 50.

42. Martin Gilens, *Why Americans Hate Welfare: Race, Media, and the Politics of Antipoverty Policy* (Chicago: University of Chicago, 1999) shows that negative public opinion concerning welfare in the United States is largely due to the misperception that such programs primarily serve Black Americans (when they in fact serve mostly whites) and to racist beliefs that label Black people as "undeserving."

43. Heather McGhee, *The Sum of Us: What Racism Costs Everyone and How We Can Prosper Together* (New York: One World, 2021), 28.

44. McGhee, *The Sum of Us*, 44.

45. McGhee, *The Sum of Us*, xix.

46. W. E. B. Du Bois, "The Position of the Negro in the American Social Order: Where Do We Go from Here?," *Journal of Negro Education* 8, no. 3 (July 1939): 564. See also Du Bois, "Colored World," 104.

47. Heather McGhee, along with Ian Haney López and Anat Shenker-Osorio, cofounded the Race-Class Narrative Project, a research and advocacy group that contends that a "winning narrative" for progressives in the US electoral context is one that fuses race and class, rather than avoiding talk of race *or* speaking about race without any

reference to economic inequality. Based on focus group and survey research on political messaging, they have developed a narrative structure that they believe has the best chance at convincing "conflicted" voters (those often mischaracterized as "moderate") to support progressive candidates and policies. The narrative's key features include overtly discussing race, "framing racism as a tool to divide and thus harm all of us," and stressing that cross-racial solidarity is an effective way to elect new leaders who "work for all of us." Race-Class Narrative Summary (2018). https://ianhaneylopez.com/race-class-narrative. Their research on political messaging finds that for conflicted voters (of which there are many), "the race-class message also proved stronger than the main progressive alternatives, either staying silent about race to focus on class, or leading with racial justice" detached from any reference to the division between "the "1% and the rest of us." Ian Haney López, *Merge Left: Fusing Race and Class, Winning Elections, and Saving America* (New York: New Press, 2019), xxi; Ian Haney López, "Shor Is Mainly Wrong About Racism (Which Is to Say, About Electoral Politics)," Oct. 11, 2021. https://gen.medium.com/shor-is-mainly-wrong-about-racism-which-is-to-say-about-electoral-politics-77692910255c.

48. W. E. B. Du Bois, "Social Planning for the Negro, Past and Present," *Journal for Negro Education* 5, no. 1 (January 1936): 125.

49. Singh, *Black Is a Country,* 218. The official M4BL platform is not socialist, but their policy proposals aim to dramatically reshape the contemporary regime of racial capitalism in favor of workers' rights, robust social supports, and the redistribution of wealth downward, as evidenced by their "Economic Justice" proposals: https://m4bl.org/policy-platforms/economic-justice/. Moreover, many of their proposed Economic Justice measures are race specific, such as the creation of state and federal job programs with living wages for the most "economically marginalized Black people," even as they are tied to the goal of "economic justice for all." See Siddhant Issar, "Listening to Black Lives Matter: Racial Capitalism and the Critique of Neoliberalism," *Contemporary Political Theory* 20, no. 1 (2020): 48–71, which shows how M4BL's demand for reparations in particular makes use of a "racial capitalism" framework that challenges the still-prevalent tendency on the left to cast political action on behalf of subordinated racialized populations as impediments to class struggle.

50. Hannah Arendt, "Thoughts on Politics and Revolution," in *Crises of the Republic* (New York: Harcourt Brace & Company, 1972), 203.

51. Wendy Brown, "Where Is the Sex in Political Theory?," *Women & Politics* 7, no. 1 (Spring 1987): 18–19.

52. Anne Braden, Transcript, *Anne Braden: Southern Patriot,* dir. Anne Lewis and Mimi Pickering (2012). https://newsreel.org/transcripts/Anne-Braden-Southern-Patriot-transcript.pdf.

53. Susan B. Goldberg and Cameron Levin, "Toward a Radical White Identity" (2009). https://www.awarela.org/our-models.

54. Mark R. Warren, *Fire in the Heart: How White Activists Embrace Racial Justice* (Oxford: Oxford University Press, 2010), 82.

55. adrienne maree brown, *Pleasure Activism: The Politics of Feeling Good* (Chico, CA: AK Press, 2019). Ebook.
56. W. E. B. Du Bois, "The Concept of Race," in *Dusk of Dawn,* 66–67.
57. Du Bois, "The Concept of Race," 66.

Bibliography

"The 1619 Project," edited by Nikole Hannah-Jones, Mary Elliott, Jazmine Hughes, and Jake Silverstein. *New York Times Magazine*. August 18, 2019. https://www.nytimes.com/interactive/2019/08/14/magazine/1619-america-slavery.html.

Ahmed, Sara. "The Nonperformativity of Antiracism." *Meridians: Feminism, Race, Transnationalism* 7, no. 1 (2006): 104–26.

Alcoff, Linda. "The Future of Whiteness." In *Living Alterities: Phenomenology, Embodiment, Race*, edited by Emily S. Lee, 151–65. Albany: State University of New York Press, 2014.

Alexander, Michelle. *The New Jim Crow*. New York: New Press, 2010.

Allen, Theodore W. *The Invention of the White Race*. Vol. 1. London: Verso Books, 2012 (1994).

Allen, Theodore W. *The Invention of the White Race*. Vol. 2. London: Verso Books, 2012 (1997).

Allen, Theodore W. "Letter of Support." In *Revolutionary Youth and the New Working Class: The Praxis Papers, the Port Authority Statement, the RYM Documents and Other Lost Writings of SDS*, edited by Carl Davidson, 163–67. Pittsburgh, PA: Changemaker Productions, 2011.

Allen, Theodore W. "Summary of the Argument of *The Invention of the White Race*," 1998. http://www.elegantbrain.com/edu4/classes/readings/race-allen.html.

Anderson, Carol. *White Rage: The Unspoken Truth of Our Racial Divide*. New York: Bloomsbury Publishing, 2016.

Anderson, Elijah. "'The White Space.'" *Sociology of Race and Ethnicity* 1, no. 1 (2015): 10–21.

Apel, Dora. "'Hands Up, Don't Shoot': Surrendering to Liberal Illusions." *Theory and Event* 17, no. 3 (July 2014).

Arendt, Hannah. "Thoughts on Politics and Revolution." In *Crises of the Republic*, 199–234. New York: Harcourt Brace & Company, 1972.

Arnesen, Eric. "Whiteness and the Historians' Imagination." *International Labor and Working Class History* 60 (Fall 2001): 3–32.

Arnold, Edwin. *What Virtue There Is in Fire: Cultural Memory and the Lynching of Sam Hose*. Athens: University of Georgia Press, 2009.

Auerbach, Jonathan, and Russ Castronovo. "Introduction: Thirteen Propositions About Propaganda." In *The Oxford Handbook of Propaganda Studies*, edited by Jonathan Auerbach and Russ Castronovo, 1–16. Oxford: Oxford University Press, 2013.

Baigell, Matthew. "Territory, Race, Religion: Images of Manifest Destiny." *Smithsonian Studies in American Art* 4, no. 3/4 (1990): 2–21.

Baker, Courtney R. *Humane Insight: Looking at Images of African American Suffering and Death*. Urbana: University of Illinois Press, 2015.

Balfour, Lawrie. *Democracy's Reconstruction: Thinking Politically with W. E. B. Du Bois*. Oxford: Oxford University Press, 2011.

Bell, Derrick. *Faces at the Bottom of the Well: The Permanence of Racism*. New York: Basic Books, 1992.

Bell, Derrick. "The Final Civil Rights Act." *California Law Review* 79, no. 3 (1991): 597–611.

Bell, Derrick. "White Superiority in America: Its Legal Legacy, Its Economic Costs." *Villanova Law Review* 33 (1988): 767–79.

Bernstein, Lenny, and Joel Achenbach. "A Group of Middle-Aged Whites Is Dying at a Startling Rate." *Washington Post*. November 2, 2015. https://www.washingtonpost.com/national/health-science/a-group-of-middle-aged-american-whites-is-dying-at-a-startling-rate/2015/11/02/47a63098-8172-11e5-8ba6-cec48b74b2a7_story.html.

Berry, Mary-Francis. "'Reckless Eyeballing': The Matt Ingram Case and the Denial of African American Sexual Freedom." *Journal of African American History* 93, no. 2 (Spring 2008): 223–34.

Best, Stephen. *The Fugitive's Properties: Law and the Poetics of Possession*. Chicago: University of Chicago Press, 2004.

Bhambra, Gurminder K. "Brexit, Trump and Methodological Whiteness: On the Misrecognition of Race and Class." *British Journal of Sociology* 68, no. S1 (2018): S214–32.

Blow, Charles. "'The Lowest White Man.'" *New York Times*. January 11, 2018.

Blum, Edward J. *W. E. B. Du Bois: American Prophet*. Philadelphia: University of Pennsylvania Press, 2007.

Blumer, Herbert. "Race Prejudice as a Sense of Group Position." *Pacific Sociological Review* 1, no. 1 (Spring 1958): 3–7.

Boddie, Elise C. "Racial Territoriality." *UCLA Law Review* 58, no. 401 (2010): 401–63.

Boggs, James. *Racism and the Class Struggle: Further Pages from a Black Worker's Notebook*. New York: Monthly Review Press, 1970.

Bonacich, Edna. "Class Approaches to Race and Ethnicity." *Insurgent Sociologist* 10, no. 2 (Fall 1980): 9–23.

Bonds, Anne, and Joshua Inwood. "Beyond White Privilege: Geographies of White Supremacy and Settler Colonialism." *Progress in Human Geography* 40, no. 6 (2016): 715–33.

Bouie, Jamelle. "The Joy of Hatred." *New York Times*. July 19, 2019. https://www.nytimes.com/2019/07/19/opinion/trump-rally.html.

Bouie, Jamelle. "What If Bundy Ranch Were Owned by a Bunch of Black People?" *Slate*. April 15, 2014. http://www.slate.com/blogs/weigel/2014/04/15/bundy_ranch_and_bureau_of_land_management_standoff_what_right_wingers_anger.html.

Braden, Anne. Transcript, *Anne Braden: Southern Patriot*. Directed by Anne Lewis and Mimi Pickering. 2012. https://newsreel.org/transcripts/Anne-Braden-Southern-Patriot-transcript.pdf.

Brodeur, Michael Andor. "Our Memes, Ourselves: The Year in Things." *Boston Globe*. December 23, 2018. https://www.bostonglobe.com/arts/2018/12/20/our-memes-our-selves-year-things/MtTpjtyap9fejL6eg2YikN/story.html.

brown, adrienne maree. *Pleasure Activism: The Politics of Feeling Good*. Chico, CA: AK Press. 2019. Ebook.

Brown, Emma. "On the Anniversary of Brown v. Board, New Evidence That U.S. Schools Are Resegregating." *Washington Post*. May 17, 2016. https://www.washingtonpost.com/news/education/wp/2016/05/17/on-the-anniversary-of-brown-v-board-new-evidence-that-u-s-schools-are-resegregating/.

Brown, Mark B. "James Baldwin and the Politics of White Identity." *Contemporary Political Theory* 20, no. 1 (2020): 1–22.

Brown, Stacia L. "Looking While Black." *New Republic*. April 30, 2015. https://newrepub
lic.com/article/121682/freddie-grays-eye-contact-police-led-chase-death.

Brown, Wendy. "Where Is the Sex in Political Theory?" *Women & Politics* 7, no. 1 (Spring 1987): 3–23.

Buchanan, Larry, Quoctrung Bui, and Jugal K. Patel. "Black Lives Matter May Be the Largest Movement in U.S. History." *New York Times*. July 3, 2020. https://www.nytimes.com/interactive/2020/07/03/us/george-floyd-protests-crowd-size.html.

Burch, Audra D. S., Weiyi Cai, Gabriel Giandoli, Morrigan McCarthy, Jugal K. Patel, and Scott Reinhard. "How Black Lives Matter Reached Every Corner of the United States." *New York Times*. June 16, 2020. https://www.nytimes.com/interactive/2020/06/13/us/george-floyd-protests-cities-photos.html.

Butler, Judith. "Endangered/Endangering: Schematic Racism and Racial Paranoia." In *Reading Rodney King, Reading Urban Uprising*, edited by Robert Gooding-Williams, 15–22. New York: Routledge, 1993.

Capeci Jr., Dominic J., and Jack C. Knight. "Reckoning with Violence: W. E. B. Du Bois and the 1906 Atlanta Race Riot." *Journal of Southern History* 62, no. 4 (November 1996): 727–66.

Carby, Hazel V. "The Limits of Caste." *London Review of Books*. August 2020. https://www.lrb.co.uk/the-paper/v43/n02/hazel-v.-carby/the-limits-of-caste.

Carby, Hazel V., and Adam Shatz, "The Colour Line in the Americas." *LRB Conversations* podcast. January 12, 2021. https://www.lrb.co.uk/podcasts-and-videos/podcasts/lrb-conversations/the-colour-line-in-the-americas.

Carby, Hazel V. *Race Men*. Cambridge, MA: Harvard University Press, 1998.

Carnes, Nicholas, and Noam Lupu. "It's Time to Bust the Myth: Most Trump Voters Were Not Working Class." *Washington Post*. June 5, 2017. https://www.washingtonpost.com/news/monkey-cage/wp/2017/06/05/its-time-to-bust-the-myth-most-trump-voters-were-not-working-class/.

Carnes, Nicholas, and Noam Lupu. "The White Working Class and the 2016 Election." *Perspectives on Politics* 19, no. 1 (March 2021): 55–72.

Caron, Christina. "A Black Yale Student Was Napping, and a White Student Called the Police." *New York Times*. May 9, 2018. https://www.nytimes.com/2018/05/09/nyregion/yale-black-student-nap.html.

Case, Anne, and Angus Deaton, "Rising Morbidity and Mortality in Midlife Among White Non-Hispanic Americans in the 21st Century." *PNAS* 112, no. 49 (November 2015): 15078–83. https://doi.org/10.1073/pnas.1518393112.

Chang, Ailsa, Rachel Martin, and Eric Marrapodi. "Summer of Racial Reckoning." *NPR*. August 16, 2020. https://www.npr.org/2020/08/16/902179773/summer-of-racial-reckoning-the-match-lit.

Chen, Chris. "The Limits of Capitalist Equality: Notes Toward an Abolitionist Antiracism." *Endnotes* 3 (September 2013). https://endnotes.org.uk/issues/3/en/chris-chen-the-limit-point-of-capitalist-equality.

Chokshi, Niraj. "Trump Voters Driven by Fear of Losing Status, Not Economic Anxiety, Study Finds." *New York Times*. April 24, 2018. https://www.nytimes.com/2018/04/24/us/politics/trump-economic-anxiety.html.

Chudy, Jennifer. "Many Whites Are Protesting with Black Lives Matter. How Far Will Their Support Go?" *Washington Post*. June 15, 2020. https://www.washingtonpost.com/politics/2020/06/15/many-whites-are-protesting-with-black-lives-matter-how-far-will-their-support-go/.

Chudy, Jennifer, and Hakeem Jefferson. "Support for Black Lives Matter Surged Last Summer. Did It Last?" *New York Times.* May 22, 2021. https://www.nytimes.com/2021/05/22/opinion/blm-movement-protests-support.html.

Coates, Ta-Nehesi. "Cliven Bundy and the Tyranny All Around Us." *The Atlantic.* April 22, 2014. https://www.theatlantic.com/politics/archive/2014/04/clive-bundy-and-the-tyranny-all-around-us/361039/.

Coates, Ta-Nehesi. "The First White President." *The Atlantic.* October 2017. https://www.theatlantic.com/magazine/archive/2017/10/the-first-white-president-ta-nehisi-coates/537909/.

Coleman, Nancy. "Why We're Capitalizing 'Black.'" *New York Times.* July 5, 2020. https://www.nytimes.com/2020/07/05/insider/capitalized-black.html.

The Combahee River Collective. "The Combahee River Collective Statement." In *Home Girls: A Black Feminist Anthology,* edited by Barbara Smith, 272–81. New York: Kitchen Table – Women of Color Press, 1983.

Cone, James H. *The Cross and the Lynching Tree.* Maryknoll, NY: Orbis Books, 2011.

Connolly, William. *Pluralism.* Durham, NC: Duke University Press, 2005.

Cook, Lindsey. "U.S. Education: Still Separate and Unequal." *US News and World Report.* January 28, 2015. https://www.usnews.com/news/blogs/data-mine/2015/01/28/us-education-still-separate-and-unequal.

Cooper, Anna Julia. *A Voice from the South.* 1892. https://docsouth.unc.edu/church/cooper/cooper.html.

Coulthard, Glen. *Red Skin, White Masks: Rejecting the Colonial Politics of Recognition.* Minneapolis: University of Minnesota Press, 2014.

Cox, Daniel, Rachel Lienesch, and Robert P. Jones. "Beyond Economics: Fears of Cultural Displacement Pushed the White Working Class to Trump." *Public Religion Research Institute.* May 9, 2017. https://www.prri.org/research/white-working-class-attitudes-economy-trade-immigration-election-donald-trump/.

Craig, Maureen A., and Jennifer A. Richeson. "More Diverse Yet Less Tolerant? How the Increasingly Diverse Racial Landscape Affects White Americans' Racial Attitudes." *Personality and Social Psychology Bulletin* 40, no. 6 (2014): 750–61.

Craig, Maureen A., and Jennifer A. Richeson. "On the Precipice of Majority-Minority America: Perceived Status Threat from the Racial Demographic Shift Affects White Americans' Political Ideology." *Psychological Science* 25, no. 6 (June 2014): 1189–97.

Daly, Mary C., Bart Hobijn, and Joseph H. Pedtke. "Disappointing Facts About the Black-White Wage Gap." *FRBSF Economic Letter.* September 2017. https://www.frbsf.org/economic-research/publications/economic-letter/2017/september/disappointing-facts-about-black-white-wage-gap/.

Daum, Courtenay W. "Counterpublics and Intersectional Radical Resistance: Agitation as Transformation of the Dominant Discourse." *New Political Science* 39, no. 4 (2017): 523–37.

Davis, Angela. *Abolition Democracy: Beyond Empire, Prisons, and Torture.* New York: Seven Stories Press, 2005.

Davis, Angela. *Freedom Is a Constant Struggle: Ferguson, Palestine, and the Foundations of a Movement.* Chicago: Haymarket Books, 2016.

Davis, Angela. "Masked Racism: Reflections on the Prison Industrial Complex." *Colorlines.* September 10, 1998. https://www.colorlines.com/articles/masked-racism-reflections-prison-industrial-complex.

Davis, Angela. *The Meaning of Freedom: And Other Difficult Dialogues*. San Francisco: City Lights Publishers, 2012.

Davis, Angela. *Are Prisons Obsolete?* New York: Seven Stories Press, 2003.

Davis, Ben. "Monuments Across the United States Re-Emerged as Targets of Rage over a Weekend of Widespread Protest." *Artnet News*. June 1, 2020. https://news.artnet.com/art-world/monuments-across-the-united-states-re-emerged-as-targets-of-fury-over-a-weekend-of-widespread-protest-1876542.

Davis, Mike. "Not a Revolution—Yet." *Verso Books Blog*. November 15, 2016. http://www.versobooks.com/blogs/2948-not-a-revolution-yet.

Dawson, Michael C. "Hidden in Plain Sight: A Note on Legitimation Crises and the Racial Order." *Critical Historical Studies* 3, no. 1 (Spring 2016): 143–61.

Dawson, Michael C., and Megan Ming Francis. "Black Politics and the Neoliberal Order." *Public Culture* 28, no. 1 (2015): 23–62.

Delmont, Matthew F. *Why Busing Failed: Race, Media, and the National Resistance to School Desegregation*. Berkeley: University of California Press, 2016.

DiAngelo, Robin. *White Fragility: Why It's so Hard for White People to Talk About Racism*. Boston: Beacon Press, 2018.

Douglas, Andrew J. *W. E. B. Du Bois and the Critique of Competitive Society*. Athens: University of Georgia Press, 2019.

Douglass, Frederick. Address to the Massachusetts Anti-Slavery Society. Quoted in *The Liberator* 12, no. 7 (February 18, 1842). http://fair-use.org/the-liberator/1842/02/18/the-liberator-12-07.pdf.

Douhat, Ross. "The Dying of the Whites." *New York Times*. November 7, 2015. https://www.nytimes.com/2015/11/08/opinion/sunday/the-dying-of-the-whites.html.

Dray, Phillip. *At the Hands of Persons Unknown: The Lynching of Black America*. New York: Random House, 2002.

Dreher, Rod. "Why Trump Matters." *American Conservative*. November 6, 2015.

Du Bois, W. E. B. "The African Roots of War." *The Atlantic*. May 1915. https://www.theatlantic.com/magazine/archive/1915/05/the-african-roots-of-war/528897/.

Du Bois, W. E. B. "Apologia." 1954. http://www.webdubois.org/dbSAST-Apologia.html. —

Du Bois, W. E. B. "Black and White Workers." In *The Emerging Thought of W. E. B. Du Bois: Essays and Editorials from the Crisis*, edited by Henry Lee Moon, 274–76. New York: Simon and Schuster, 1972.

Du Bois, W. E. B. "The Black Man and the Unions." In *The Emerging Thought of W. E. B. Du Bois: Essays and Editorials from the Crisis*, edited by Henry Lee Moon, 158–59. New York: Simon and Schuster, 1972.

Du Bois, W. E. B. *Black Reconstruction in America: An Essay Toward a History of the Part Which Black Folk Played in the Attempt to Reconstruct Democracy in America, 1860–1880*. Oxford: Oxford University Press, 2007 (1935).

Du Bois, W. E. B. "The Class Struggle." In *The Emerging Thought of W. E. B. Du Bois: Essays and Editorials from the Crisis*, edited by Henry Lee Moon, 269–70. New York: Simon and Schuster, 1972.

Du Bois, W. E. B. "Colonialism, Democracy, and Peace After the War." In *Against Racism: Unpublished Essays, Papers, Addresses*, edited by Herbert Aptheker, 229–36. Amherst: University of Massachusetts Press, 1985.

Du Bois, W. E. B. "The Color Line Belts the World." *Collier's*. October 20, 1906.

Du Bois, W. E. B. "The Colored World Within." In *Dusk of Dawn: An Essay Toward an Autobiography of the Race Concept*, 88–110. Oxford: Oxford University Press, 2007 (1940).

Du Bois, W. E. B. "The Concept of Race." In *Dusk of Dawn: An Essay Toward an Autobiography of the Race Concept*, 49–67. Oxford: Oxford University Press, 2007 (1940).

Du Bois, W. E. B. "Criteria of Negro Art." 1926. http://www.webdubois.org/dbCriteriaN Art.html.

Du Bois, W. E. B. "The Damnation of Women." In *Darkwater: Voices from Within the Veil*, 78–89. Oxford: Oxford University Press, 2007 (1920).

Du Bois, W. E. B. "The Denial of Economic Justice to Negroes." In *W. E. B. Du Bois Speaks: Speeches and Addresses 1920–1963*, edited by Philip S. Foner, 55–58. New York: Pathfinder Press, 1971.

Du Bois, W. E. B. "The Development of a People." *Ethics* 123, no. 3 (April 2013 [1904]): 525–44.

Du Bois, W. E. B. "Dives, Mob and Scab, Limited." In *The Emerging Thought of W. E. B. Du Bois: Essays and Editorials from the Crisis*, edited by Henry Lee Moon, 161. New York: Simon and Schuster, 1972.

Du Bois, W. E. B. "Education in the Last Decades of the Nineteenth Century." In *Dusk of Dawn: An Essay Toward an Autobiography of the Race Concept*, 13–25. Oxford: Oxford University Press, 2007 (1940).

Du Bois, W. E. B. *The Gift of Black Folk: The Negroes in the Making of America*. Oxford: Oxford University Press, 2014 (1924).

Du Bois, W. E. B. "The Hands of Ethiopia." In *Darkwater: Voices from Within the Veil*, 28–36. Oxford: Oxford University Press, 2007 (1920).

Du Bois, W. E. B. "Karl Marx and the Negro." *The Crisis* 40, no. 3 (March 1933): 55–56.

Du Bois, W. E. B. Letter from W. E. B. Du Bois to Grace Goens, September 13, 1961. W. E. B. Du Bois Papers (MS 312). Special Collections and University Archives, University of Massachusetts Amherst Libraries. https://credo.library.umass.edu/view/full/mums 312-b153-i208.

Du Bois, W. E. B. "Marxism and the Negro Problem." *The Crisis* 40, no. 5 (May 1933): 103–4, 118.

Du Bois, W. E. B. "My Evolving Platform for Negro Freedom." In *What the Negro Wants*, edited by Rayford W. Logan, 27–57. Chapel Hill: University of North Carolina Press, 1944.

Du Bois, W. E. B. "The Negro and Communism." In *W. E. B. Du Bois: A Reader*, edited by David Levering Lewis, 583–93. New York: Henry Holt and Co., 1995.

Du Bois, W. E. B. "The Negro and Radical Thought." In *The Emerging Thought of W. E. B. Du Bois: Essays and Editorials from the Crisis*, edited by Henry Lee Moon, 265–68. New York: Simon and Schuster, 1972.

Du Bois, W. E. B. "The Negro and Social Reconstruction." In *Against Racism: Unpublished Essays, Papers, Addresses*, edited by Herbert Aptheker, 103–58. Amherst: University of Massachusetts Press, 1985.

Du Bois, W. E. B. "A Negro Nation Within a Nation." *Black Past*. 1934. https://www.blackp ast.org/african-american-history/speeches-african-american-history/1934-w-e-b-du-bois-negro-nation-within-nation/.

Du Bois, W. E. B. "Of the Culture of White Folk." *Journal of Race Development* 7, no. 4 (April 1917): 434–47.

Du Bois, W. E. B. "Of the Ruling of Men." In *Darkwater: Voices from Within the Veil*, 65–76. Oxford: Oxford University Press, 2007 (1920).

Du Bois, W. E. B. "Of Work and Wealth." In *Darkwater: Voices from Within the Veil*, 40–50. Oxford: Oxford University Press, 2007 (1920).

Du Bois, W. E. B. "A Pageant in Seven Decades." In *W. E. B. Du Bois Speaks: Speeches and Addresses 1890–1919*, edited by Philip S. Foner, 21–72. New York: Pathfinder Press, 1970.

Du Bois, W. E. B. "The Perfect Vacation." *The Crisis* 40, no. 8 (August 1931).

Du Bois, W. E. B. "The Plot." In *Dusk of Dawn: An Essay Toward an Autobiography of the Race Concept*, 1–3. Oxford: Oxford University Press, 2007 (1940).

Du Bois, W. E. B. "The Position of the Negro in the American Social Order: Where Do We Go from Here?" *Journal of Negro Education* 8, no. 3 (July 1939): 551–70.

Du Bois, W. E. B. "Propaganda and World War." In *Dusk of Dawn: An Essay Toward an Autobiography of the Race Concept*, 111–33. Oxford: Oxford University Press, 2007 (1940).

Du Bois, W. E. B. "Revolution." In *Dusk of Dawn: An Essay Toward an Autobiography of the Race Concept*, 134–62. Oxford: Oxford University Press, 2007 (1940).

Du Bois, W. E. B. "The Right to Work." In *Du Bois: Writings*, edited by Nathan Huggins, 1235–38. New York: Library of America, 1986.

Du Bois, W. E. B. "Science and Empire." In *Dusk of Dawn: An Essay Toward an Autobiography of the Race Concept*, 26–48. Oxford: Oxford University Press, 2007 (1940).

Du Bois, W. E. B. "'The Servant in the House.'" In *Darkwater: Voices from Within the Veil*, 53–58. Oxford: Oxford University Press, 2007 (1920).

Du Bois, W. E. B. "The Shape of Fear." *North American Review* 223, no. 831 (June–August 1926): 291–304.

Du Bois, W. E. B. "Social Equality and Racial Intermarriage." *World Tomorrow* (March 1922): 83–84.

Du Bois, W. E. B. "Social Planning for the Negro, Past and Present." *Journal for Negro Education* 5, no. 1 (January 1936): 110–25.

Du Bois, W. E. B. *The Souls of Black Folk*. Oxford: Oxford University Press, 2007 (1903).

Du Bois, W. E. B. "The Souls of White Folk." In *Darkwater: Voices from Within the Veil*, 15–25. Oxford: Oxford University Press, 2007 (1920).

Du Bois, W. E. B. "Triumph." *The Crisis* 2, no. 5 (September 1911): 195.

Du Bois, W. E. B. "The White World." In *Dusk of Dawn: An Essay Toward an Autobiography of the Race Concept*, 68–87. Oxford: Oxford University Press, 2007 (1940).

Du Bois, W. E. B., and Martha Gruening. "The Massacre of East St. Louis." *The Crisis* 14, no. 5 (September 1917): 219–38.

Ehrenfreund, Max, and Scott Clement. "Economic and Racial Anxiety: Two Separate Forces Driving Support for Donald Trump." *Washington Post*. March 22, 2016. https://www.washingtonpost.com/news/wonk/wp/2016/03/22/economic-anxiety-and-racial-anxiety-two-separate-forces-driving-support-for-donald-trump/.

Eligon, John, and Audra D. S. Burch. "After a Summer of Racial Reckoning, Race Is on the Ballot." *New York Times*. October 30, 2020. https://www.nytimes.com/2020/10/30/us/racial-justice-elections.html.

Ellis, Mary Louise. *"Rain Down Fire": The Lynching of Sam Hose*. PhD dissertation, Florida State University, 1992.

Erickson, Peter. "Seeing White." *Transition* 67 (1995): 166–85.

Fanon, Frantz. *Black Skin, White Masks,* translated by Ruchard Philcox. New York: Grove Press, 2008 (1952).

Farley, Anthony Paul. "The Apogee of the Commodity." *DePaul Law Review* 53 (2003–04): 1229–46.

Feagin, Joe. *The White Racial Frame: Centuries of Racial Framing and Counter-Framing.* New York: Taylor & Francis, 2009.

Fearnow, Benjamin. "Video: White Woman Calls Police on Black Family's BBQ for 'Trespassing' in Oakland Park." *Newsweek.* May 10, 2018. https://www.newsweek.com/lake-merritt-bbq-barbecue-video-oakland-racist-charcoal-east-bay-black-family-919355.

Fields, Barbara J. "Ideology and Race in American History." In *Region, Race, and Reconstruction: Essays in Honor of C. Vann Woodward,* edited by J. Morgan Kausser and James M. McPherson, 143–77. New York: Oxford University Press, 1982.

Fields, Barbara J. "Slavery, Race, and Ideology in the United States of America." *New Left Review* 181 (May–June 1990): 95–118.

Fields, Barbara J. "Whiteness, Racism, and Identity." *International Labor and Working-Class History* 60 (Fall 2001): 48–56.

Fields, Barbara J., and Karen E. Fields. "Did the Color of His Skin Skill Philando Castille?" *Jacobin.* July 3, 2016. https://www.jacobinmag.com/2016/07/racecraft-barbara-karen-fields-philando-castile.

Fields, Karen E., and Barbara J. Fields. "How Race Is Conjured: An Interview with Barbara J. Fields and Karen E. Fields." *Jacobin.* June 29, 2015. https://www.jacobinmag.com/2015/06/karen-barbara-fields-racecraft-dolezal-racism/.

Fields, Karen E., and Barbara J. Fields. *Racecraft: The Soul of Inequality in American Life.* London: Verso Books, 2012.

Flaccus, Gillian. "Ammon Bundy Testifies in Second Oregon Standoff Trial." *U.S. News.* February 28, 2017.

Flatley, Jonathan. "'What a Mourning': Propaganda and Loss in Du Bois's *Souls of Black Folk.*" In *Affective Mapping: Melancholia and the Politics of Modernism,* 105–57. Cambridge, MA: Harvard University Press, 2008.

Fowler, Hayley. "Hampton Inn Worker Calls Police on Black Guests at Hotel Pool in NC, Video Shows." *News and Observer.* June 30, 2020. https://www.newsobserver.com/news/state/north-carolina/article243897702.html.

Francis, Megan Ming. "The Battle for the Hearts and Minds of America." *Souls: A Critical Journal of Black Politics, Culture, and Society* 13, no. 1 (2011): 46–71.

Freud, Sigmund. "Instincts and Their Vicissitudes." In *The Standard Edition of the Complete Psychological Works of Sigmund Freud,* vol. 14, translated by James Strachey, 111–40. London: Hogarth Press, 1957.

Frey, William H. "U.S. White Population Declines and Generation 'Z-Plus' Is Minority White, Census Shows." *Brookings.* June 22, 2018. https://www.brookings.edu/blog/the-avenue/2018/06/21/us-white-population-declines-and-generation-z-plus-is-minority-white-census-shows/.

Garza, Alicia. "A Herstory of the #BlackLivesMatter Movement by Alicia Garza." *Feminist Wire.* October 7, 2014. https://www.thefeministwire.com/2014/10/blacklivesmatter-2/.

Garza, Alicia. *The Purpose of Power: How We Come Together When We Fall Apart.* New York: One World, 2020.

Getachew, Adom. *Worldmaking After Empire: The Rise and Fall of Self-Determination.* Princeton, NJ: Princeton University Press, 2019.

Giddings, Paula. "Missing in Action: Ida B Wells, the NAACP and the Historical Record." *Meridians* 1, no. 2 (Spring 2001): 1–17.

Gilens, Martin. *Why Americans Hate Welfare: Race, Media, and the Politics of Antipoverty Policy.* Chicago: University of Chicago, 1999.

Gillman, Susan, and Alys Eve Weinbaum, eds. *Next to the Color Line: Gender, Sexuality and Du Bois.* Minneapolis: University of Minnesota Press, 2007.

Gilmore, Ruth Wilson. "Abolition Geography and the Problem of Innocence." In *Futures of Black Radicalism*, edited by Gaye Theresa Johnson and Alex Lubin, 225–40. New York: Verso, 2017.

Gilmore, Ruth Wilson. *Golden Gulag: Prisons, Surplus, Crisis, and Opposition in Globalizing California.* Berkeley: University of California Press, 2007.

Gilmore, Ruth Wilson. "From the Military Industrial Complex to the Prison Industrial Complex." *Recording Carceral Landscapes.* Creative Commons. May 2005. https://poin tsforponder.files.wordpress.com/2012/10/gilmore-nd2.pdf.

Gilmore, Ruth Wilson. "Transcript: In Conversation with Ruth Wilson Gilmore." University College London. June 2020. https://www.ucl.ac.uk/racism-racialisation/tra nscript-conversation-ruth-wilson-gilmore.

Gilmore, Ruth Wilson, and James Kilgore. "The Case for Abolition." June 19, 2019. https:// www.themarshallproject.org/2019/06/19/the-case-for-abolition.

Gilroy, Paul. *The Black Atlantic: Modernity and Double Consciousness.* Cambridge, MA: Harvard University Press, 1993.

Goldberg, Susan B., and Cameron Levin. "Toward a Radical White Identity." 2009. https:// www.awarela.org/our-models.

Goldstein, Dana. "One Reason School Segregation Persists: White Parents Want It That Way." *Slate.* July 15, 2016. https://slate.com/human-interest/2016/07/when-white-pare nts-have-a-choice-they-choose-segregated-schools.html.

Goldstein, Dana. "Where Civility Is a Motto, a School Integration Fight Turns Bitter." *New York Times.* November 12, 2019. https://www.nytimes.com/2019/11/12/us/how ard-county-school-redistricting.html.

Golub, Mark. "Remembering Massive Resistance to School Desegregation." *Law and History Review* 31, no. 3 (August 2013): 491–530.

Gooding-Williams, Robert. "Autobiography, Political Hope, Racial Justice." *Du Bois Review* 11, no. 1 (2014): 159–75.

Gooding-Williams, Robert. "Look! A Negro!" In *Reading Rodney King/Reading Urban Uprising*, edited by Robert Gooding-Williams, 157–77. New York: Routledge, 1993.

Gordon, Lewis. "Critical 'Mixed Race'?" *Social Identities* 1, no. 2 (August 1995): n.p.

Gould, Elise. "Black-White Wage Gaps Are Worse Today Than in 2000." Economic Policy Institute. February 27, 2020. https://www.epi.org/blog/black-white-wage-gaps-are-worse-today-than-in-2000/.

Green, Emma. "It Was Cultural Anxiety That Drove White Working Class Voters to Trump." *The Atlantic.* May 9, 2017. https://www.theatlantic.com/politics/archive/2017/ 05/white-working-class-trump-cultural-anxiety/525771/

Greene, Peter. "White Flight, Without the Actual Flight." *Forbes.* November 12, 2019. https://www.forbes.com/sites/petergreene/2019/11/12/white-flight-without-the-act ual-flight/?sh=74f00c6253c6.

Griffin, Farah Jasmine. "Black Feminists and Du Bois: Respectability, Protection, and Beyond." *Annals of the American Academy of Political and Social Science* 586 (March 2000): 28–40.

Gunier, Lani, and Gerald Torres. *The Miner's Canary: Enlisting Race, Resisting Power, Transforming Democracy*. Cambridge, MA: Harvard University Press, 2003.

Gusterson, Hugh. "From Brexit to Trump: Anthropology and the Rise of Nationalist Populism." *American Ethnologist* 44, no. 2 (2017): 209–14.

Hale, Grace Elizabeth. *Making Whiteness: The Culture of Segregation in the South, 1890–1940*. New York: Pantheon Books, 1999.

Hall, Stuart. "Race, Articulation, and Societies Structured in Dominance." In *Black British Cultural Studies: A Reader*, edited by Houston A. Baker Jr., Manthia Diawara, and Ruth H. Lindeborg, 16–60. Chicago: University of Chicago Press, 1996.

Hannah-Jones, Nikole. "It Was Never About Busing." *New York Times*. July 12, 2019. https://www.nytimes.com/2019/07/12/opinion/sunday/it-was-never-about-busing.html.

Hannah-Jones, Nikole. "Segregation Now." *Pro Publica*. April 16, 2014. https://www.propublica.org/article/segregation-now-full-text.

Harriot, Michael. "White Caller Crime: The Worst Wypipo Police Calls of All Time." *The Root*. May 15, 2018. https://www.theroot.com/white-caller-crime-the-worst-wypipo-police-calls-of-1826023382.

Harris, Cheryl. "Whiteness as Property." *Harvard Law Review* 106, no. 8 (June 1993): 1701–91.

Harris, Cheryl. "Whitewashing Race, Scapegoating Culture." *California Law Review* 94, no. 3 (2006): 907–43.

Hartman, Andrew. "The Rise and Fall of Whiteness Studies." *Race Class* 46, no. 2 (2004): 22–38.

Hartman, Saidiya. "Introduction". to W. E. B. Du Bois, *The Suppression of the African Slave Trade to the United States of America, 1638–1870*, xxv–xxx. Oxford: Oxford University Press, 2007 (1896).

Hartman, Saidiya. *Scenes of Subjection: Terror, Slavery, and Self-Making in 19th Century America*. Oxford: Oxford University Press, 1997.

Hawkins, T. D. Letter from T. D. Hawkins to W. E. B. Du Bois, November 15, 1930. W. E. B. Du Bois Papers (MS 312). Special Collections and University Archives, University of Massachusetts Amherst Libraries. https://credo.library.umass.edu/view/full/mums312-b054-i107.

Henderson, Taja-Nia Y., and Jamila Jefferson-Jones. "#LivingWhileBlack: Blackness as Nuisance." *American University Law Review* 69, no. 3 (2020): 863–914.

Hernandez, Dan, and Joseph Langdon. "Federal Rangers Face Off Against Armed Protesters in Nevada 'Range War.'" *The Guardian*. April 13, 2014.

Higginbotham, Evelyn Brooks. "African-American Women's History and the Metalanguage of Race." *Signs* 17, no. 2 (Winter 1992): 251–74.

Hochschild, Arlie Russell. *Strangers in Their Own Land: Anger and Mourning on the American Right*. New York: New Press, 2016.

Hooker, Juliet. "Black Lives Matter and the Paradoxes of U.S. Black Politics: From Democratic Sacrifice to Democratic Repair." *Political Theory* 44, no. 4 (2016): 448–69.

Hooker, Juliet. *Theorizing Race in the Americas: Douglass, Sarmiento, Du Bois and Vasconcelos*. Oxford: Oxford University Press, 2017.

hooks, bell. *Black Looks: Race and Representation*. Boston: South End Press, 1992.

hooks, bell. "Representing Whiteness in the Black Imagination." In *Displacing Whiteness: Essays in Social and Cultural Criticism*, edited by Ruth Frankenberg, 338–46. Durham, NC, and London: Duke University Press, 1997.

HoSang, Daniel Martinez. "'We Have No Master Race': Racial Liberalism and Political Whiteness." In *Racial Propositions: Ballot Initiatives and the Making of Postwar California*, 13–23. Berkeley: University of California Press, 2010.

Howell, Junia, Marie Skoczylas, and Shatae DeVaughn. "Living While Black." *American Sociological Association Contexts* 18, no. 2 (2019): 68–69.

Hudak, John. "A Reality Check on 2016's Economically Marginalized." Brookings. November 16, 2016. https://www.brookings.edu/blog/fixgov/2016/11/16/economic-marginalization-realitycheck/?utm_campaign=Brookings+Brief&utm_source=hs_email&utm_medium=email&utm_content=37763319.

Ignatiev, Noel. "The Point Is Not to Interpret Whiteness but to Abolish It." 1997. https://blog.pmpress.org/2019/09/16/the-point-is-not-to-interpret-whiteness-but-to-abolish-it/.

Ignatin, Noel. "Black Worker, White Worker: Understanding and Fighting White Supremacy." Sojourner Truth Organization Electronic Archive. 1972. http://www.sojournertruth.net/bwww.html.

Ignatin, Noel. "Letter to Progressive Labor." In *Revolutionary Youth and the Working Class: Lost Writings of SDS*, edited by Carl Davidson, 148–63. Pittsburgh, PA: Changemaker Productions, 2011.

Ince, Onur Ulas. "Primitive Accumulation and Global Land Grabs." *Rural Sociology* 79, no. 1 (2014): 104–31.

Ingersoll, William T. Oral History Interview of W. E. B. Du Bois, ca. June 1960. W. E. B. Du Bois Papers (MS 312). Special Collections and University Archives, University of Massachusetts Amherst Libraries. https://credo.library.umass.edu/view/full/mums312-b237-i137.

Inwood, Joshua F. J., and Anne Bonds. "Property and Whiteness: The Oregon Standoff and the Contradictions of the U.S. Settler State." *Space and Polity* 21, no. 3 (2017): 253–68.

Issar, Siddhant. "Listening to Black Lives Matter: Racial Capitalism and the Critique of Neoliberalism." *Contemporary Political Theory* 20, no. 1 (2020): 48–71.

Issar, Siddhant. "Theorising 'Racial/Colonial Primitive Accumulation': Settler Colonialism, Slavery, and Racial Capitalism." *Race & Class* 63, no. 1 (2021): 23–50.

Jackson, Lauren Michelle. "What's Missing from 'White Fragility.'" *Slate*. September 4, 2019. https://slate.com/human-interest/2019/09/white-fragility-robin-diangelo-workshop.html.

Jacobs, Julia. "The 'Black Lives Matter' Street Art that Contains Multitudes." *New York Times*. July 16, 2020. https://www.nytimes.com/2020/07/16/arts/design/black-lives-matter-murals-new-york.html.

James, Joy. *Transcending the Talented Tenth: Black Leaders and American Intellectuals*. New York: Routledge, 1997.

Jardina, Ashley. *White Identity Politics*. Cambridge: Cambridge University Press, 2019.

Johnson, Walter. "Brute Ideology." *Dissent* 61, no. 4 (Fall 2014): 127–32.

Johnson, Walter. *Soul by Soul: Life Inside the Antebellum Slave Market*. Cambridge, MA: Harvard University Press, 1999.

Kaba, Mariame. *We Do This Til We Free Us: Abolitionist Organizing and Transforming Justice*. Chicago: Haymarket Books, 2021.

Keeler, Jacqueline. "On Calvin Bundy's 'Ancestral Rights.'" *The Nation.* April 29, 2014. https://www.thenation.com/article/archive/cliven-bundys-ancestral-rights/

Kelley, Robin D. G. "The Rest of Us: Rethinking Settler and Native." *American Quarterly* 69, no. 2 (June 2017): 267–76.

Kelley, Robin D. G. "What Did Cedric Robinson Mean by Racial Capitalism?" *Boston Review.* January 12, 2017. https://bostonreview.net/articles/robin-d-g-kelley-introduct ion-race-capitalism-justice/.

Kendi, Ibram X. *How to Be an Antiracist.* New York: One World Books, 2019.

Kerr-Ritchie, J. R. "Review of Edward J. Blum, *W. E. B. Du Bois: American Prophet.*" *Journal of African American History* 94, no. 1 (Winter 2009): 123–25.

Khazan, Olga. "Middle-Aged White Americans Are Dying of Despair." *The Atlantic.* November 4, 2015. https://www.theatlantic.com/health/archive/2015/11/boomers-deaths-pnas/413971/.

Kirschke, Amy Helene. "Art in *Crisis* During the Du Bois Years." In *Protest and Propaganda: W. E. B. Du Bois, The Crisis, and American History,* edited by Amy Helene Kirschke and Phillip Luke Sinitiere, 49–117. Columbia: University of Missouri Press, 2019.

Klarman, Michael J. *Unfinished Business: Racial Equality in American History.* Oxford: Oxford University Press, 2007.

Kolchin, Peter. "Whiteness Studies: The New History of Race in America." *Journal of American History* 89, no. 1 (June 2002): 154–73.

Kristof, Nicholas. "When Whites Just Don't Get It." Parts 1–7. *New York Times.* 2014–16.

Krugman, Paul. "Despair, American Style." *New York Times.* November 9, 2015. https://www.nytimes.com/2015/11/09/opinion/despair-american-style.html.

Kurtzleben, Danielle, and Miles Parks. "Trump Defends 'Beauty' of Confederate Memorials." *NPR.* August 17, 2017. https://www.npr.org/2017/08/17/544137751/trump-defends-beauty-of-confederate-memorials.

Kushner, Rachel. "Is Prison Necessary? Ruth Wilson Gilmore Might Change Your Mind." *New York Times.* April 17, 2019. https://www.nytimes.com/2019/04/17/magazine/pri son-abolition-ruth-wilson-gilmore.html.

Latour, Bruno. "What Is Iconoclash?" In *Iconoclash: Beyond the Image Wars in Science, Religion, and Art,* edited by Bruno Latour and Peter Weibel, 16–40. Cambridge, MA: MIT Press, 2002.

Lebron, Christopher J. *The Making of Black Lives Matter: A Brief History of an Idea.* Oxford: Oxford University Press, 2017.

Lewis, David Levering. *W. E. B. Du Bois: Biography of a Race, 1868–1919.* New York: Henry Holt and Co., 1993.

Lewis, David Levering. *W. E. B. Du Bois: The Fight for Equality and the American Century, 1919–1963.* New York: Henry Holt and Co., 2000.

Lewis, George. *Massive Resistance: The White Response to the Civil Rights Movement.* London: Hodder Arnold, 2016.

Lipsitz, George. *The Possessive Investment in Whiteness.* Philadelphia: Temple University Press, 1998.

Lizza, Ryan. "What We Learned About Trump Supporters This Week." *New Yorker.* August 13, 2016. https://www.newyorker.com/news/daily-comment/what-we-learned-about-trumps-supporters-this-week.

Locke, Jill. "Little Rock's Social Question: Reading Arendt on School Desegregation and Social Climbing." *Political Theory* 41, no. 4 (August 2013): 533–61.

López, Ian Haney. *Merge Left: Fusing Race and Class, Winning Elections, and Saving America*. New York: New Press, 2019.

López, Ian Haney. "Shor Is Mainly Wrong About Racism (Which Is to Say, About Electoral Politics)." October 11, 2021. https://gen.medium.com/shor-is-mainly-wrong-about-racism-which-is-to-say-about-electoral-politics-77692910255c.

Luis-Brown, David. *Waves of Decolonization: Discourses of Race and Hemispheric Citizenship in Cuba, Mexico, and the United States*. Durham, NC: Duke University Press, 2008.

Luxemburg, Rosa. *The Accumulation of Capital*, translated by Agnes Schwarzschild. London: Routledge and Kegan Paul, 1951 (1913).

Mackin, Glenn. "Black Lives Matter and the Concept of the Counterworld." *Philosophy & Rhetoric* 49, no. 4 (2016): 459–81.

Major, Brenda, Alison Blodorn, and Gregory Major Blascovich. "The Threat of Increasing Diversity: Why Many White Americans Support Trump in the 2016 Presidential Election." *Group Processes & Intergroup Relations* 21, no. 6 (2018): 931–40.

Marable, Manning. *W. E. B. Du Bois: Black Radical Democrat*. 2nd ed. New York: Routledge, 2016.

Marcus, Ezra. "Will the Last Confederate Statue Standing Turn Off the Lights?" *New York Times*. June 23, 2020. https://www.nytimes.com/2020/06/23/style/statue-richmond-lee.html.

Martinot, Steve, and Jared Sexton. "The Avant-Garde of White Supremacy." *Social Identities* 9, no. 2 (2003): 169–81.

Marx, Karl. "Marx to Sigfrid Meyer and August Vogt in New York, April 9, 1870." In *The Civil War in the United States: Karl Marx and Friedrich Engels*, edited by Andrew Zimmerman, 203–5. New York: International Publishers, 2016.

Marx, Karl. "Marx, on Behalf of the International Working Men's Association, Letter to President Abraham Lincoln." In Karl Marx and Friedrich Engels, *The Civil War in the United States*, edited by Andrew Zimmerman, 154–55. New York: International Publishers, 2016.

Marx, Karl. "The North American Civil War." In Karl Marx and Friedrich Engels, *The Civil War in the United States*, edited by Andrew Zimmerman, 39–48. New York: International Publishers, 2016.

McAdam, Doug. "The Framing Function of Movement Tactics: Strategic Dramaturgy in the American Civil Rights Movement." In *Comparative Perspectives on Social Movements: Political Opportunities, Mobilizing Structures, and Cultural* Framings, edited by Doug McAdam, John D. McCarthy, and Mayer N. Zald, 338–55. Cambridge: Cambridge University Press, 1996.

McGhee, Heather. *The Sum of Us: What Racism Costs Everyone and How We Can Prosper Together*. New York: One World, 2021.

McGill, Ralph. "W. E. B. Du Bois." *Atlantic Monthly*. November 1965. https://www.theatlantic.com/past/docs/unbound/flashbks/black/mcgillbh.htm.

McIntosh, Kriston, Emily Moss, Ryan Nunn, and Jay Shambaugh. "Examining the Black-White Wealth Gap." Brookings Institute. February 27, 2020. https://www.brookings.edu/blog/up-front/2020/02/27/examining-the-black-white-wealth-gap/.

McIntosh, Peggy. "White Privilege and Male Privilege: A Personal Account of Coming to See Correspondences Through Work in Women's Studies." *Peace and Freedom* (July/August 1988).

McNamarah, Chan Tov. "White Caller Crime: Racialized Police Communication and Existing While Black." *Michigan Journal of Race and Law* 24 (2019): 335–415.

Melamed, Jodi. "Racial Capitalism." *Critical Ethnic Studies* 1, no. 1 (Spring 2015): 76–85.

Mervosh, Sarah. "How Much Wealthier Are White School Districts Than Nonwhite Ones? $23 Billion, Report Says." *New York Times.* February 27, 2019. https://www.nytimes.com/2019/02/27/education/school-districts-funding-white-minorities.html.

Mervosh, Sarah, Simon Romero, and Lucy Tompkins. "Reconsidering the Past, One Statue at a Time." *New York Times.* June 17, 2020. https://www.nytimes.com/2020/06/16/us/protests-statues-reckoning.html.

Middlebrook, Jeb Aram. "The Ballot Box and Beyond: On the (Im)Possibilities of White Antiracist Organizing." *American Quarterly* 62, no. 2 (June 2010): 233–52.

Miller, Mark Crispin. Introduction to Edward Bernays's *Propaganda*, 9–33. New York: Ig Publishing, 2004.

Mills, Charles. "Global White Ignorance." In *Routledge International Handbook of Ignorance Studies,* edited by Matthias Gross and Linsey McGoey, 217–27. New York: Routledge, 2015.

Mills, Charles. *The Racial Contract.* Ithaca, NY: Cornell University Press, 1997.

Mills, Charles. "The Racial Polity." In *Blackness Visible: Essays on Philosophy and Race,* 119–38. Ithaca, NY: Cornell University Press, 1998.

Mills, Charles. "W. E. B. Du Bois: Black Radical Liberal." In *The Political Companion to W. E. B. Du Bois,* edited by Nick Bromwell, 19–56. Lexington: University Press of Kentucky, 2018.

Mills, Charles. "White Ignorance." In *Race and Epistemologies of Ignorance,* edited by Shannon Sullivan and Nancy Tuana, 13–38. Albany: State University of New York Press, 2007.

Mirzoeff, Nicholas. "Tactics of Appearance for Abolition Democracy #BlackLives Matter." *Critical Inquiry.* 2018. https://criticalinquiry.uchicago.edu/tactics_of_appearance/.

Moreton-Robinson, Aileen. *The White Possessive: Property, Power, and Indigenous Sovereignty.* Minneapolis: University of Minnesota Press, 2015.

Morgan, Edmund. *American Slavery, American Freedom.* New York: W. W. Norton & Co., 1975.

Morrison, Toni. *Playing in the Dark: Whiteness and the Literary Imagination.* New York: Vintage Books, 1992.

Moten, Fred, and Stefano Harvey, "The University and the Undercommons: Seven Theses." *Social Text* 22, no. 2 (2004): 101–15.

Movement for Black Lives (M4BL) Platform. 2020. https://m4bl.org/policy-platforms/.

Mueller, Jennifer. "Racial Ideology or Racial Ignorance? An Alternative Theory of Racial Cognition." *Sociological Theory* 38, no. 2 (2020): 142–69.

Mullen, Bill V. *Un-American: W. E. B. Du Bois and the Century of World Revolution.* Philadelphia: Temple University Press, 2015.

Mullen, Bill V. "A World to Win: Propaganda and African American Expressive Culture." In *The Oxford Handbook of Propaganda Studies,* edited by Jonathan Auerbach and Russ Castronovo, 49–66. Oxford: Oxford University Press, 2013.

Munro, John. "Roots of Whiteness." *Labour/La Travail* 54 (Fall 2004): 175–92.

Murch, Donna. "Ferguson's Inheritance." *Jacobin.* August 5, 2015. https://www.jacobinmag.com/2015/08/ferguson-police-black-lives-matter/.

Murdock, Sebastian. "White Woman Threatened to Call Cops on 8-Year-Old Girl Selling Water." *HuffPost.* June 23, 2018. https://www.huffpost.com/entry/

white-woman-sees-black-girl-selling-water-allegedly-calls-police_n_5b2e94a5e4b00 295f15cf35f.

Mutz, Diana C. "Status Threat, not Economic Hardship, Explains the 2016 Presidential Vote." *Proceedings of the National Academy of Sciences* 115, no. 19 (March 2018): E4330–39. https://www.pnas.org/content/115/19/E4330.

Myers, Ella. *Worldly Ethics: Democratic Politics and Care for the World.* Durham, NC: Duke University Press, 2013.

Mzezewa, Tariro. "The Woman Who Took Down a Confederate Flag on What Came Next." *New York Times.* June 14, 2020. https://www.nytimes.com/2020/06/14/us/polit ics/bree-newsome-bass-confederate-flag.html.

Nagourney, Adam. "A Defiant Rancher Savors the Audience that Rallied to His Side." *New York Times.* April 24, 2014. https://www.nytimes.com/2014/04/24/us/politics/ rancher-proudly-breaks-the-law-becoming-a-hero-in-the-west.html.

Nazaryan, Alex. "School Segregation in America Is as Bad Today as It Was in the 1960s." *Newsweek.* March 22, 2018. https://www.newsweek.com/2018/03/30/school-segregat ion-america-today-bad-1960-855256.html.

Nazaryan, Alex. "Whites Only: School Segregation Is Back, From Birmingham to San Francisco." *Newsweek.* May 2, 2017. https://www.newsweek.com/2017/05/19/race-schools-592637.html.

Nichols, Robert. "Disaggregating Primitive Accumulation." *Radical Philosophy* 194 (November/December 2015): 18–28.

Nietzsche, Friedrich. *On the Genealogy of Morals and Ecce Homo*, translated and edited by Walter Kaufmann. New York: Vintage Books, 1989.

Nsele, Zamansele. Interview with Frank Wilderson III, "Part I: 'Afropessimism' and the Rituals of Anti-Black Violence." *Mail & Guardian.* June 24, 2020. https://mg.co.za/arti cle/2020-06-24-frank-b-wilderson-afropessimism-memoir-structural-violence/.

Nsele, Zamansele. Interview with Frank Wilderson III, "Part II: 'Afropessimism' and the Rituals of Anti-Black violence." *Mail & Guardian.* June 27, 2020. https://mg.co.za/fri day/2020-06-27-part-ii-afropessimism-and-the-rituals-of-anti-black-violence/.

Oliver, Melvin, and Thomas Shapiro. *Black Wealth/White Wealth: A New Perspective on Racial Inequality.* 2nd ed. New York: Routledge, 2006.

Olson, Joel. *The Abolition of White Democracy.* Minneapolis: University of Minnesota Press, 2004.

Olson, Joel. "W. E. B. Du Bois and the Race Concept." *Souls* 7, no. 3–4 (2005): 118–28.

O'Neil, Tim. "Look Back: Race Hatred, Workforce Tensions Explode in East St. Louis in 1917." *St. Louis Post Dispatch* (St. Louis, Missouri). September 21, 2014. https://www. stltoday.com/news/local/history/race-hatred-workforce-tensions-explode-in-east-st-louis-in-1917/article_9bfa1b5d-c627-5dc7-b1da-6d58993f3ecb.html.

Onwuachi-Willig, Angela. "Policing the Boundaries of Whiteness: The Tragedy of Being 'Out of Place' from Emmet Till to Trayvon Martin." *Iowa Law Review* 102, no. 1113 (2017): 1113–85.

Pachirat, Timothy. *Every Twelve Seconds: Industrialized Slaughter and the Politics of Sight.* New Haven, CT: Yale University Press, 2011.

Painter, Nell Irvin. *The History of White People.* New York: W. W. Norton and Company, 2011.

Painter, Nell Irvin. "What Whiteness Means in the Trump Era." *New York Times.* November 12, 2016. https://www.nytimes.com/2016/11/13/opinion/what-whiteness-means-in-the-trump-era.html.

Painter, Nell Irvin. "Why 'White' Should Be Capitalized." *Washington Post*. July 22, 2020. https://www.washingtonpost.com/opinions/2020/07/22/why-white-should-be-capi talized/.

Park, Alex. "The St. Louis Area Has a Long History of Shameful Racial Violence." *Mother Jones*. August 18, 2014. https://www.motherjones.com/politics/2014/08/riot-east-st-louis-ferguson-history-race/.

Parker, Kim, Juliana Menasce Horowitz, and Monica Anderson. "Amid Protests, Majorities Across Racial and Ethnic Groups Express Support for the Black Lives Matter Movement." Pew Research Center. June 12, 2020. https://www.pewresearch.org/social-trends/2020/06/12/amid-protests-majorities-across-racial-and-ethnic-groups-expr ess-support-for-the-black-lives-matter-movement/.

PBS Thirteen: Media with Impact. "The Rise and Fall of Jim Crow." 2002. https://www. thirteen.org/wnet/jimcrow/tools_unwritten.html.

Perhamus, Lisa M., and Clarence W. Joldersma. "What Might Sustain the Activism of This Moment? Dismantling White Supremacy, One Monument at a Time." *Journal of Philosophy of Education* 54, no. 5 (2020): 1314–32.

Peters, Tacuma. "Revisiting *Black Reconstruction*: Chattel Slavery, Native Lands, and the Color Line." Paper presented at the Western Political Science Association meeting, Vancouver, BC, 2017.

Petitjean, Clément. "Prisons and Class Warfare: An Interview with Ruth Wilson Gilmore." August 2, 2018. https://www.versobooks.com/blogs/3954-prisons-and-class-warfare-an-interview-with-ruth-wilson-gilmore.

Pew Research Center. "An Examination of the 2016 Electorate, Based on Validated Voters." August 9, 2018. https://www.pewresearch.org/politics/2018/08/09/an-exam ination-of-the-2016-electorate-based-on-validated-voters/.

Pickens, William "A Roman Holiday." In *Negro Anthology*, edited by Nancy Cunard, 32–35. London: Wishart & Co., 1934.

Pierson, Paul. "Listening to Louisiana: What 'Climbing the Empathy Wall' Can (and Can't) Tell Us About the Populist Right." *British Journal of Sociology* 68, no. 1 (2017): 133–37.

Pinn, Anthony B. "Reading Du Bois Through Religion and Religious Commitment." *Journal of Religion* 94, no. 3 (July 2014): 370–82.

Platt, Verity. "Why People Are Toppling Monuments to Racism." *Scientific American*. July 3, 2020. https://www.scientificamerican.com/article/why-people-are-toppling-monuments-to-racism/.

Posnock, Ross. "The Distinction of Du Bois: Aesthetics, Pragmatism, Politics." In Ross Posnock, *Color and Culture: Black Writers and the Making of the Modern Intellectual*, 111–45. Cambridge, MA: Harvard University Press, 2000.

Purdy, Jedediah. "The Bundys and the Irony of American Vigilantism." *New Yorker*. January 5, 2016.

Rabaka, Reiland. "The Souls of White Folk: W. E. B. Du Bois's Critique of White Supremacy and Contributions to Critical White Studies." *Journal of African American Studies* 11 (2007): 1–15.

Race-Class Narrative Project. "Race-Class Narrative Summary." 2018. https://ianhaneylo pez.com/race-class-narrative.

Rancière, Jacques. *Dis-agreement: Politics and Philosophy*, translated by Julie Rose. Minneapolis: University of Minnesota Press, 1999.

Rankine, Claudia. "The Condition of Black Life is One of Mourning." *New York Times.* June 22, 2015. https://www.nytimes.com/2015/06/22/magazine/the-condition-of-black-life-is-one-of-mourning.html.

Ransby, Barbara. *Making All Black Lives Matter: Reimagining Freedom in the 21st Century.* Oakland: University of California Press, 2018.

Reed, Adolph. *W. E. B. Du Bois and American Political Thought: Fabianism and the Color Line.* New York: Oxford University Press, 1997.

Robinson, Cedric J. *Black Marxism: The Making of the Black Radical Tradition.* Chapel Hill: University of North Carolina Press, 2000 (1983).

Roda, Allison, and Amy Stuart Wells. "School Choice Policies and Racial Segregation: Where White Parents' Good Intentions, Anxiety, and Privilege Collide." *American Journal of Education* 119, no. 2 (February 2013): 261–93.

Roediger, David. "Accounting for the Wages of Whiteness: US Marxism and the Critical History of Race." In *Wages of Whiteness and Racist Symbolic Capital,* edited by Wulf D. Hund, Jeremy Krikler, and David R. Roediger, 9–26. Munster: LIT Verlag, 2010.

Roediger, David. *How Race Survived U.S. History.* New York: Verso Books, 2010.

Roediger, David. *The Wages of Whiteness: Race and the Making of the American Working Class.* Rev. ed. London: Verso, 2007 (1991).

Roediger, David. "Who's Afraid of the White Working Class?" *Los Angeles Review of Books.* May 17, 2017.

Rogers, Melvin. "Propaganda and Rhetoric: On W. E. B. Du Bois' 'Criteria of Negro Art.'" In *The Darkened Light of Faith: Race, Democracy, and Freedom in African American Political Thought.* Book manuscript forthcoming from Princeton University Press.

Rogin, Michael. "American Political Demonology: A Retrospective." In *Ronald Reagan, the Movie, and Other Episodes in Political Demonology.* Berkeley: University of California Press, 1987.

Rosenberg, Eli. "A Black Former White House Staffer Was Moving into a New Apartment. Someone Reported a Burglary." *Washington Post.* May 1, 2018. https://www.washingtonpost.com/news/post-nation/wp/2018/05/01/a-black-former-white-house-staffer-was-moving-into-a-new-apartment-someone-reported-a-burglary/.

Rothstein, Richard. "The Racial Achievement Gap, Segregated Schools, and Segregated Neighborhoods—A Constitutional Insult." *Race and Social Problems* 7, no. 1 (March 2015): 21–30.

Rothwell, Jonathan T., and Pablo Diego-Rosell. "Explaining Nationalist Political Views: The Case of Donald Trump." August 2016. http://papers.ssrn.com/sol3/papers.cfm?abstract_id=2822059.

Rowe, John Carlos. *Literary Culture and U.S. Imperialism: From the Revolution to WWII.* Oxford: Oxford University Press, 2000.

Royall, Sam. " 'The Well-Meaning White People': A Comparative Case Study of the White Anti-Racist Organizing Models of the Southern Student Organizing Committee and Alliance of White Anti-Racists Everywhere, Los Angeles." Senior thesis, Occidental College, 2018. https://www.oxy.edu/sites/default/files/assets/UEP/Comps/Sam%20Royall_The%20Well-Meaning%20White%20People.pdf.

Sandberg, Cara. "The Story of *Parents Involved in Community Schools.*" Student paper, UC Berkeley School of Law, 2011. https://www.law.berkeley.edu/files/The_Story_of_Parents_Involved_Sandberg.pdf.

Saxton, Alexander. *The Rise and Fall of the White Republic: Class Politics and Mass Culture in Nineteenth-Century America.* London: Verso Books, 1990.

Schaffner, Brian N., Matthew MacWilliams, and Tatishe Nneta. "Understanding White Polarization in the 2016 Vote for President: The Sobering Role of Racism and Sexism." *Political Science Quarterly* 133, no. 1 (2018): 9–34.

Selvin, Claire, and Tessa Solomon. "Toppled and Removed Monuments: A Continually Updated Guide to Statues and the Black Lives Matter Protests." *ARTnews*. June 11, 2020. https://www.artnews.com/art-news/news/monuments-black-lives-matter-guide-120 2690845/.

Serwer, Adam. "The Nationalist's Delusion." *The Atlantic*. November 20, 2017. https://www.theatlantic.com/politics/archive/2017/11/the-nationalists-delusion/546356/.

Sexton, Jared. *Amalgamation Schemes: Antiblackness and the Critique of Multiracialism*. Minneapolis: University of Minnesota Press, 2005.

Sexton, Jared. "Racial Profiling and the Societies of Control." In *Warfare in the American Homeland: Policing and Prison in a Penal Democracy*, edited by Joy James, 197–218. Durham, NC: Duke University Press, 2007.

Shaw, Randy. "How Black Lives Matter Is Building New Activist Strategies in a New Era," *UC Press Blog*. July 7, 2020. https://www.ucpress.edu/blog/51174/how-black-lives-matter-is-building-new-activist-strategies-in-a-new-era/.

Shelby, Tommie. *We Who Are Dark*. Cambridge, MA: Harvard University Press, 2007.

Shuford, John. "Four Du Boisian Contributions to Critical Race Theory." *Transactions of the Charles S. Peirce Society* 37, no. 3 (2001): 301–37.

Sides, John, Michael Tesler, and Lynne Vavreck. *Identity Crisis: The 2016 Presidential Campaign and the Battle for the Meaning of America*. Princeton, NJ: Princeton University Press, 2018.

Siegler, Kirk. "Roots of U.S. Capitol Insurrectionists Run Through American West." *NPR*. January 12, 2021. https://www.npr.org/2021/01/12/955665162/roots-of-u-s-capitol-insurrectionists-run-through-american-west.

Silver, Nate. "The Mythology of Trump's Working Class Support." *FiveThirtyEight*. May 3, 2016. https://fivethirtyeight.com/features/the-mythology-of-trumps-working-class-support/.

Singh, Nikhil. "On Race, Violence, and So-Called Primitive Accumulation." *Social Text* 34, no. 3 (September 2016): 27–50.

Singh, Nikhil Pal. *Black Is a Country: Race and the Unfinished Struggle for Democracy*. Cambridge, MA: Harvard University Press, 2004.

Singh, Nikhil Pal, and Thuy Linh Tu. "Morbid Capitalism." *N + 1*, no. 30 (Winter 2018): 101–15.

Sinitiere, Phillip Luke. "W. E. B. Du Bois's Prophetic Propaganda: Religion and *The Crisis* 1910–1934." In *Protest and Propaganda: W. E. B. Du Bois, the Crisis and American History*, edited by Amy Helene Kirschke and Phillip Luke Sinitiere, 190–207. Columbia: University of Missouri Press, 2019.

Smith, Shawn Michelle. *Photography on the Color Line: W. E. B. Du Bois, Race, and Visual Culture*. Durham, NC: Duke University Press, 2004.

Snow, David A., and Robert D. Benford. "Master Frames and Cycles of Protest." In *Frontiers in Social Movement Theory*, edited by Aldon D. Morris and Carol McClurg Mueller, 133–55. New Haven, CT: Yale University Press, 1992.

Spade, Dean. "Solidarity, Not Charity: Mutual Aid for Mobilization and Survival." *Social Text* 38, no. 1 (March 2020): 131–51.

Spillers, Hortense. "Mama's Baby, Papa's Maybe: An American Grammar Book." *Diacritics* 17, no. 2 (1987): 64–81.

Stanley, Sharon. "The Enduring Challenge of Racial Integration." *Du Bois Review* 12, no. 1 (2015): 5–24.

Stevens, Matt. "When Kamala Harris and Joe Biden Clashed on Busing and Segregation." *New York Times*. July 31, 2019. https://www.nytimes.com/2019/07/31/us/politics/kam ala-harris-biden-busing.html.

Students for a Democratic Society. "Huey Newton Talks to the Movement." *The Movement*. August 1968. https://omeka.library.kent.edu/special-collections/items/show/3176.

Sullivan, Shannon. *Good White People: The Problem with Middle Class White Anti-Racism*. Albany: State University of New York Press, 2014.

Sullivan, Shannon. *Revealing Whiteness: The Unconscious Habits of Racial Privilege*. Bloomington: Indiana University Press, 2006.

Tardon, Raphael. "Richard Wright Tells Us: The White Problem in the United States." *Action*. October 24, 1946.

Tavernese, Sabrina. "Why the Announcement of a Looming White Minority Makes Demographers Nervous." *New York Times*, November 22, 2018. https://www.nytimes. com/2018/11/22/us/white-americans-minority-population.html.

Taylor, Keeanga-Yamahtta. *From #BlackLivesMatter to Black Liberation*. Chicago: Haymarket Books, 2016.

Tesler, Michael. "The Floyd Protests Will Likely Change Public Attitudes About Race and Policing. Here's Why." *Washington Post*. June 5, 2020. https://www.washingtonpost. com/politics/2020/06/05/floyd-protests-will-likely-change-public-attitudes-about-race-policing-heres-why/.

Tharps, Lori L. "The Case for Black with a Capital B." *New York Times*. November 18, 2014. https://www.nytimes.com/2014/11/19/opinion/the-case-for-black-with-a-capi tal-b.html.

Thomas, Deja, and Juliana Menasce Horowitz. "Support for Black Lives Matter Has Decreased Since June but Remains Strong Among Black Americans." Pew Research Center. September 16, 2020. https://www.pewresearch.org/fact-tank/2020/09/16/supp ort-for-black-lives-matter-has-decreased-since-june-but-remains-strong-among-black-americans/.

Toscano, Alberto. "'America's Belgium': W. E. B. Du Bois on Race, Class, and the Origins of World War I." In *Cataclysm 1914: The First World War and the Making of Modern World Politics*, edited by Alexander Anievas, 236–57. Leiden: Brill, 2015.

Ture, Kwame, and Charles V. Hamilton. *Black Power: The Politics of Liberation*. New York: Vintage Books, 1992 (1967).

Valdez, Inés. *Transnational Cosmopolitanism: Kant, Du Bois, and Justice as a Political Craft*. Cambridge: Cambridge University Press, 2019.

Valentino, Nicholas A., Fabian G. Neuner, and L. Matthew Vandenbroek. "The Changing Norms of Racial Political Rhetoric and the End of Racial Priming." *Journal of Politics* 80, no. 3 (July 2018): 757–71.

Wallace-Wells, Benjamin. "Why the Bundys and Their Heavily Armed Supporters Keep Getting Away with It." *New Yorker*. August 25, 2017. https://www.newyorker.com/ news/news-desk/why-the-bundys-and-their-heavily-armed-supporters-keep-gett ing-away-with-it.

Walley, Christine J. "Trump's Election and the 'White Working Class': What We Missed." *American Ethnologist* 44, no. 2 (2017): 231–36.

Wang, Jackie. *Carceral Capitalism*. South Pasadena, CA: Semiotexte, 2018.

Warren, Mark R. *Fire in the Heart: How White Activists Embrace Radical Justice.* Oxford: Oxford University Press. 2010.

Watts, Eric King. "Cultivating a Public Voice: W. E. B. Du Bois and the 'Criteria of Negro Art.'" *Rhetoric & Public Affairs* 4, no. 2 (Summer 2001): 181–201.

Weinbaum, Alys Eve. "Interracial Romance and Black Internationalism." In *Next to the Color Line: Gender, Sexuality and Du Bois,* edited by Susan Gillman and Alys Eve Weinbaum, 96–123. Minneapolis: University of Minnesota Press, 2007.

Wells, Ida B. "Lynch Law in Georgia." In *The Light of Truth: Writings of an Anti-Lynching Crusader,* edited by Mia Bay, 313–34. New York: Penguin Books, 2014.

Wells, Ida B. "A Red Record." In *The Light of Truth: Writings of an Anti-Lynching Crusader,* edited by Mia Bay, 218–312. New York: Penguin Books, 2014.

West, Cornel. "Black Strivings in a Twilight Civilization." In *The Cornel West Reader,* 87–118. New York: Basic Books, 1999.

White, Dan. "Hope, Mutual Aid, and Abolition." *UC Santa Cruz News.* February 16, 2021. https://news.ucsc.edu/2021/02/kaba-mlk-coverage-2021.html.

Wilderson III, Frank. *Afropessimism.* New York: W. W. Norton & Co., 2020.

Wilderson III, Frank. "Afro-Pessimism and the End of Redemption." Franklin Humanities Institute. 2016. https://humanitiesfutures.org/papers/afro-pessimism-end-redemption/.

Wilderson III, Frank. "The Black Liberation Army and the Paradox of Political Engagement." April 2014. https://illwill.com/the-black-liberation-army-the-paradox-of-political-engagement.

Wilderson III, Frank. "Gramsci's Black Marx: Whither the Slave in Civil Society?" *Social Identities* 9, no. 2 (2003): 225–40.

Wilderson III, Frank. *Red, White, & Black: Cinema and the Structure of U.S. Antagonisms.* Durham, NC: Duke University Press, 2010.

Wilkerson, Isabelle. *Caste: The Origins of our Discontents.* New York: Random House, 2020.

Willer, Robb, Matthew Feinberg, and Rachel Wetts. "Threats to Racial Status Promote Tea Party Support Among White Americans." May 4, 2016. http://ssrn.com/abstract=2770186.

Williams, Apryl. "Black Memes Matter: #LivingWhileBlack with Becky and Karen." *Social Media and Society* (December 2020): 1–14.

Williams, Joan C. "The Democrats' White People Problem." *The Atlantic.* December 2018. https://www.theatlantic.com/magazine/archive/2018/12/the-democrats-white-people-problem/573901/.

Wilson, Erika K. "Monopolizing Whiteness." *Harvard Law Review* 134 (May 2021): 2382–448.

Winters, Joseph R. *Hope Draped in Black: Race, Melancholy, and the Agony of Progress.* Durham, NC: Duke University Press, 2016.

Wolfe, Patrick. "Settler Colonialism and the Elimination of the Native." *Journal of Genocide Research* 8, no. 4 (2006): 387–409.

Woodley, Jenny. *Art for Equality: The NAACP's Cultural Campaign for Civil Rights.* Lexington: University Press of Kentucky, 2014.

Woodward, C. Vann. "The Price of Freedom." In *What Was Freedom's Price?,* edited by David Sansing, 93–113. Columbia: University Press of Missouri, 1978.

Yancy, George. *Black Bodies, White Gazes: The Continuing Significance of Race.* Lanham, MD: Rowman & Littlefield, 2008.

Yancy, George. "Introduction: Flipping the Script." In *Look, A White! Philosophical Essays on Whiteness,* 1–16. Philadelphia: Temple University Press, 2012.

Yoganathan, Nimalan. "Black Lives Matter Movement Uses Creative Tactics to Confront Systemic Racism." *The Conversation.* July 30, 2020. https://theconversation.com/black-lives-matter-movement-uses-creative-tactics-to-confront-systemic-racism-143273.

Zietz, Joshua. "Does the White Working Class Really Vote Against Its Own Interests?" *Politico.* December 31, 2017. https://www.politico.com/magazine/story/2017/12/31/trump-white-working-class-history-216200/.

Zimmer, Ben. "Talk of Whitelash Revives 1960s Term." *Wall Street Journal.* November 16, 2016. https://www.wsj.com/articles/talk-of-a-whitelash-revives-a-1960s-term-1479479174.

Index

For the benefit of digital users, indexed terms that span two pages (e.g., 52–53) may, on occasion, appear on only one of those pages.